# A BLACK QUEER HISTORY

## OF THE UNITED STATES

# A BLACK QUEER HISTORY

## OF THE UNITED STATES

C. RILEY SNORTON AND DARIUS BOST

BEACON PRESS, BOSTON

BEACON PRESS
24 Farnsworth Street
Boston, Massachusetts
www.beacon.org

Beacon Press books
are published under the auspices of
the Unitarian Universalist Association of Congregations.

29 28 27 26    8 7 6 5 4 3 2 1

This book is printed on acid-free paper that meets the uncoated paper
ANSI/NISO specifications for permanence as revised in 1992.

Text design and composition by Kim Arney

*Library of Congress Cataloging-in-Publication
Data is available for this title.*
ISBN: 978-0-8070-0855-3; e-book: 978-0-8070-0856-0;
audiobook: 978-0-8070-2215-3

The authorized representative in the EU for product safety and
compliance is Easy Access System Europe 16879218, Mustamäe tee 50,
10621 Tallinn, Estonia: http://beacon.org/eu-contact.

# CONTENTS

# AUTHORS' NOTE

I t's hard to pinpoint when we met but our first real hangout was in Miami, Florida, at S.P.A.C.E., a retreat for Black queer writers in 2015. Working on *Evidence of Being: The Black Gay Cultural Renaissance and the Politics of Violence* and *Black on Both Sides: A Racial History of Trans Identity*, we found that we shared language and a common orientation to history being, among many things, a political tool. We knew each other's work but hadn't yet had the opportunity to get to know each other personally. We both grew up in smaller towns in the Carolinas, both had professional lives prior to entering the academy, both love a kickback and a cookout, and both view friendship as a cherished form of relation. Writing this book offered us the time and space to learn about and from each other. We found ourselves writing on each other's couches, watching documentary films together, and reading each other's book recommendations. And talking about our families, our different expressions of Black queer masculinity, and the state of the world.

We began writing this book with a sense that any history of Black queer people in the United States requires grappling with the meanings of each word in the title and the additional layers of meanings they produce when taken together. History is another form of storytelling, and we approach historical figures and events in this book with a keen interest in reviving strategies and recovering and amplifying wisdom for our collective present and future.

As *Black* and *queer* specify the kind of history that follows, we take care with identifying when these terms function as verbs as well as nouns. Across the book, we view blackness and queerness as identities and identifications describing people, places, and communities, as aesthetic, political, and spiritual practices, as ways of seeing and thinking, as structures of feeling, and as conditions for living.

We also wrote this book as interdisciplinary scholars of Black, queer, and trans studies, and our archival practices are always shaped by a desire to learn more about our usable past. As a survey, this book is necessarily not exhaustive, and any omissions are not meant to indicate a lack of importance or esteem. Some people we discuss will be more familiar than others, and some well-known histories are narrated differently through a Black, queer, and trans lens. We resist limiting what a Black queer history can be, opting to think and write about how blackness, queerness, and transness indelibly shapes America's national culture—often through confrontations with the state.

Just as social movements exist through collective action, this social history is an expression of our collaboration and solidarity. We invite you to continue this work by remembering the histories—personal and otherwise—that make Black queer and trans living more possible.

# INTRODUCTION

B lack gay filmmaker, cultural critic, and university professor Marlon Riggs was born in Fort Worth, Texas, in 1954. He received his bachelor of arts degree in history from Harvard University and his master of arts degree in journalism with a specialization in documentary film from the University of California–Berkeley. Riggs wrote, produced, and directed eight films and videos, winning Emmy and Peabody awards for his work. His works explored issues of race, sexuality, and representation in the United States. His later films and videos explored issues of homosexuality and HIV/AIDS amid the culture wars of the 1990s, making him a target of the conservative politicians and the Christian right. When his film *Tongues Untied* aired on PBS in 1991, Republican primary candidate Pat Buchanan released an ad targeting his opponent George H. W. Bush using reedited clips from the film. Condemned as pornographic, the film became a talking point on the floor of Congress and among right-wing Christian activists because Riggs received federal funds for its completion.

Riggs's final film, *Black Is . . . Black Ain't: A Personal Journey Through Black Identity* (1994), subverts monolithic notions of blackness.[1] He conducts interviews with prominent community members discussing their diverse upbringings and understandings of the term, shows how regional and group differences produced distinct Black vernaculars and forms of cultural expression, and presents various political and cultural ideologies espoused by Black leaders. Riggs's emphasis on the diverse meanings and expressions of blackness was deeply personal. It created an opening for him to be included in the Black community as a Black gay man dying of AIDS. African American communities were slow to respond to the AIDS crisis in their communities. The case prevalence increased rapidly among Blacks in the 1980s and '90s, making them the most affected racial group by 1996. Due to the stigma attached to homosexuality and injection drugs, Black Americans distanced themselves from the community members most affected by the disease. Though African American responses to AIDS changed when the virus began to impact heterosexuals, Black leaders' and community members' failure to mobilize around the pandemic early on allowed it to take hold in Black communities. The film was completed posthumously due to Riggs's death from AIDS, making the disease one driving force in his "personal journey" to define what "Black" is.

While most of the film traces what the term connotes across a range of communities—a phenotype, a political identity, a cultural marker, to name a few meanings—early in the documentary Riggs turns to the dictionary to meditate on what "Black" denotes. He states, "For the longest, of course, being Black wasn't always beautiful. A sixteenth-century Oxford English Dictionary provides a clue to the word's meaning before we redefined it." He included the following definitions:

- Black: deeply stained with dirt; soiled, dirty, foul.
- Having dark or deadly purposes, malignant.
- Black: pertaining to, or involving death; deadly, baneful, disastrous, sinister.
- Iniquitous, atrocious, horrible, wicked.
- Black, indicating disgrace, censure, liability to punishment.[2]

Later in the film, Riggs discusses how African Americans redefined the terms like *Black* that were used to malign them: "All of those words, when we took them into our own culture, became, I think, affirmations of who we are. Rather than ways which society at large put us down."[3] Riggs referred to the common practice among marginalized groups of reappropriating terms used to marginalize them. Black became a term of political empowerment in the mid-1960s as expressed in the slogan, "Black is beautiful."

In the following scene, Riggs reflects on the AIDS epidemic in the 1990s that demanded Black-identified people to, once again, embrace

a word that had been used against them and use it to affirm who
they are:

> AIDS is central to the catalyst that's pushing me to deal with iden-
> tity on the global perspective. The connection between AIDS and
> black folks and black folks' identity is metaphoric. Both of them
> are a struggle against the odds in the face of adversity, in the face of
> possible extinction. How do we keep ourselves together as a people
> in the face of all of our differences? How do we maintain a sense
> of communal selfhood, if you will? Who is in the community and
> who's not? I mean there has been a history of excluding other black
> folk from community in this country to the detriment I think of our
> empowerment as an overall people.[4]

Riggs recognized that AIDS, that dirty word that pertained to
death, was associated with iniquity, which had come to mark Black
people with dark and deadly purposes and made them liable to punishment—that *AIDS* was akin to the word *black* before it was redefined by the community. Yet, the stigma of AIDS prevented the
Black community from affirming the value of those affected and seeing
mobilization against the disease as a source of empowerment for the
community overall.

Riggs had witnessed how Haitian refugees seeking asylum in the
US became trapped in Guantanamo Bay prison camps after three
hundred of them tested positive for AIDS in the early '90s. They were
not allowed treatment in the US because immigration laws banned
HIV-positive people from entering US territory. He saw that in the
early 1990s, sub-Saharan Africans made up nine million of the total
AIDS cases out of a global total of fourteen million. Million-dollar
corporations in the West refused to allow companies in Africa to
manufacture the antiretrovirals at costs that would not bankrupt
sub-Saharan nations' already fragile (read: exploited) economies. He
saw the difficulties the Black church had dealing with the AIDS crisis
because it would force them to rethink the theologies that deemed
homosexuality, injection drug use, and nonprocreative sex as immoral.

Riggs foresaw how AIDS would reignite US myths of predatory
Black male sexuality. In 1997, just two years after the film was released,

AIDS would turn the HIV-positive Black man, Nushawn Williams, into a "public health threat."[5] Williams had unprotected sex with numerous young women, nine of whom contracted HIV. His name circulated in mass media despite laws protecting the confidentiality of people with AIDS. For Riggs, AIDS had, like issues past, unsettled the matter of Black identity and had become another word the community had to embrace and redefine if they were going to continue to beat "the odds in the face of adversity, in the face of possible extinction."[6] Black people's failure to unify in a moment when Black-identified people faced the possibility of extinction prompted many of the questions that guided Riggs's personal cinematic journey.

Riggs's exploration of the meaning of Black identity required not only new questions about how to grapple with differences within the community in the present. It also prompted him to look backward toward the "history of excluding other black folk from the community in this country to the detriment . . . of our empowerment as an overall people."[7] In essence, Riggs's journey to define what "Black is" pushed him to reconsider what Black was. The concerns Riggs's film raised about the past guide our journey toward *A Black Queer History of the United States*.

We explore the rifts that developed within the community as it sought to rescue Black identity away from its prior meanings. We look for those who were forced to remain in the closet, removed from public-facing roles, or ignored as political constituents in the moments when blackness was being redefined. We search for individuals and groups that became "othered" in the process of developing "a sense of communal selfhood."[8] As with the Black people with AIDS stigmatized in the 1990s, we seek out those whose identities became stained with dirt, soiled, and indicative of disgrace. We view the marginalization of people with AIDS within Black communities as the culmination of neglect of the needs and desires of LGBTQ people throughout the modern Black freedom movement. Our findings show that this neglect was detrimental to the freedom of Black people overall.

We begin with this example because the invention of the racial category "Black" as a denigrated caste serves as the foundation of a Black queer history in the United States and as a reason for the illusive nature of this history. In 1619, British settlers captured "20 and odd"

Africans from a Portuguese warship and transported them to colonial America to labor as indentured or lifetime servants.[9] European settlers' need for labor propelled further theft and trade of Africans. The transatlantic slave trade homogenized diverse African tribes, evacuating them of their past identities by turning them into commodities. Through a series of laws that made slavery a permanent condition specific to Africans, settlers transformed them into a blackened caste. As a European invention used to justify white settler domination and Black subjugation, blackness became an identity fixed to the bodies of bonded people. This condition of fixity, devaluation, and subjugation served as the historical backdrop to colonial and, later, US constructions of gender and sexuality. Somehow, Black people found opportunities for gender and sexual exploration in the face of and in resistance to the dominant class that tried to exploit, regulate, and control their bodies.

We consider the ellipses in Riggs's title as referencing the numerous, unnamed possibilities of gender and sexual exploration and liberation that were unrecognized or marginalized as a result of histories of Black racial and sexual domination. *A Black Queer History of the United States* provides a more expansive view of blackness in the US that is inclusive of a range of gender expressions and sexual desires, both named and unnamed, including Black queer and trans figures whose lives were recorded in the historical record and those who, by force and/or by choice, remain elusive. This history also names gender and sexual arrangements and practices that may be heterosexual but are considered deviations from white middle-class norms of marriage and family. Pursuing the openings initiated by Riggs, this volume offers a Black queer history of the US that contests dominant historical accounts that assume blackness was and is straight and gender normative.

One way to think of blackness in an expansive way, and to consider how it defies any easy categorization, is to play with naming. Whether "Black" is a last name, a drag name, or a reference to icon status, playing with names allows us to speculate about what Black is, was, will be, and ain't. In the remainder of the introduction, we focus on the narratives of four Black queer and gender-variant people to open this book's discussion of alternative ways of seeing, framing, and naming a Black queer past. We begin by examining the career of professional female impersonator Phil Black to redefine Black as genderqueer resistance and to demonstrate how the civil rights of Black queer people were marginalized in mainstream visions of US democracy. Phil Black shows us how the ordinary act of buying shoes can open up considerations of working-class solidarity, the history of anti-cross-dressing laws, and alternatives to civil rights strategies of integration. We then examine the life and death of Black trans woman Georgia Black to demonstrate that histories—what we know and how we talk about the past—create and reflect systems of value. Our historical account of Georgia Black seeks to unsettle those systems that devalue Black queer existence.

We look at the larger-than-life figure Joan Jett Blakk, a drag queen who ran for president twice in the 1990s. We show how Black queer performers have used their platform to expose how mainstream US political theater often pays lip service to the causes of marginalized US populations and how spectacular queer performances of blackness might transform mainstream US politics. Finally, we return to Riggs's film with a focus on Black queer feminist scholar-activist Angela Davis. Her status as a Black historical icon has prevented us from acknowledging her queerness. More than demonstrating an alliance between Black, feminist, and queer thought, Davis's talking-head interviews make visible the unmarked intersections of Black history, thereby disrupting the gendered and heteronormative assumptions that govern how we see and know the Black past.

### (PHIL) BLACK AS GENDERQUEER RESISTANCE

> You got to make a living, you got to make a living
> the best way we can.
>
> —*Black Is . . . Black Ain't*

Born in Pittsburgh in the early 1900s, Phil Black began his career as a female impersonator in 1924 as a headliner in vaudeville theater. Dressed as a woman, Black would go to "cake walks" with a friend and win first prize as the best couple. He also attended local Halloween parties masquerading as a woman.[10] Friends encouraged him to pursue female impersonation professionally, and he soon became a regular at the Little Paris Club, a small Black-owned and -patronized neighborhood club in the Upper Hill District of Pittsburgh. There, he became a sought-after performer among locals and in surrounding cities. During the Hill District's peak from the 1920s to the 1950s, Black female impersonators were regulars at local nightclubs and appeared in community parades. Black female impersonators' visibility in the Hill District and other Black entertainment districts across the US has become the subject of debates among historians about the degree of African American acceptance of gender and sexual difference in the years following the Great Migration of African Americans to the urban North. Did Black working-class communities like those in the Hill District embrace Black queerness as integral to the community, or were female impersonators who graced the stage only accepted as exotic entertainment? Phil Black's openness about his identity as a gay man and the presence of other gender-nonconforming people on the street suggest that drag queens were more than entertainment in the Hill District.

Phil Black's acceptance in his Black community was not only a matter of inclusion. His gender and sexual difference also spoke to Black working-class communities' resistance to the gender and sexual regulation of Black elites. Working-class communities' embrace of figures like Phil Black symbolized a larger resistance to the gender and sexual norms imposed by Black leaders in an attempt to show African Americans' moral worthiness for full US citizenship. Black homosexuals came to represent all the elements of working-class culture that civil rights leaders identified as obstacles to citizenship.[11] In 1929, in one of the first sermons in the African American church to address homosexuality, Adam Clayton Powell Sr., minister of the Abyssinian Baptist Church in Harlem, named homosexuality as one of the vices that debased the race.[12] He characterized homosexuality as an individual pursuit of pleasure that overshadowed one's obligations to the Black community. Homosexuality stood in for the broader urban culture that clashed with the ethic of self-sacrifice and community responsibility.

Powell's published sermon immediately followed the Committee of Fourteen's vice report, which deemed Harlem the most vice-ridden neighborhood in New York City.[13] Organized in 1905 to fight prostitution at commercial establishments, the committee reported that

Harlem's nightclubs and speakeasies had become the focal point of commercialized prostitution. In an interview in the *New York Times*, the chairman of the committee, Dr. James Pederson, stated, "Harlem has been found to present this problem in its most acute form, due in large measure to the inability of white police officers to understand and win the confidence and cooperation of the densely populated negro district." He further reported that police commissioner Grover A. Whalen and the "leading citizens of Harlem" were working with the committee to correct "these fundamental difficulties."[14] That Harlem's "leading citizens" were working with the committee and the police to curb vice in Harlem spoke to Black leaders' efforts to regulate Black working-class sexuality and the spaces where entertainers like Phil Black might perform.

Despite Powell's and other Black leaders' efforts to discipline the Black working class to prepare them for citizenship, Black working-class communities resisted the gender and sexual norms prescribed by middle-class African Americans. After Powell's sermon, the increased popularity of drag balls, which attracted several thousand spectators and performers annually, serves as evidence of this resistance. Phil Black, first a symbol of the openness of African American culture in Pittsburgh, became a leader among this resistance in Harlem. After establishing a name for himself in Pittsburgh and Atlantic City, he moved to New York City and became an important figure in the drag ball scene. He left his greatest legacy as the chief promoter of the Funmakers Ball, an annual Thanksgiving night masquerade party that attracted thousands of attendees. Started in the 1940s, his Harlem ball drew mostly Black queens and was considered one of the most significant events of drag society. It continued until the 1960s.

In its description of the 1957 ball, the Harlem-based Black newspaper *New York Age* focused on how the ball broke down barriers of race and gender:

> When I say the barriers are down, I mean all the barriers, honey. Racial barriers, for one. With all the noise the White Citizens Council have been making they haven't been able to destroy the integration policies of the gay world. There were many of our white "sisters" who attended this ball and some of the most ravishing white men

arrive bearing Black, beige and brown gay boys on their arms and vice versa. It's all most democratic. There's another barrier which comes down on the night of our ball. It gets most confusing who is who and what is what in the ladies and gentlemen's rest rooms. At the Rockland Palace the other night, there were more shes in the he room and more hes in the she room than you could shake a hip at.[15]

Facing violent white resistance to racial integration and increasing state repression of homosexuals and cross-dressers amid the Cold War, the Funmakers Ball provided an irreverent space of racial, gender, and sexual boundary-crossings that further demonstrated the resistance of Harlem's Black working class to the gender and sexual norms imposed by civil rights ideology.

Unlike the vision of integration promised by *Brown v. Board of Education*, which required compliance with US gender and sexual norms, the Funmakers Ball espoused a vision of integration that incorporated gender nonconformity and queer interracial desire. Justices in *Brown v. Board* viewed integration as a pathway for Black children to conform to the social norms and cultural values of the nation, including sexual restraint and an aversion to homosexuality.[16] After the *Brown* decision, Black queerness was replaced in Black public discourse and popular culture with heteronormative values.[17] A 1963 protest exemplified the threat Phil Black's genderqueer vision of democracy posed to civil rights ideology. A group of fifteen protesters under the name Committee of Racial Pride picketed the ball. They viewed drag and homosexuality as blights on the Black community and an import brought into Harlem by white visitors from downtown.[18] The picketers carried signs reading "Rear Admirals Stay Downtown" and "Queer Thanksgiving Featuring Faggot Turkeys." Locals physically assaulted some attendees, leading to the cancellation of the 1964 ball. Already navigating the policing and surveillance of white-dominant law enforcement and the "noise" of the White Citizens Council, Black and other drag performers now had to contend with a civil rights ideology that sought to remove homosexuals and drag queens from public view.

What civil rights leaders did not consider was how drag performance was a means to make one's living and how their regulation of public space reproduced histories of racial domination and discrimination. As late as 1953, Black trans woman Carlett Brown was arrested in Boston for wearing a "woman's coat-suit ensemble." Brown responded, "I feel that female impersonators are being denied their right to life, liberty, and the pursuit of happiness when they are arrested for wearing female clothes—especially when they are minding their own business."[19] Brown's emphasis on "minding their own business" suggested that female impersonation was not intrinsically spectacular or socially threatening, and that it was a means of making a living. It was female impersonators who were under threat, and the undue scrutiny of the police turned them into a spectacle. A person dressed in men's clothing and trying on women's shoes may have been punished under the cross-dressing laws that date back to the mid-nineteenth century. These local laws, often a part of broader vice campaigns, emerged after the end of slavery and coincided with Jim Crow laws. Anti-cross-dressing laws were enforced to protect the interests of property-owning white men and to, as sociologist Clare Sears has argued, "impose their vision of social order onto city space."[20] Anti-gay and anti-trans sentiment intensified across the nation in the mid-twentieth century, inciting the use of these cross-dressing laws to police queer and trans people.

Phil Black sewed all his own clothes, though he would shop for accessories. In a 1969 interview, he recalled a moment early in his career when he went out to buy shoes to match his gowns. As he was trying on the shoes, he noticed people staring at him and remembered that he was trying on women's shoes while wearing men's clothing. He explained to the onlookers that he was merely buying them for his act as a female impersonator. According to Black, his honesty proved effective, and the people left him alone. He added that the store manager was so pleased to serve a performer that he asked for a picture and displayed it in the shop window for a long time. After that, Black let shop owners know who he was and what he did for a living.[21] Black's routine shopping for work clothing casually defied the law. Breaking segregation laws was a civil rights strategy, especially in spaces of public accommodation. Black's was not a deliberate effort to change the law but merely to make his living.

The scrutiny he faced and his vulnerability to arrest demonstrate how the vision of social order imposed on city space by property-owning white men in the nineteenth century had lasting effects on the everyday lives and labor of Black queer people in the mid-twentieth century. Anti-cross-dressing laws made performers like Black more conspicuous and available for policing and regulation. Police often cited the "three items of clothing" rule that required people to wear three articles of gender-appropriate clothing or face arrest.[22] Drag performers' hypervisibility in the public sphere stood in stark contrast to their invisibility in mainstream civil rights ideology. Civil rights ideology omitted drag performers from public discourse and popular culture to prove that Black people could adjust to the gender and sexual norms of American society. Though civil rights struggles in the North sought to disrupt the vision of social order imposed by white men, Black activist protests of the Funmakers Ball further imposed that same vision by forcibly removing Black female impersonators from public view. The photograph of Phil Black in the shop window serves as a reminder of the alternative visions of democracy that are hidden in plain sight. It serves as a reminder of his role in creating a vision of desegregation that crossed racial, gender, and sexual boundaries.

### (GEORGIA) BLACK AND HISTORY AS A MAKER OF VALUE

As a child, the church did offer a sense of belonging, you know, I mean a sense of community. And that's important, I think, for anyone who wants to be nurtured in an environment, an environment of support and love, uh, in coming together.

—*Black Is . . . Black Ain't*

Georgia Black was, by all accounts, a community pillar in Sanford, Florida. Monica Roberts, the late activist archivist known to her communities as the trans griot, explains how Georgia, twice widowed, became Georgia Black in her second marriage to Muster Black in 1919. With her second husband, Black moved to Sanford, where she ran a boarding house and did domestic work for many of the wealthy families in Sanford. She was also a mother, a leader of the local Women's Missionary Society, and as her son William "Willie" Sabb describes, "a tower of strength and a tireless worker for her church," St. James A.M.E.[23] A doctor's visit became the catalyst for years of sensationalist speculation in the press. It was more than forty years before the Health Insurance Portability and Accountability Act, or HIPAA, became national law in 1996, which might have offered her a reasonable expectation of privacy. As Georgia Black learned of her cancer diagnosis, her family, the town, and shortly thereafter, a national audience became privy to the incongruity of her sex assignment at birth and the woman known and respected by her community.

Although some sources suggest that Black was born in 1906, her son maintained that she died at fifty-six in 1951, making her date of birth sometime in 1895. Born in Charleston, South Carolina, she escaped fieldwork and did domestic work to support herself. In Winter Gardens, Florida, Georgia met her first husband, Alonzo Sabb, with whom she adopted Willie, her cousin's son, as a young boy. After a tragic logging accident that killed Alonzo Sabb, Georgia arranged for Willie to live with her in Sanford where she was working. Georgia remarried World War I veteran Muster Black about a year later. Mr. Black died of dropsy in 1925. Georgia never remarried. After her second husband's death she converted their family home to a boarding house and immersed herself in church work and raising her son.

According to *Ebony*'s reporters, Georgia Black's story was a "bizarre and moving drama which had its finale in a simple grave at Sanford's Burton Cemetery."[24] *Ebony*'s feature, "The Man Who Lived 30 Years as a Woman," first published in October of 1951, then republished in *Ebony*'s thirtieth-anniversary edition in 1975, and again in its sibling publication, *Jet*, in 1989, was the first in a series of national media stories focused on Black trans people to appear in Johnson Publishing Company's imprints. Throughout the 1950s, and typically advertised in the top right-hand corner, *Ebony* frequently covered "nonconventional" Black life, including "exposés" on nudism and dwarfism, as well as reports of racial and gender "passing." Even with its sensationalist tone, suggesting, for example, that Black was "one of the most incredible stories in the history of sexual abnormalities," *Ebony* could not help but tell the story of how Georgia Black was beloved by various and disparate communities in Sanford, reporting that at her funeral, "lining the sidewalks of the Dixie town that once barred Jackie Robinson from its stadium, Negro and white mourners rubbed elbows, bowed heads and shed genuine tears."[25]

The timing of *Ebony*'s article was in part a consequence of various actors—her pastor, employers, family, and friends—trying to block sensational media coverage of Georgia Black's life as she was dying. This is not to suggest that her gender was widely embraced after her physician, Dr. Orville Barks, reported her sex assignment. Many treated her as a curiosity—dropping by the hospital and later by the home of her in-laws, Malakai and Lugenia Black, to "catch a glimpse of her."[26] In an article published on March 8, 1951, Sanford Police Chief Roy G. Williams reported to the press that although "Georgia has a good reputation as a church worker," the police department planned to investigate the causes of death of her two husbands. At a moment of intense vulnerability and failing health, Black was interrogated by the police and the press. In her interview with *Ebony*, she defends herself against the rumors and allegations, stating simply, "I never done nuthin wrong in my life." And in response to the doctor's (and the public's) incredulity about her character and quality of life, Black explained, "The doctor says he didn't see how I coulda married, but I don't pay no 'tention to that doctor. My husbands and me had a peaceful, lovely life."[27]

Two years after his mother's death, Willie Sabb sought to correct public memory and address the misconceptions forwarded in the press. In the article "My Mother Was a Man," published in the June 1953 issue of *Ebony*, Sabb described his mother as generous, law-abiding, and loving. Sabb's narrative weaved her story with the town of Sanford and with his own, ending with "I loved her with all my heart and shall cherish her memory as long as I live. She will always be Mom to me." In his desire to replace her posthumous notoriety with his loving memory of her, Sabb underscores a critical aspect of what history is and does. Narratives about the past make and reflect systems of value.

Moreover, Georgia Black's life becomes an important example of the complex forms of belonging that we discuss throughout *A Black Queer History of the United States*. Even as *Ebony* and other media outlets characterized the fact that Black was and could be loved as counterintuitive, perhaps even unthinkable because she was a woman who might in today's language be understood as "trans," this history refuses those logics. At the same time, this book is interested in the complexities of belonging—in and across various communities, in time and geography, and more often than not, under fragile, negotiated, and impermanent circumstances.

### (JOAN JETT) BLAKK'S DRAG OF US POLITICS

History is more than chains on your ankles and knowing this black leader and knowing that black leader, it's much more to history than that.

—*Black Is . . . Black Ain't*

In 1991, the Chicago chapter of Queer Nation asked founding member Terence Smith, an activist and drag queen who performed under the stage name Joan Jett Blakk, to run against then-uncontested incumbent mayor Richard M. Daley. With humor and verve, Joan Jett Blakk and her team, whom he described as a "gaggle of drag queens" campaigned along the streets of downtown Chicago, earning media coverage and votes.[28] Blakk lost the election but accomplished the aims of his campaign. Blakk explains, "We just wanted to increase gay visibility and fight a rising homophobia here in Chicago, but do it in a not-so-tense way that everyone could have fun with."[29] Queer Nation turned to Blakk again in 1992, and on his thirty-fifth birthday—the first day he became legally eligible to run—he announced his candidacy for president, saying at his party/press conference, "If a bad actor can be elected president, why not a good drag queen?"[30] A pointed critique of the popularity of Ronald Reagan and a reading of George Bush Sr.'s first term as more of the same, Blakk's platform was a radical divergence, promising the end of police, the military, and privatized health care.

Smith started performing in 1974 and took his stage name from the popular rock band Joan Jett and the Blackhearts, finding inspiration in the performances of Divine, David Bowie, and Grace Jones. Blakk's 1992 presidential campaign is widely considered a master class in the critical possibilities of camp, an aesthetic style or sensibility that places emphasis on theatricality, humor, and irony. As Joe Jeffreys explains, "The drag persona Smith wields as Blakk simultaneously explores and exploits notions of gender, race, and sexuality; his presidential candidacy and stunt of penetrating the floor of the Democratic National Convention in full drag concurrently interrogates the politics of performance and the performance of politics (not to mention the politics of drag and the drag of politics)."[31]

Blakk made US history as the first drag queen and first openly gay Black man to run for political office. Six months into his 1992 campaign, Blakk, outfitted in a red, white, and blue miniskirt, addressed the attendees of the Democratic National Convention. Securing a round-trip ticket to New York City through an engagement at the Limelight nightclub and attending the convention on a press pass from Gay Cable News, Blakk preempted Governor Mario Cuomo's speech, as he delivered this statement from the DNC floor:

[I'm] Joan Jett Blakk, the only drag queen presidential candidate in the United States. And I'm down here on this floor saying, "Hi" to all of America. Why look, "Hi America!" [Waves á la Queen Elizabeth to the entirety of Madison Square Garden. Mario Cuomo ceases speaking and the crowd cheers.] And they said, "Hi" back. In fact they had to stop talking. Look at all these people. Hi y'all. So here we are bringing Queer issues to the campaign. Right here, right now, in a dress! Are you ready for this? I don't know if I am.[32]

While Blakk would read his platform before the Limelight audience later that night, this brief moment of address—coming on the heels of more than two days of on-the-ground campaign organizing, caused quite a stir. In the Republican National Convention that followed, conservative presidential hopeful Pat Buchanan criticized Blakk in his speech before Republican delegates as "the greatest single exhibition of crossdressing in American political history." From the Democratic National Convention, Blakk also claimed for his own the several delegates who casted for "other," explaining that he was "clearly the only 'other' on that floor."[33]

Blakk ran for president again on the Queer Nation Party ticket in 1996 against incumbent president Bill Clinton, updating the campaign slogan from Lick Bush! (in '92) to Lick Slick Willie! Following the 1992 campaign, Smith moved to San Francisco and continued to flourish as an activist and artist, joining the noted stage troupe Pomo

Afro Homos (an abbreviation of Postmodern African American Homosexuals) and launching the talk show *Late Night with Joan Jett Blakk*, which featured guests of interest to the LGBTQ community. In 1999, Smith announced Blakk's plan to run against incumbent mayor Willie Brown for San Francisco mayor.

In an interview published in *Chicago Outlines*, Blakk responds to the question "What's your long-range plan for the United States?" in this way:

> I want to make America the beautiful again. They use that line all the time but they don't know what they are talking about. I think in a lot of different ways we can bring beauty back into people's lives. It's all become too serious . . . but if I'm elected it's going to mean major major fun. I'd love everybody to be happy. That and to beautify are my long range plans.[34]

Blakk injected humor and play into the tenor of American political discourse, with Smith deftly manipulating the spectacle of Black (queer) sexuality, making use of his drag persona to garner attention for anti-racist, abolitionist, and queer politics.

### ANGELA DAVIS'S QUEER PRESENCE

> I think we have such an obsession with naming ourselves because during most of history . . . we've been named by somebody else.
>
> —*Black Is . . . Black Ain't*

Angela Davis appears in Riggs's film *Black Is . . . Black Ain't* as a conspicuous figure. She is, after all, an icon. After being appointed as an assistant professor of philosophy at the University of California, Los Angeles, in 1969, then governor of California Ronald Reagan targeted Davis for her affiliation with the Communist Party. She was initially fired by the University Board of Regents, but a court found her firing illegal. However, UCLA's administration fired her later for using inflammatory language. Her status as an icon was cemented after her involvement with the defense fund of incarcerated activist-intellectuals the Soledad Brothers landed her in jail for eighteen months.

On August 7, 1970, the teenage brother of one of the Soledad Brothers used a gun registered to Davis to take several people hostage in a courtroom. His desperate attempt to secure his sibling's freedom ended in a standoff with the police. Four people were killed, including the court judge. Fearful of the government that had already targeted her because of her beliefs, Davis went into hiding and landed on the FBI's 10 Most Wanted list. When the FBI captured her that year, President Richard Nixon congratulated them for seizing a "dangerous terrorist."[35] The FBI charged Davis with murder, kidnapping, and conspiracy, and denied her bail. During her time in prison, activists rallied around her cause, believing that she had been unfairly targeted due to her political beliefs. The "Free Angela" campaign garnered international attention, and the buttons, posters, and other materials with images of Davis donning an afro became a lasting symbol of revolutionary movements against state violence, Western imperialism, and the prison-industrial complex.

On June 4, 1972, Davis was acquitted and continued speaking out against government repression and for prison abolition. She returned to the academia and published an autobiography and several influential books about the intersections of gender, race, and class, including the seminal *Women, Race, and Class*. In October 1980, Davis gave a keynote speech at the historic "Becoming Visible" conference, a gathering of two hundred Black lesbians in San Francisco, considered the first Black lesbian conference in the United States. In an interview with *Out* magazine, Davis credited women of color feminism and her research on queer blues women with giving her a new vocabulary for making gender and sexuality central to her politics, and for understanding the personal as political.[36]

*Black Is . . . Black Ain't* began circulating three years before Davis "came out" publicly as a lesbian. In the film, Davis discussed the stigma attached to Black identity, relaying a story about her hair texture in her youth and how the struggles of Black Power groups in the 1960s encouraged communities to embrace Black identity and phenotypical features as a source of racial pride. "In the sixties, we began to say 'Black is beautiful.' That was a slogan that indicated a politics of struggle." Davis also spoke as a Black feminist critic and scholar by teaching viewers about the gender imbalance within this politics of struggle: "When we said 'Black is beautiful' [. . .] that meant the Black man is beautiful. There is this tendency now to want to constantly rehabilitate the Black man as patriarch, and I have problems with positing that as the goal of the community."[37]

While Davis's interview focused on race and gender inequality in the 1960s and 1970s Black liberation movements—the movements that made her an icon—queer sexuality also informed her contributions to the film. We claim Davis's contributions as Black queer feminism in the same way that we claim the contributions of Combahee River Collective and Kitchen Table: Women of Color Press cofounder Barbara Smith, who is featured prominently in the film as well. In a memorable moment in Riggs's film, Smith addressed the audience directly, expressing her feelings about being marginalized because of her sexuality:

> Many people would say that I am not a member of the black community. In fact, many of the people who are viewing this would say, "She says she's a lesbian, oh no, that doesn't cut it." But the thing is I know I'm a part of the black community in every single way that is important.[38]

In a 2019 interview, Smith further recalled the vitriolic response she received from the predominantly Black audience at Howard University in 1979 after she read excerpts from her landmark critical essay "Toward a Black Feminist Criticism," which called for a queer reading of Black women's literature and asserted the significance of Black lesbian representation to the lived experiences of Black lesbians.[39] The audience response was so harsh that it left even Black lesbian feminist warrior poet Audre Lorde speechless. Psychiatrist Frances Cress Welsing, who had argued that racism was a global phenomenon sparked by white people's fear of their minority status, was in the audience. She said she expressed pity for Smith being a homosexual, stating that homosexuality was the "death of the race."[40] Smith's experience demonstrated how much lesbianism was vilified in Black communities in the late 1970s and 1980s. These Black scholars viewed lesbianism as threatening to the emerging field of Black studies, which was rooted in the same Black liberation struggles Davis discussed in the film. This example also reflected Black political debates about whether gender and sexual minorities could speak for Black America.

By including Davis in the film, Riggs reveals the irony of the question of who can speak for Black America, since one of the most iconic figures in Black liberation struggles is a lesbian. Beyond the question of identity, Davis's appearance reminds us that the state has historically perceived Black queer feminists as dangerous. Though she was not on trial because she is a lesbian, the anti-war, anti-capitalist, anti-prison stance of Black lesbian feminists has long challenged the values of the US nation-state. Davis continues to appear as a threat to the state due to her outspoken criticism of Israel's colonial occupation of Palestine and the United States' complicity in it. In 2019, Alabama's Birmingham Civil Rights Institute announced that Davis would be given the Fred Shuttlesworth Human Rights Award, an honor even more noteworthy because she is a native of Birmingham and grew up in the "Dynamite Hill" neighborhood heavily targeted by segregationists in the 1940s, '50s, and '60s. However, the institute rescinded her award due to her outspoken support of the boycott, divestment, and sanctions campaign against Israel.[41] Though the organization eventually issued a public apology and reinstated the award, this controversy shows how Davis continues to be associated with "terror," this time through her support of Palestinian human rights.

The appearances of Davis, Smith, and bell hooks (also a key architect of Black queer feminism) in *Black Is . . . Black Ain't* make visible how Black queer Americans have often been critical of the US nation-state in hopes of holding it to its highest democratic values. Throughout this book, we show how the marginalization of Black queer voices in America poses questions about content and form. Put differently, Black queer repression has been as much about what we have to say to and about the country as what national culture legislates about our identities. Our goal in this volume, then, is not to merely include the contributions of Black queer people to US history but to show how they have held and continue to hold the nation accountable to its highest ideals, including its founding principles: life, liberty, and the pursuit of happiness. This is some of what *Black Is* to a *Black Queer History of the United States*.

Additionally, we are writing this volume amid a wave of anti-queer and anti-trans legal and extralegal violence that has left Black queer, trans, and gender-nonconforming people especially vulnerable. We recognize that our efforts to recover the Black queer past might be mistaken as a sign of liberal progress—as an attempt to show how far we have come and how much we have accomplished despite the odds. Readers might also interpret it as a tool for Black queer empowerment. We discourage any attempt to use this volume to detract from the task of social and political transformation of the systemic inequality that continues to make us vulnerable. We hope this history can be used as a tool for teaching transgression—that it reminds readers that linear narratives of progress are fictional and that the horizon of liberation for what *Black is and will be* has a usable past.

### CHAPTER OVERVIEW

Part I, "Proofs of Existence," addresses the difficulties of writing a history of queer and trans people in the United States when their histories are marginal in the archives. Within those marginal mentions, the racial and sexual dominance of Black people have featured so prominently that the dominant approach among African American historians has been to document these histories and resistance to them. Historians have sought to counter the pervasive stereotypes of Black people as sexually available or hypersexual by marginalizing aspects of the African American experience that might confirm these stereotypes. European settlers' perceptions of Blacks as sexually nonnormative have prompted historians to disregard important instances when gender and sexual non-normativity have been central to the individual and collective liberation of Black people. The first four chapters of the book confront this dilemma by centering gender and sexual freedom as significant, but marginalized, aspects of Black liberation. We also examine the ways that the historical archive limits the legibility of acts such as cross-dressing to escape enslavement as expressions of gender and sexual, as well as racial, freedom.

Chapter 1, "The Erotic Life of Colonialism and Slavery," begins our search for a usable past with the arrival of African captives to the shores of colonial America. European settlers' conversion of Africans to Black—a denigrated class destined for permanent enslavement—rested on gender and sexual stereotypes. Sexual stereotypes of African captives confined them to a condition of racial inferiority and sexual non-normativity. The dominant discourse of Puritanism relied on these stereotypes to bolster white settlers' claims to normalcy and morality. Despite their claims to morality, settlers deployed gender and sexual violence in the forms of rape, concubinage, and forced breeding as tools of regulation and domination of the enslaved.

Focusing solely on the sexual domination of the enslaved prohibits a discussion of the pleasurable and consensual aspects of their erotic lives. This discussion has remained marginal in historical scholarship on slavery because there is little evidence of expressions of gender and sexual freedom among the enslaved. Moreover, the heterosexism of African American studies has prevented a more thorough discussion of queer expression and gender subversion in the antebellum period. We confront this gap in the historical scholarship by turning to creative fiction that queerly reimagines the erotic lives of the enslaved. We read for representations of queer sexuality in Jewelle Gomez's *The Gilda Stories* (1991) and Robert Jones's *The Prophets* (2021).

Chapter 2, "By Any Other Name," begins with the story of Ellen Craft, who escaped to freedom with her husband by appearing as his male master. Craft's story is paired with William Cathay/Cathay Williams's, who served in the US military as a girl and a man. The modern categories of queer and trans did not exist at this time, so these terms cannot be easily applied to these instances of gender subversion. We consider instead how the impulse to categorize gender and sexual expression reveals broader cultural anxieties about the instability of identity categories in the United States. Moving from the nineteenth century to the mid-twentieth century, we consider the lives of entertainer Josephine Baker and playwright Lorraine Hansberry. Baker's public persona concealed her internal conflicts about homosexuality. Hansberry used pseudonyms to hide her participation in lesbian culture and politics amid the heterosexism of the Civil Rights Movement.

Chapter 3, "On the Outs," revises the dominant model of gay liberation—the individual act of coming out—by considering how gender and sexual stereotypes have maintained the "color line" in the twentieth century. To resist the stereotypes, Black leaders created a Black racial closet from which gender and sexual minorities could come out and risk marginalization or remain in for the furtherance of racial equality. We use the examples of artists and activists such as Harlem Renaissance poet Countee Cullen; sociologist and Du Bois protégé Augustus Granville Dill; civil rights leaders Pauli Murray, Bayard Rustin, and James Baldwin; trans advocate and "ex-GI" Delisa Newton; and lesbian feminist poet Audre Lorde. We show how coming out or being outed has resulted in marginalization, conditional acceptance, or dismissal of prominent Black queer intellectuals in the Black freedom movement. These moments of confining queerness to the racial closet culminated in marginalization of the stigmatized members of the Black community who were dying of AIDS. We also revise the dominant conception of coming out by highlighting how, throughout the twentieth century, segregationists, liberals, and conservatives have outed Black people, heterosexual and homosexual, as queer because of their deviation from white middle-class norms of marriage and family. We use Linda Taylor as an example, whose complicated life served as the basis for the "welfare queen" stereotype.

Chapter 4, "Werk!," centers on the creative contributions of Black queer and trans communities. While confined to the racial closet and facing the potentially deadly consequences of such confinement, Black queer and trans musicians and performers have created forms of cultural expression that have been critical to their survival. These creatives did not acquiesce to their marginal positions in the nation and in Black culture. Their creative work served as forms of cultural resistance to the racism, heterosexism, and transphobia that plagued the nation. The chapter highlights Black queer and trans creative contributions to a range of genres: Ma Rainey and Bessie Smith to the blues, Willmer "Little Axe" Broadnax to gospel, Sir Lady Java and Ava Betty Brown to dance and performance, Frankie Knuckles to house music, and Tim'm T. West to hip-hop. The chapter encourages us to view these artists as important contributors to the history of Black music and consider queerness and transness as intrinsic to Black sound.

Part II, "We Cannot Live Without Our Lives," marks a shift from our examination of how centering the voices, contributions, and experiences of Black queer and trans artists, activists, and intellectuals revises dominant understandings of key moments in African American history and culture. Instead, it examines race as an often-unmarked category in the modern LGBTQ rights movement. Race, in this instance, describes how identity categories like gay, lesbian, and transgender—the organizing forces behind this movement for gender and sexual equality—have been associated, implicitly and explicitly, with white people. The comparisons between the legal right to marry interracially and the right to same-sex marriage exemplify this. Racial justice movements have served as precedents for the modern LGBTQ liberation movement, unintentionally neglecting those who are racial *and* gender and sexual minorities.

Marginalizing those who face discrimination and violence on multiple fronts is not merely a matter of exclusion. Centering queer and trans communities of color in the modern LGBTQ rights movement exposes the limitations of some of its dominant strategies, namely the extension of rights through legislation. Communities of color face systemic inequality, meaning that racism, homophobia, and transphobia do not require racist, homophobic, or transphobic actors to discriminate against people. Rather, these systems of inequality are embedded in US institutions such as the legal system and law enforcement. Therefore, changing the law to achieve equality and using carceral solutions to punish racist, homophobic, or transphobic actors will not eliminate the systems of inequality that Black queer and trans people endure.

The disproportionate numbers of African Americans in prisons and jails and ongoing brutality toward Black citizens by police officers demonstrate how relying on laws and law enforcement might enhance racial inequality while advancing gender and sexual equality. The remaining two chapters explore these concerns by examining how, despite the influence of the Black civil rights and Black Power movements on the modern LGBTQ rights movement, the implied whiteness of and racism in the LGBTQ movement prompted the creation of separate Black queer and trans organizations in the post-Stonewall era. Even in cases where race does not appear to inform important legal decisions pertaining to LGBTQ rights, race is nevertheless present. Focusing on the LGBTQ rights movement in the 1990s and early decades of the 2000s, we demonstrate how pursuing legislative change cannot eliminate the multiple harms faced by Black queer and trans communities.

Chapter 5, "Coming Together," describes how, from the 1950s to the late 1980s, LGBTQ people came together to transform the conditions of their lives. It begins with the series of trans protests in the 1960s that served as the precursor to the Stonewall rebellion in 1969. It then focuses on the lesbian and gay protests and organizations in the 1970s as catalysts for the creation of Black lesbian and gay organizations. The post-Stonewall emphasis on public protest and social transformation represented by the Pride March in 1970 coincided with the politicization of women and trans of color feminist organizations in the post–civil rights and Black Power eras. The latter half of the chapter describes the formation, mission, and major contributions of Black lesbian feminist, Black lesbian and gay, and AIDS organizations in the 1970s, '80s, and '90s.

Chapter 6, "Survival Is Not a Luxury," examines how Black LGBTQ communities have been impacted by late-twentieth and twenty-first-century legal reform efforts led by white gays and lesbians, and by mass mobilizations led by Black civic leaders, clergy, and grassroots activists. The increasing emphasis on marriage equality and hate crime legislation left Black queer and trans people on the margins of the LGBTQ movement. Black heterosexual communities responded to the legislative changes led by white queer communities with conservatism. The chapter also includes a discussion of the Million Man, Million Woman, and Reignite the Legacy marches in the late 1990s and early 2000s. We assess how gender and sexuality featured in these Black mass mobilizations and how these marches reinscribed heterosexual and gender norms by emphasizing the role of the family and the church as the most powerful institutions in the Black community. We conclude by looking at the coterminous legalization of gay marriage and emergence of the Black Lives Matter movement, showing how Black queer and trans people have been "squeezed between and invisible in" these movements.

## PART I

# PROOFS OF EXISTENCE

### CHAPTER ONE

# THE EROTIC LIFE OF COLONIALISM AND SLAVERY

I n 1619, the Portuguese slaving ship *São João Bautista* set sail for New Spain, which is present-day Mexico, with three hundred fifty Africans. When the ship arrived, it delivered less than half of the original number at Vera Cruz. An estimated one hundred Africans died during the trans-Atlantic voyage. While at sea, the *Bautista* was also attacked and looted by two English ships, the *White Lion* and the *Treasurer*, which absconded with roughly thirty Africans. In August of 1619, the *White Lion* and, a few days later, the *Treasurer* docked at Port Comfort on the southern tip of the Virginia peninsula and sold in exchange for food the at least twice-stolen human cargo. Some enslaved Africans were transported to Jamestown and sold again. Recorded in Virginia's first muster (or census) in 1620, the "colony's thirty-two Africans: fifteen male and seventeen female" along with four Indians appeared under the heading, "Others Not Christians in the Service of the English."[1] In describing the thirty-two Africans and four Native people in terms of their position "in the service of the English" and as "Others Not Christians," the Virginia muster reveals in language how settler colonialism and racial slavery informed and reinforced ideas about difference and power that would contribute to America's national character.[2] In combining racial, national, and religious differences, the census articulates a distinction between the European settlers and a new caste of slaves.

Beliefs about gender and sexuality also sharpened this distinction. Enslaved Africans and Indigenous people were often caricatured as gender and sexual deviants whose being and expression threatened white puritanical culture. This colonial projection was a rhetorical cover for the violent forms of physical and sexual abuse, genocidal acts, and other forms of sexual and racial terror that characterized the settler-colonial and slaving project.

To be clear, we are not suggesting that the first documented instance of slavery is the origin of blackness or queerness in America. It is not even the first recorded instance of Africans in the Americas. Some historians and anthropologists trace African presence as far back as the early 1300s, drawing on archaeological evidence and colonial records to reveal a rich history of African and Indigenous exchange well before the arrival of Christopher Columbus or the *Mayflower*.[3] But this chapter is not about finding origins but rather about access points to Black erotic life in early America. To ask a question about the erotic life of colonialism and slavery (and freedom) means extending the scope of traditional sources and finding other methods to explore intimacy, contact, feeling, and power. As cultural critic Omise'eke Natasha Tinsley explains, in the crosscurrents of the Atlantic Ocean, the term *mati*, which means both "my girl" and "shipmate," illustrates how captive Africans "resisted the commodification of their bought and sold bodies by feeling and feeling for" each other during the Middle Passage.[4] Considering erotic contact in the sex-segregated holds of slaving ships becomes a counterweight—although the scale is never balanced—to the copious documentation of sexual conquest and rape between ship captains, traders, and captives.[5]

Under racial slavery, sexualized violence was an imminent threat for the enslaved irrespective of gender. Archives and first-person accounts from the formerly enslaved provide evidence of the erotic aspects of white women's abuse of enslaved women, even as research has primarily focused on white men's sexual domination of enslaved women through practices of rape, forced "breeding," and concubinage. In her autobiography, *Incidents in the Life of a Slave Girl* (1861), Harriet Jacobs provides a vivid picture of this difficult and painful history, as her memoir contains evidence of white women's role in sexual abuse and white men's use of rape to dominate enslaved men.[6] Although scholars have been slower to explore the sexual abuse of male slaves, a growing number of scholars of slavery, including Thomas Foster and Aliyyah Abdur-Rahman, have called attention to the victimization of enslaved men by white women and men. Testimony to the American Freedmen's Inquiry Commission, convened in 1863, suggests that light-skinned enslaved men were fetishized as sexually desirable in ways that mirror the literature on light-skinned enslaved women. Simply put, sexuality was a privileged domain for exercising control over the enslaved.

Although abuse and violation were pervasive features of the lives of the enslaved, they did not represent the totality of enslaved people's erotic lives. Tinsley's method of reading language to access queer intimacies not captured in the archives of slavery is a model for the discussion that follows. As historians Treva B. Lindsey and Jessica Marie Johnson argue, "The ability to feel through sensory stimulation such as erotic touch is a tool of survival and an affective act of asserting one's humanity."[7] Focusing on erotic life during the time of slavery also means tracing how conceptions of normalcy, morality, criminality, and legal personhood were forged through and alongside racial and sexual categories. Racial slavery rendered the distinction between "free" and "enslaved" porous for Black people living in antebellum America.

The political implications of reading historical materials—whether documentary or literary—for feeling are complicated yet crucial to this Black queer history of the United States. Here we attend to queer-affirming spiritual practices, sex and sex work among free and enslaved Africans, and the ways early American concepts of gender and sexuality shaped the language of abolition. Our aim is to provide a fuller account of Black queer and erotic life in colonial and antebellum America, even as the "record" of queer erotic contact between and among the enslaved finds its fullest expression in the imaginative works of twentieth and twenty-first century Black queer writers.

### SEXUALITY, POWER, AND THE PECULIAR INSTITUTION

"God, gold, and glory" is a pithy phrase historians use to describe the motivations of early European settlement in the Americas. Fleeing religious persecution in Europe and establishing personal wealth in the so-called New World became dominant motivations of a colonial personality, even as there were differences—in circumstances, in belief systems, in nationality—among European settlers. Though Christianity threaded the legal and social fabric of most American colonies, doctrinal arguments in support of abolition were generally met with ambivalence. As John Hope Franklin explains, "While the earliest justification offered by Europeans for the recognition of Negro slavery was the salvation of the souls, this seems to have been of secondary importance to the colonists in the New World. There were no strong evangelical churches at the outset, and the furtherance of Christianity was viewed by the majority with considerable indifference."[8]

For Puritanical theologians, there was also no real consensus about whether slavery was immoral. Differences in perspective frequently pivoted on the question of whether enslaved people could be converted, and consequentially if, as Christians, they must be emancipated. Some religious leaders argued and believed that enslaved Africans had no souls, which further rationalized the existence and perpetuation of slavery and worked to the advantage of the merchant and planter classes. According to their beliefs, the survival and prosperity of Puritans was a sign of God's approval. Puritanical prosperity doctrine, as a religiously inflected rationalization for conquest, informs the nineteenth-century concept of manifest destiny and a view of white settlement as natural and inevitable.[9]

In the transition from British colony to settler colonial state, slavery drove a wedge between American settlers and Great Britain prior to the formal abolition of slavery in either country. The Stamp Act of 1765, in which the British parliament instituted taxes on a range of transactions in the colonies, was an early inciting incident in what would become the American Revolutionary War. Over the next ten years or so, colonists' rage blossomed into a declaration of principles, commonly referred to as the Declaration of Independence. April 19, 1775, marked the onset of an eight-year war with the British over the nascent nation's self-determination. In response to the American insurrection, some British officials offered manumission to enslaved people if they joined the British army. In a deleted passage of the Declaration of Independence, Thomas Jefferson, the future US president, Continental Congress delegate from Virginia, and enslaver of hundreds of Africans, wrote about the seeming contradictions of the British strategy:

He has waged cruel war against human nature itself, violating its most sacred rights of life and liberty in the persons of a distant people who never offended him, captivating & carrying them into slavery in another hemisphere or to incur miserable death in their transportation thither. This piratical warfare, the opprobrium of infidel powers, is the warfare of the Christian King of Great Britain. Determined to keep open a market where Men should be bought & sold, he has prostituted his negative for suppressing every legislative attempt to prohibit or restrain this execrable commerce. And that this assemblage of horrors might want no fact of distinguished die, he is now exciting those very people to rise in arms among us, and to purchase that liberty of which he has deprived them, by murdering the people on whom he has obtruded them: thus paying off former crimes committed against the Liberties of one people, with crimes which he urges them to commit against the lives of another.[10]

Jefferson's use of the language of sexual commerce—"prostituted his negative"—to describe what he viewed as Great Britain's hypocritical practices underscores how sexuality functions as a narrative vehicle and discourse of power. In suggesting that slavery was forced upon the colonies, Jefferson frames the "Christian King" and British government as opportunists for offering emancipation to the enslaved in exchange for military service. It should be noted that Jefferson experienced a decline in the number of those he personally enslaved due to the enactment of such a strategy in Virginia, which may have contributed to the vibrant tone of Jefferson's allegations. Certainly, Africans in the Americas—enslaved, fugitive, and free, as well as abolitionists, carried a critique and similar charge of hypocrisy against American revolutionaries who participated in, supported, or were complicit with the maintenance and perpetuation of slavery, even as they opined and pursued different conditions for "life, liberty, and pursuit of happiness." For these revolutionaries not to recognize this as a contradiction was both financially expedient and a form of ideological warfare. Moral ambivalence and social indifference to slavery and Indigenous genocide were constitutive to America's early national character.

Although Jefferson's remarks were not included in the version of the Declaration of Independence signed by his fellow delegates on July 4, 1776, the peculiar intimacies of slavery were a pervasive though often veiled topic of American political discourse. The first use of the term *peculiar institution* to refer to slavery is attributed to Southern politician John C. Calhoun in 1838.[11] Calhoun began his political career as a House of Representatives member from the state of South Carolina in 1810. Over the course of his political career, he would serve as secretary of state, secretary of war, US senator, and vice president in the administrations of both John Quincy Adams and Andrew Jackson, although he resigned from Jackson's administration with only a few months left in his term. A career politician, warmonger, and avid defender of slavery, Calhoun described the peculiar institution as a safeguard against another bloody war, suggesting, "A mysterious Providence had brought together two races, from different portions of the globe, and placed them together in nearly equal numbers in the Southern portion of this Union. . . . Under no other relation could they co-exist together. To destroy it was to involve a whole region in slaughter, carnage, and desolation; and, come what will, we must defend and preserve it."[12] In short time, the term *peculiar institution* became widespread, as it became a shorthand for a perspective on slavery that recast plantations as Southern "communities" that contributed to the stability of the economy and the union. Far from harmonious as Calhoun repeatedly described it, plantations depended on violence and intimacy to maintain order, and gender and sexuality were critical domains for the exercise of planter control.[13]

Anti-slavery writers and orators often appealed to gender norms to make a case against racial slavery. In addition to condemning the moral and economic reasons proffered by slavery's supporters, abolitionist arguments focused on the implications of disallowing and invalidating marriages between the enslaved. In 1835, for example, antislavery orator and writer Reverend David Root defined slavery's impact on the enslaved in terms of reducing "them to the necessity of universal concubinage, by denying to them the civil rights of marriage; thus breaking up the dearest relations of life and encouraging universal prostitution."[14] In Root's formulation, marriage is positioned as a response to the ways slavery rendered the enslaved as sexually available and violable. Continuing his line of thought, Root also suggests that slavery works "[t]o set up between parents and childeren [*sic*] an authority higher than the impulse of nature and the laws of God; which breaks up the authority of the father over his offspring, and at pleasure separates the mother at a return less distance from her child; thus abrogating the dearest laws of nature; thus outraging all decency and justice, and degrading and oppressing thousands upon thousands of beings created like themselves in the image of the Most High God."[15] In framing fatherly authority as a "law of nature," Root makes more evident that for some abolitionists, opposing slavery was part of a larger platform to ensure men's rights. As abolitionist Charles K. Whipple wrote, in 1858, "It is the obvious duty as well as the right of a husband to provide for the defence, and security, and comfort, and happiness of his wife. But slavery not only disregards this duty and this right, but undertakes to reverse them."[16] By this logic, "slavery both removed the natural rights of men, and perverted the sexuality of those in slavery, depicting [. . .] enslaved men as victims."[17] Slavery was certainly a key context for defining gender in racial terms, but such claims about perversion—organized around a patriarchal idealization of masculinity and heterosexual norms—barely scratched the surface of the various ways gender and sexuality were put to use during the time of slavery.

Heteronormative and patriarchal sentiments expressed in anti-slavery arguments, such as the ones mentioned directly above, also obscured how gender and sexuality mediated the distinction between blackness and whiteness in free as well as slaving states and territories. Harriett E. Wilson's autobiographical novel, *Our Nig; or, Sketches from the Life of a Free Black* (1859) offers a window into how amalgamation, which in the nineteenth century typically referred to interracial sexual contact, posed a threat to idealizations of white femininity.[18] *Our Nig* follows the life of the protagonist, Frado, a working-class Black woman living in antebellum New England. It portrays how gender and race were deeply entangled concepts that produced different experiences of gender for Black and white women. The protagonist's mother, a poor white woman whose offspring, according to the one-drop rule—a legal statute dating back to 1662—defined her mixed-race children as Black, is socially ostracized. To support her family, Frado becomes an indentured servant at six years old. She is subject to physical, emotional, and psychological abuse at the hands of the mistresses of the Bellmont estate where she is employed. Black feminist scholar Patrice D. Douglass describes the implications of Mrs. Bellmont's treatment of Frado when she writes:

> As Mrs. Bellmont grooms Mary [her daughter] for proper womanhood, the aesthetic presentation of Frado is stripped to racially mark their distinctive sexualities. Frado may understand the removal of her hair and tattered garments as reducing her to "anything but an enticing object"; however, Mrs. Bellmont is knowingly conditioning her as a particular type of sexually available object, an irrefutable Black female. As such, as a condition of her service, Frado was ordered to darken her skin, where "no matter how powerful the heat . . . she was never permitted to shield her skin from the sun." The intention behind this order was clear: "she was not many shades darker than Mary now," thus the Blackening of Frado was an imposition upon her gender and sexual capacity.[19]

To highlight the difference between white women and free Black (and mixed-race) women, Mrs. Bellmont creates the circumstances through which Frado is visually marked and treated as a foil to her daughter Mary's developing femininity. Though free, Frado is marked by racial slavery's visualizing paradigm and subjected to forms of psychic and material violence to ensure that she is excluded from social participation as a white (or white-presenting) woman.

Sexuality is never not an expression of power, and the articulation of sexuality in antebellum America also made erotic contact between European settlers and Africans at best a transactional affair. Mediated through sex work and embedded in the underpinnings of slavery, interracial erotic contact was often figured in financial terms. The racist trope of Africans as sexually available and hypersexual shaped how Black people's bodies and sexualities were perceived. Sexual violence was an ordinary feature of slavery, as enslavers sought complete control over enslaved people's lives. The trans-Atlantic and domestic slave trade produced racialized and gendered ways of viewing the enslaved according to their sexual availability and reproductive capacities. Far from a purely financial affair, the slave trade was also a mechanism for enslavers to obtain people for their sexual gratification. As literary critic Aliyyah Abdur-Rahman argues, one could regard rape as a metaphor for slavery, wherein "the vulnerability of all enslaved black persons to nearly every conceivable violation produced a collective 'raped' subjectivity."[20]

While being vulnerable to sexualized power was an indiscriminate feature of the lives of the enslaved, it differed in its application. Enslaved women and men were frequently coerced into sexual contact in so-called "breeding" programs. Enslaved women's reproductive capacities also made them vulnerable to rape by their enslavers, overseers, or slave drivers. Any children who resulted from these abusive, coercive practices would become additional property for the enslaver. Infant mortality among the enslaved was high due to malnutrition, over-exhaustion, and other hazardous conditions of pregnancy and childbirth. In terms of the legal records of these abuses, historian Emily Owens describes the significance of the use of the word *cruel* in antebellum Louisianian courts, arguing that the term is best understood as legal jargon to refer to cases that include sexual violence. As Owens also explains, any legal disputes that referred to the violation of the enslaved were framed in terms of the enslavers' "damage to property, or was a question of who was entitled to inflict harm, rather than a question of the limits of violence."[21]

Although accounts of sexual coercion between enslavers and the enslaved are often framed in terms of property, the ideology of one person possessing and exerting total control over another underlines how sexual vulnerability and violability shaped the lives of enslaved people. Rape, mutilation, including the castration of males, and other forms of sexual torture were used as punishments. Enslaved people could be punished with or without "cause," and for those recaptured, there were no bounds on what kind of physical and sexual abuse they might endure.[22] Historian Thomas Foster describes why the rape and sexual violation of enslaved men has largely been underarticulated in historical accounts. Sexual abuse by male enslavers of enslaved men did not produce offspring and consequently was less traceable. This is also true of any nonreproductive coercive sexual acts in antebellum America. Contact between mistresses and enslaved women is virtually absent in historical accounts. The racial stereotyping of enslaved men as hypersexual also obscured their vulnerability and violability. As

Foster explains, "For centuries, our culture has tended to view rape in archetypal ways as the violent sexual assault of a white woman by a stranger, most often a man of color and/or lower status. The early American legal system established sexual assault as a gendered crime, one that by definition covered only free women. In application of the law, its coverage was even narrower, with biases, especially along lines of race and status, influencing outcomes."[23]

White women were viewed as passive subjects in need of protection. Historian Stephanie E. Jones-Rogers explains how British law and the colonial and, later, state statutes, which took it as their model, largely rendered white women's sexual predation invisible. As Jones-Rogers argues,

> Contrary to what many historians have presumed, enslaved people defined sexual violence in ways that moved well beyond the male perpetrator/female victim paradigm. When they talked about these acts, they very deliberately included white women in their remembrances. Enslaved people focused on white women's complicity in and acceptance of white men's sexual violation of their bodies. They spoke of white women's physical violence against them for refusing to relent to white men's sexual violations. And on rare occasions, they described white women's potentially coercive sexual relations with enslaved men and their initiation of and involvement in incidents of forced breeding.[24]

Harriet Jacobs provides a textured account of the pervasiveness of sexual violence during slavery, including incidents of white women's complicity with sexual violence and sexual abuse between male enslavers and enslaved men. Self-published under the pseudonym Linda Brent in 1861, *Incidents in the Life of a Slave Girl* was initially regarded by scholars as a work of fiction until more of the author's life was borne out by archival evidence. In describing the sexual terror she experienced at the hands of her enslavers, Dr. and Mrs. Flint, Jacobs recounts how her white mistress could neither offer her protection nor seem to believe that Jacobs was worthy of it. Driven by jealousy, anger, and suspicion, Mrs. Flint initiated a series of schemes to trick Jacobs into a false confession of a sexual relationship with the doctor, requiring her to recount every detail of his sexual advances under oath and threat of spiritual damnation. Mrs. Flint would also speak to Jacobs in the middle of the night as if she was her husband, the doctor, to see how Jacobs might respond. Eventually, Mrs. Flint confronted her husband, Dr. Flint, in Jacobs's presence, falsely alleging that Jacobs had accused him of sexual predation. Of the mistress, Jacobs summates, "She pitied herself as a martyr; but she was incapable of feeling for the condition of shame and misery in which her unfortunate, helpless slave was placed."[25]

In the penultimate chapter of *Incidents*, Jacobs relays the story of Luke, an enslaved man with whom she was "somewhat acquainted."[26] When Luke was inherited by his enslaver's disabled son, he became the son's primary caretaker. Jacobs describes Luke's new enslaver as "prey to the vices growing out of the 'patriarchal institution'" and "deprived of the use of his limbs, by excessive dissipation. . . . whose despotic habits were greatly increased by exasperation at his own helplessness."[27] As Abdur-Rahman explains, "The vice to which this passage alludes is the young master's homosexuality which, it is important to note, is not treated here as sexual orientation or as an identity that is natural to him. Instead, the master's homosexual inclinations are attributed to the extreme wealth of his family and the unbounded freedom of white masculine privilege."[28]

Jacobs refers to the sexual dimensions of Luke's abuse, including how he was whipped daily "for the most trivial occurrence" and some days "not allowed to wear any thing [*sic*] but his shirt, in order to be in readiness to be flogged."[29] Relaying such details as Luke's lower bodily exposure and that her last memory of Luke before she escaped slavery was of him chained to the son's bedside are examples of what Jacobs describes as "the strangest freaks of despotism."[30] Even as she describes these sadomasochistic scenes of Luke's sexualized domination, Jacobs also writes about her own practice of redaction, describing certain details "too filthy to be repeated."[31] This account of Luke's abuse "reveals the cultural practices and psychic maneuvers by which domination created and carried on in slavery helped to shape white American identity in the US."[32] Here the master's race, gender, class, disability, and sexuality contribute to and are shaped by the culture of slavery. As Abdur-Rahman further explains, "Through the young master's rigorous disavowal of his dependence on and desire for his male slave—facilitated by the predominant cultural practice of denying dependence and projecting illicit desires onto black bodies—Luke's own body becomes the site and sign of his master's (homo)sexuality."[33]

*Incidents* also gives other examples of the erotic lifeworld of the enslaved, which, while circumscribed by slavery, was not completely subsumed by slavery's operations of sexualized power. Jacobs describes a romantic relationship with a free Black man willing to purchase her freedom and her later taking on a white lover, with whom she had a child. Of the white lover, Jacobs describes their sexual relationship as a "deliberate calculation." She relates, "It seems less degrading to give one's self, than to submit to compulsion. There is something akin to freedom in having a lover who has no control over you, except that which he gains by kindness and attachment."[34] If choosing a lover becomes a way to experience an approximation of freedom under slavery's regime of bodily control, as Jacobs suggests, how did Black queer erotics figure into and against slavery's regime of violent intimacy? How did enslaved people find ways of expressing queer intimate connection? And what are the implications of this?

### BLACK QUEER EROTICS, SPIRITUALITY, AND IMAGINING FREEDOM AS SEXUAL PRACTICE

Scholar and activist Gloria Wekker's study of mati women in Suriname highlights how sexuality can also be a practice of preserving African traditions, beliefs, and ways of knowing. For Wekker, Black sexuality is an "orientation to reality . . . more or less colored by the cultural heritage from Africa."[35] In her research, Wekker details how mati relationships diverge from lesbianism in several important ways. Mati women form intimate relationships and build kin networks with people, regardless of gender, and these social bonds are tied to a communal sense of financial well-being. Noting that matisma is sociocentric, such that the social group is revered over the individual, Wekker underscores how matters of gender and sexuality make and reflect the social worlds in which they are lived. Mati practices are linked with the Surinamese religion Winti, a syncretization of multiple African religions. Among Winti practitioners, personhood is viewed as a combination of different gendered beings and environmental elements. Mati sexuality and erotic practices are regarded as manifestations of differently gendered gods, or winti, who act as the matis' guardian angels and call forth desire for, jealousy of, or repulsion for other people. Matis' understandings of their romantic relationships and kin networks also makes evident how, for some queer people in the African diaspora, gender and sexuality are more about practice—spiritual and otherwise—than identity.

The distinction between practice-based and identity-based understandings of gender and sexuality is also a key concern for anyone interested in locating queer and trans presence in the past. Before or without a modern language of gender and sexuality, and without a record organized to preserve it, something akin to Black queer life surely must have existed. These concerns have been taken up fulsomely by creative writers, who offer rich portraits of Black queer sexual practices in antebellum America. Often fusing fantasy with the neo–slave narrative genre, Black queer writers invite their readers to imagine alternative frameworks for the experience of erotic contact among the enslaved. For example, Jewelle Gomez's *The Gilda Stories* (1991) follows a Black lesbian vampire across three centuries of American life.[36] By beginning the book in 1850 Louisiana, Gomez explains that she sought to write "a character who escapes from her deep sense of helplessness as a slave and gains the ultimate power over life and death. She becomes a witness over time to the injustices that humans visit upon one [an]other."[37] Readers are introduced to the Girl—as she is called before she becomes a vampire and takes the name of one of her makers—just after she has escaped enslavement in Mississippi and evaded assault by killing an overseer. Found by a white woman who is the madam of a brothel and a vampire, the Girl is both intrigued and unsure of the woman's intentions. In an early scene in the novel, as the Girl begins to realize that she and the woman, named Gilda, can communicate without language, the protagonist begins to assess the vampire's ways of being: "Her face was painted in colors like a mask, but she wore men's breeches and a heavy jacket."[38]

> The Girl thought for a moment: This is a man! A little man! Gilda laughed out loud at the idea in the Girl's head and said, "No, I'm

a woman." Then without speaking aloud she said, "I am a woman, you know that. And you know I am a woman as no other you have known, nor has your mother known, in life or death. I am a woman as you are, and more."[39]

More than a scene of misrecognition, Gomez describes how the construct of gender is shaped by colonial understandings of race and sexuality. Gilda's response, "I am a woman as you are," speaks to the disparaged claim of womanhood for Black women and lesbians, underscoring how both categories were excluded from the symbolic parameters of proper femininity.

Set eleven years before the advent of the American Civil War, the Girl comes of age in a Louisiana brothel, becoming an assistant and companion to Bird, an Indigenous woman and vampire. Bird teaches the Girl to read and to speak multiple languages, and when the first Gilda chooses the true death, Bird completes the ritual to make the Girl a vampire as well, who is then called Gilda. Bird and the Girl/Gilda attempt to preserve their heritages, both of which are put under active erasure. Intimacy finds expression in the novel through teaching and learning from each other, in scenes where they are called upon to protect one another and the others they love, and in erotic congress. Across the span of the novel, the Girl/Gilda takes numerous female lovers—a selfish white vampire named Elanor, a Black civil rights activist named Aurelia, and an elder Black vampire named Effie. Across two centuries, the Girl/Gilda comes into community—queer and vampire, often unspoken—which is also her way of coming into herself. *The Gilda Stories* imagines Black lesbianism before such language existed. Here practice precedes identity, as practice informs and shapes how identity is articulated and lived over time.

Robert Jones Jr.'s *The Prophets* combats the archival erasure of Black queer life by, in the words of Patrice Douglass, "rendering plausible and possible a scenario of love that was written out of existence by the power and violence of archival telling."[40] Set on a fictional plantation in Mississippi, the story centers on Isaiah and Samuel, two enslaved men and field hands who find temporary refuge in and with each other. Readers are brought into their romantic plot as they read the interior ruminations of the two men, which, in addition to their reflections and the implications of their desire for one another, offer a stark contrast to the way their lives are marked by commodification, exploited labor, and a refusal of their humanity. An early scene in the novel brings queer erotics to the foreground, as Isaiah and Samuel find a clandestine moment with each other in the haystacks. The history of their sexual contact offers another way of thinking about how time occurs on the plantation. As Jones writes:

> It was different from the first kiss—how many seasons ago was that now; sixteen or more? It was easier to count those than the moons, which sometimes didn't show up because they could be temperamental like that. Isaiah remembered that it was when the apples had been fuller and redder than they had ever been before or since—where they stumbled, and shame had kept them from looking into each other's eyes. Now Isaiah moved in close and let his lips linger on Samuel's. Samuel recoiled only a little. His uncertainty had found cover beneath repetition. The struggle that had once made him want to choke Isaiah as much as his self was in remission. There were only traces of it now, insignificant battles in the far corners of his eyes, maybe a smidgen at the back of his throat. But it was overcome by other things.[41]

Anchored by touch and the seasons, Isaiah's internal reflections on time trace the development in intimacy between his lover and himself. Shame, misrecognition, exhaustion, ambivalence, and ecstasy appear in the interior moments of this intimate scene. Jones invites his readers to imagine not only how Black queer erotics could occur between the enslaved but also how such clandestine encounters are themselves a form of resistance to the plantocratic ideal of total control. As the title suggests, *The Prophets* places Black queer sexuality in relation to African spirituality. Isaiah and Samuel are descendants of the Kosongo people, known for their gender fluidity. Queer sexuality—though not named as such—becomes an African inheritance and a way of maintaining and preserving a heritage, which has been caricatured, criminalized, and otherwise put under erasure. Like Jacobs's reminiscences in *Incidents*, *The Prophets* attends to some of the erotic actions, or what Jacobs calls "deliberate calculations," that enslaved people took in relation to their sexual vulnerability.

As Jacobs described it, to choose not to submit to compulsion is to find something akin to freedom. By focusing on the erotic lives of the enslaved in neo–slave narratives, Black queer authors provide opportunities to think about how enslaved people made use of gender and sexuality as forms of resistance, whether in finding clandestine opportunities for reunion or in making different meanings for themselves about how they relate to their bodies. Fictional characters like Gilda, Isaiah, and Samuel invite us to imagine a more complicated terrain of sexual expression for the enslaved, not only in terms of their erotic practices but in terms of the un- and under-documented vastness of their interior worlds.

### CONCLUSION

Colonial and early American concepts of race, gender, and sexuality developed in relation to Puritanical and Christian norms, racial slavery, and settler colonialism. Sodomy laws and the criminalization of homosexuality in the colonies and in the colonial militia, which were established in 1714, were not abolished until 1925. Even as homosexuality was illegal and socially condemned in colonial and antebellum America, racial slavery provided a cover for enslavers to attempt to exercise total control over the people they enslaved. Harriet Jacobs's description of Luke's sexual abuse and torture at the hands of his enslaver is but one example of how queerness was projected onto blackness in the context of the violent intimacies permissible on the plantation.

Records of Black queer expression in early America are linked to the preservation of African heritage, as with mati relationships forged in the hold of the ship, and to other forms of survival, financial and otherwise. To highlight narratives of Black queer erotic contact, we turned to neo–slave narratives to address the problem of the archive. Through fiction, Black queer writers in the twentieth and twenty-first centuries bring forward textured accounts of Black queer erotics in relation to spirit, embodied practices, and limited expressions of autonomy.

Racial slavery yoked Black gender and sexuality with deviance, and in the next chapter, we continue to focus on the legacies of slavery and resistance that informed Black queer and trans ways of living at the twilight of slavery and into the twentieth century.

### CHAPTER TWO

# BY ANY OTHER NAME

When fifteen-year-old Ann Maria Weems fled her enslavers in Washington, DC, she did so as a coachman named Joe Wright, steering the horses of a white doctor's carriage to freedom. According to abolitionist William Still's account,

> The doctor's horse and carriage stood waiting before the White House. . . . It being understood that 'Joe' was to act as coachman in passing out of Washington, at this moment he was called for, and in the most polite and natural manner, with the fleetness of a young deer, he jumped into the carriage, took the reins and whip, whilst the doctor and William Penn [an alias of another Underground Railroad operator] were cordially shaking hands and bidding adieu. This done, the order was given to Joe, 'drive on.' Joe bravely obeyed.[1]

Wright, after posing as the servant of the abolitionist doctor on the multiday trip from DC to Philadelphia, arrived at Still's home on Thanksgiving in 1855. William Still, known to have assisted nearly one thousand enslaved people in his work with the Philadelphia Anti-Slavery Society, self-published the accounts of over one hundred fugitives "determined to have liberty even at the cost of life" in *The Underground Railroad* (1872).[2] In the preface, Still notes the different ways those in pursuit of freedom "disguised in female attire" or "dressed in the garb of men" to escape their enslavers, including the stories of Weems/Wright in 1855; Clarissa Davis of Virginia, alias

Mary D. Armstead, in 1854; and William and Ellen Craft, who fled by train respectively as slave and master in 1848.

The frequency with which fugitives crossed gender to escape enslavement shows that gender is varied and changeable. Of Weems's/Wright's appearance, Still writes, "Indeed it was difficult to realize that she was not a boy, even after becoming acquainted with the facts of the case."[3] Weems/Wright would eventually land in the Buxton Settlement in Ontario, Canada, where she reconnected with her family. It is unclear who Weems/Wright may have loved or desired, and we know little to nothing about how Weems felt about living as Joe Wright while secreted away in DC or on their voyage to Philadelphia. Similarly, Still's description of Clarissa Davis's epic fugitive tale, which included hiding from slave catchers for seventy-five days before stowing away in a crate on a boat headed north, provides so few details of her masculine persona that we do not even know his name.

Racial slavery in the United States was, among many things, a peculiarly visual institution, structuring ways of seeing Black people as fugitive or enslaved but rarely as free. The numerous policies to facilitate and control slavery—the Fugitive Slave Act of 1793, the Act Prohibiting the Importation of Slaves of 1808, the Compromise of 1820, also referred to as the Missouri Compromise, to name a few, did not deter enslaved people from resisting, whether by rebelling against their enslavers, running away, or through daily acts of slowing work down on the plantation. Whether free or enslaved, Black people lived with the threat of capture. As a vast network of anti-slavery intelligence, the Underground Railroad was built with letters and telegraph wires, word of mouth, encoded messages and carefully compiled records, railroad tracks, steamship lines, and country roads with routes that went north to free states and Canada, south to the Caribbean and Mexico, and west into the United States' western territories and Native territories. Fugitives made use of an array of strategies to move toward freedom, including obscuring or changing their appearance to avoid the detection of their enslavers or slave catchers.

Literally and figuratively, racial slavery altered the conditions with which gender was represented, perceived, and lived, by radically defining Black personhood as property and as according to an individual's capacity to reproduce capital. The brutality of slavery lessened gendered distinctions between captives, as all enslaved people were measured according to the value they could produce for their enslavers. Black feminist literary critic Hortense Spillers coined the term *ungendering* to explain how gender for the enslaved might be understood more in terms of a "territory of cultural and political maneuver" under such conditions.[4] As gender for the enslaved eluded strict biological definition and determinism, for fugitives it became a strategy or tool to navigate lethal oversight.

Although there are archival traces of nineteenth-century historical figures existing at the same time as Weems/Wright who more closely align with modern conceptions of transness, such as Mary Jones of New York and Frances Thompson of Memphis, Tennessee, this chapter focuses on the frequency with which people made use of gender, race, and other (unstable) categories of social difference in antebellum America to move through and grasp beyond confinement. While we are unable to verify historical expressions of gender and sexual variation in presentist terms, this chapter discusses how Black queer and trans historical figures have taken on alternative identities to survive the racial, gender, and sexual regulations imposed on them. These regulations and violent prohibitions were frequently expressed and maintained by making recourse to the visual logics and markers of race, gender, and sex.

Scientific racism, the law, and dominant culture cast Black people, free or enslaved, as incompatible with white gender and sexual ideals. The archives under discussion here bear this trace, and this chapter highlights the implications of narratively conscripting historical figures into heterosexual and patriarchal norms. We are equally committed to asking different questions of the archives and to demonstrating how identity itself changes over time. Rather than focusing on narratives that feel more resonant with modern understandings of transness or queerness, we draw attention to the porosity of sexuality and gender as social categories and also highlight how Black historical figures developed strategies of gender and sexual transgression in pursuit of freedom. In this sense, no word or term can name and contain the politics and practices of racialized gender and sexuality.

The first section discusses examples of cross-gender performance and identification in the twilight of formal slavery and explores the mutability of gender for enslaved people, including Ellen Craft, who escaped to freedom with her husband by appearing as his master, and Cathay Williams/William Cathay, whose military record includes service as a girl and as a man. While queerness and transness in our modern idiom are focused on an internal sense of different or variant sexual and gender understanding, this chapter thinks through how structural conditions and ideologies produce "queerness" and "transness" as ways of navigating limitations. "By Any Other Name" also outlines how impulses to name and contain Black desire—between enslaved Africans, slaves and their masters, and slaves and abolitionists; and between Black women in the first half of the twentieth century—have factored into broader contestations over the meanings of blackness, gender, and sexuality in the United States.

The chapter then moves forward to the mid-twentieth century to situate dancer and actress Josephine Baker, whose public bisexuality masked her own ambivalence about queer sexualities. We read Baker alongside Black lesbian playwright Lorraine Hansberry and the broader global struggles against fascism, white supremacy, and Jim Crow segregation. For Hansberry, even as civil rights–era political visions did not allow her to openly express same-sex desire, she used a pseudonym to maintain correspondence in *The Ladder*, a publication of the early lesbian rights organization Daughters of Bilitis, and in other lesbian literary and political outlets, underscoring how her dedication to freedom struggles included struggles for gender and sexual freedom.

### CRAFTING FREEDOM WITH (UN)GENDER

In a published letter to William Lloyd Garrison, William Wells Brown recounts the four-day journey of Ellen and William Craft's escape from Macon, Georgia, in the most widely circulated anti-slavery newspaper from 1831 to 1865, *The Liberator*. In this first printed account of the fugitive tale, Ellen Craft receives considerable and, according to Black feminist scholar Daphne Brooks, unprecedented attention as "an equally heroic counterpart to that of her husband."[5] Although Brown's version of the Crafts' narrative would receive greater elaboration in subsequent retellings, the tone set in the letter remains consequential to how audiences interpret what Brown described as "one of the most interesting cases of the escape of fugitives from American slavery."[6]

> Here is a wonderful case—read it!
> PINEVILLE, (Pa.) Jan. 4, 1849.
> DEAR FRIEND GARRISON:

One of the most interesting cases of the escape of fugitives from American slavery that have ever come before the American people, has just occurred, under the following circumstances:—William and Ellen Crapt [*sic*], man and wife, lived with different masters in the State of Georgia. Ellen is so near white, that she can pass without suspicion for a white woman. Her husband is much darker. He is a mechanic, and by working nights and Sundays, he laid up money enough to bring himself and his wife out of slavery. Their plan was without precedent; and though novel, was the means of getting them their freedom. Ellen dressed in man's clothing, and passed as the master, while her husband passed as the servant. In this way they travelled from Georgia to Philadelphia. They are now out of the reach of the blood-hounds of the South. On their journey, they put up at the best hotels where they stopped. Neither of them can read or write. And Ellen, knowing that she would be called upon to write her name at the hotels, &c., tied her right hand up as though it was lame, which proved of some service to her, as she was called upon several times at hotels to 'register' her name. In Charleston, S. C., they put up at the hotel which Gov. M'Duffie and John C. Calhoun generally make their home, yet these distinguished advocates of the 'peculiar institution' say that the slaves cannot take care of themselves. They arrived in Philadelphia, in four days from the time they started. Their history, especially that of their escape, is replete with interest. They will be at the meeting of the Massachusetts Anti-Slavery Society, in Boston, in the latter part of this month, where I know the history of their escape will be listened to with great interest. They are very intelligent. They are young, Ellen 22, and Wm. 24 years of age. Ellen is truly a heroine.

> Yours, truly,
> WM. W. BROWN.

Here Brown makes use of *pass*—to refer to a false performance of identity—three times to describe the Crafts' fugitive passage, referring to Ellen as "so near white, that she can pass without suspicion for a white woman." Passing would become a recurring refrain in subsequent narrations of the Crafts' escape, and Ellen's complexion as "near white" became a focal point for abolitionists, journalists, and scholars. Ellen's color aired the taboo of miscegenation, as it also underscored the frequent occurrence of sexual violence for those held in captivity. Brown's letter to Garrison consists of three descriptive remarks about William Craft: his complexion, his "pass[ing] as the servant," and his illiteracy at the time.

As an anti-slavery orator and the author of *Running a Thousand Miles for Freedom*, William would become a pivotal, if not the primary, source on the details of their escape. According to his account, "Notwithstanding my wife being of African extraction on her mother's side, she is almost white—in fact, she is so nearly so that the tyrannical old lady to whom she first belonged became so annoyed, at finding her frequently mistaken for a child of the family . . . [that she] gave her when eleven years of age to a daughter, as a wedding present." Before their escape, Ellen was held captive by her half-sister, Eliza Collins, for whom Ellen acted as a "ladies' maid."

The difference in color between William and Ellen provides a possible explanation for her cross-gendered escape. Although she may have been expected to make use of her appearance as a white woman, her coupling with William would have brought greater scrutiny and surveillance during their fugitive journey. The legal and social prohibitions against interracial relationships, romantic or otherwise—particularly for white mistresses—was a compelling rationale for Ellen's gender transformation. This is not to imply that the appearance of homosocial interracial couplings should be understood as absent of sexual activity. As Black feminist literary critic Aliyyah Abdur-Rahman argues, slavery's "economies of desire and sexuality . . . provided a cover under which aberrant sexuality flourished . . . [as] the institution granted to all whites—slaveholders and non-slaveholders—the full-fledged legal right and unchecked personal authority to exploit, consume, and destroy the slave's psyche and body in whatever ways they chose."[7] As we discussed in the previous chapter, same-sex sexual violence and abuse was ubiquitous in antebellum America, as sexuality between whites and enslaved people often functioned as another mode of domination and control.

There are significant differences across the numerous accounts of the Crafts' fugitive passage. In her retelling in *Biography of an American Bondman*, Josephine Brown describes how Ellen conceived of the entire plan, formulating each aspect of their fugitive plot in response to William's skeptical questions.[8] Ellen proposed to cut her hair and wear men's clothes—high-heeled boots, a top hat, a covering about her mouth, a sling for her right arm, and binding around her right hand—in order to present herself as Mr. William Johnson, a "most respectable-looking gentleman."[9] *Biography of an American Bondman* includes nearly every detail of Ellen Craft's sartorial plan to become William Johnson except for a pair of green spectacles that would later be seen in the engraved portrait and frontispiece of *Running a Thousand Miles for Freedom*. Brown's depiction contradicts William Craft's later claim of authorship over the plan. In his account, published four years after Brown's, William credits himself with conceiving their elaborate plan for escape and then describes how he had to convince his wife to join him in his detailed plot. In reference to the discrepancy between Brown's and Craft's accounts, historian Barbara McCaskill argues that William's revision of the narrative "stands as an example of how Black abolitionists often wrote formerly enslaved Africans into conventional gender roles."[10]

This practice has consequential implications, as it demonstrates how heterosexual norms distorted the record of lived experiences of slavery and abolitionist practice. It also points to the severe limitations under which a Black queer history could unfold from the existent archives. In the case of the Crafts, it naturalizes and confirms the couple within a heteropatriarchal frame. Not only *Running* but also William Wells Brown's initial letter and Still's account function to secure the Crafts' status as husband and wife, against the legal and social ways that their marriage could be revoked due to their status as fugitive slaves. The use of conventional gender roles as a plot device suppresses the violence of captivity and downplays the creative and inventive ways fugitives crafted freedom with (un)gender, as an available tool. Relatedly, the heteronorming of fugitive narratives mitigates the reality that Black freedom is often expressed in terms of gender and sexuality.

William and Ellen Craft were legally married in Boston within months of the passage of the Fugitive Slave Law of 1850. Whether it was their original plan or a response to the new legislation, the Crafts fled to Canada and then to the United Kingdom where they lived in exile for nineteen years. Of England, William Craft described feeling "free from every slavish fear." In 1870 the Crafts returned to Georgia to teach and to continue locating family members lost in the domestic slave trade. Ellen Craft was buried in 1891 under her favorite tree on the Woodville Plantation in the town later renamed Richmond Hill, Georgia. William died in 1900 at their daughter's Charleston, South Carolina, home and was buried there at the Humane and Friendly Society Cemetery. There is no record of what Ellen felt about living in the world as William Johnson, besides references to her fear of being discovered. The lack of materials to address this question gestures toward the ways a Black queer history requires a different way of seeing the past. We find it important to ask these questions, even as there are no easy or accessible answers. In many ways, asking these sorts of questions of historical figures in this period produces more questions about the nature of archives and the function of history.

Nowhere is this more apparent than in the example of Private William Cathay, who on November 15, 1866, at twenty-two years old, enlisted with two companions in the US Army in St. Louis, Missouri.[11] Described by the recruiting officer as five feet, nine inches tall, with black eyes, hair, and complexion, Cathay was assigned to Company A of the Thirty-Eighth Infantry, one of several battalions of buffalo soldiers tasked with protecting settlers, controlling the Native population of the plains, capturing cattle rustlers and thieves, and guarding stagecoaches, wagon trains, and railroad crews along the Western front. Like all new recruits, Cathay was subject to a medical exam upon entry and declared by the examining surgeon to be "free from all bodily defects and mental infragility, which would, in any way, disqualify him from performing the duties of a soldier."[12] By all historical accounts, William Cathay's just under two years of military service was unremarkable. His company never saw direct battle, and rheumatism and neuralgia caused Cathay to spend several months in the infirmary. As a soldier, he was never signal out for praise or punishment, but Cathay is invariably named in military histories as the first Black woman to serve in the US Army.

In a firsthand account to the *St. Louis Daily Times* published in 1876, Cathay explained how illnesses framed their service, beginning with smallpox contracted shortly after enlisting. "[F]inally," Cathay professed, "I got tired and wanted to get off. I played sick, complained of pains in my side, and rheumatism in my knees. The post surgeon found out I was a woman and I got my discharge. The men all wanted to get rid of me after they found out I was a woman. Some of them acted real bad to me."[13] On October 14, 1868, William Cathay and two other privates were discharged at Fort Bayard on a surgeon's certificate of disability. Cathay's certificate included statements from both the company captain and the post's assistant surgeon. The captain's statement read that Cathay, since under his command, "has been . . . feeble both physically and mentally, and much of the time quite unfit for duty. The origin of his infirmities is unknown to me." The surgeon's statement claimed Cathay was of "a feeble habit. He is continually on sick report without benefit. He is unable to do military duty. . . . This condition dates prior to enlistment."[14]

Both captain and surgeon's statements refer to an unknown prior cause or condition—a foreshadowing of Cathay's denied disability-benefits claim, which brought their life into public view. As told to the *St. Louis Daily Times*, Cathay began military service as a girl when they were "carried off" to Little Rock, Arkansas by Col. William Plummer Benton of the Thirteenth Army Corps. Born near Independence, Missouri, to an enslaved mother and a freeman, Cathay was conscripted into service as a cook after their enslaver died at the beginning of the Civil War. On the circumstances of the first term of service, they shared: "I did not want to go." Under Benton, Cathay traveled through various parts of Arkansas, Louisiana, and Georgia, and was eventually sent to Washington City where they served as a cook and launderer for General Sheridan and his staff, with whom Cathay continued to travel through Virginia and Iowa until stationed in Jefferson Barracks (in St. Louis, Missouri) for some time. From enslavement to military conscription and later service, the circumstances of Cathay's disabilities are also a record of their debilitating encounter with state power.

After being discharged, Cathay lived in New Mexico, then traveled to Fort Union and later to Pueblo and Trinidad, Colorado, while working intermittently as a cook or launderer. At some point in late 1889 or early 1890, Cathay was hospitalized in Trinidad for nearly a year and a half. As DeAnne Blanton explains, "She was probably indigent when she left the hospital, so she filed in June 1891 for an invalid pension based upon her military service."[15] The original application gave Cathay's age as forty-one and made reference to military service–related deafness, rheumatism, and neuralgia. In July, Cathay submitted a supplemental affidavit, which mentioned the case of smallpox contracted at the beginning of their service. On September 9, 1891, a medical doctor acting on behalf of the Pension Bureau described Cathay as "5'7, 160 pounds, large, stout, and 49 years of age." He reported that "she could hear a conversation, and therefore was not deaf and that there were no physical changes in her joints, muscles, or tendons to indicate rheumatism or neuralgia."[16] The doctor also noted that the complainant walked with the aid of a cane, as all ten toes had been amputated. The report did not indicate the cause of the amputations, whether because it was unasked for or unknown.

The use of female pronouns in the doctor's report marks the first usage in reference to William Cathay's military service. They would be repeated in February 1892, when the Pension Bureau rejected Cathay's claim on the grounds that no disability existed. Again, the gaps and silences in the archive produce more questions than answers, and here, as in elsewhere in our book, our commitment is to hold and bear witness to the complexities and seeming contradictions that constitute an archival trace of a person whose movements might be regarded as the means of their self-protection.

We know that Cathay went by William and also by the names Kate Williams, John Williams, James Cady, and William Cather; that Cathay was married and later separated; that they spent some time in asylums; and that they made a life in several frontier towns across the US Southwest. Descriptions of what happened to Cathay following their denied disability-benefits claim vary widely. Some hypothesize that Cathay lived just one year past their denied claim. Others suggest that they established a school or boarding house in Trinidad, Colorado, or in Raton, New Mexico. Although there have been two petitions and one exhumation, no one has been able to locate Cathay's remains yet. Some petitioners seek biological proof of Cathay's multi-gendered experience. Others may be motivated by the opportunity to bury and memorialize Cathay according to their military service. In either instance, finding Cathay's remains cannot restore our sense of their agency, but we can honor their inscrutable complexity as a form of trans critique and queer protest. Rather than make definitive claims about the gendered identifications and sexual desires of Black people in the nineteenth century, we have offered examples of how blackness gave different expressions to the terms with which gender and sexuality were defined.

### EXPRESSING THE "NATURE OF OUR EXISTENCE"

Between 1910 and 1970, millions of African Americans moved from the US South to Northern, Midwestern, and Western states during the Great Migration. Whether fleeing de jure segregation and racist violence or searching for more economic and social opportunities, Black people moved great distances in hopes of a better life. The density of the urban centers made queerness more visible, while class and educational status continued to segment Black experiences in cities like New York, Chicago, and Philadelphia. Blues and vaudeville performances became meeting grounds for queer Black and "slumming" white audiences, as blues singers Gladys Bentley, Ma Rainey, Bessie Smith, and Ethel Waters, and dancer Josephine Baker, among others, drew crowds at venues like the Clam House in Harlem or the Cabin Inn in the Bronzeville area of Chicago. Visibility and mobility posed major challenges for the performers themselves. Baker, who vowed never to play a segregated venue, found more permanent residence in Paris, while many Black artists and intellectuals traveled to Europe to find more temporary reprieve from Jim and Jane Crow and later de facto forms of racially and sexually organized discrimination, oppression, and violence.

Baker, born in 1906 in St. Louis, Missouri as Freda J. McDonald, would answer to many names in her life, such as Bronze Venus, Black Pearl, and the Creole Goddess. In her iconic performances of *La Revue Nègre* in 1927, wearing a skirt of sixteen bananas and a pearl necklace, Baker, also an activist and a World War II spy, danced before audiences in what some viewed as a skillfully executed parody of white heterosexual male fantasies. Documentarian Ilana Navaro, for example, notes that Baker "transformed bananas, the ultimate racist symbols, into phallic trophies."[17] Before her rise to international celebrity in Paris, Baker performed in New York cabarets and eventually on Broadway. It was the Roaring Twenties, and Black queer life was vibrant in Harlem. Baker described her bisexuality as natural, and she found both friends and lovers among the blues singers, writers, and socialites who all called New York, and particularly Harlem, their home.

As an entertainer and public figure, Baker and her many aliases describe her complex relationship to the beauty industry, European standards of beauty, and desirability politics more generally. Her complex inhabitation of international celebrity as a Black queer woman and sexual icon offers a way to interpret her famous declaration: "If I want to become a star, I have to be scandalous," where embracing scandal became a way to endure her hypervisibility.[18] Her notoriety was one of her greater assets, allowing her to gather information for the French resistance movement while socializing with her fans, which included members of the German, Japanese, and Italian governments.

In contrast to the narrative strategies surrounding the Crafts' escape, which often functioned to frame their relationship within the bounds of heteronormativity, Baker's public queerness served as a cover for her personal contradictions. She was romantically linked with numerous women, including the visual artist Frida Kahlo. She was also married four times. With her fourth husband, Jo Bouillon, who was also queer, she adopted twelve children from nations including Finland, Belgium, France, Japan, and Venezuela, and she called them her "rainbow tribe."[19] Baker trained her children to become entertainers and raised them in public, displaying them as proof of the possibility of multiracial harmony. However, when she learned that her fifteen-year-old son, Jarry, was gay, she chastised him in front of his siblings and sent him to live with her then estranged husband, Bouillon, in Buenos Aires, Argentina. While little is known about whether Baker and Jarry ever reconciled, he, along with his brother, Jean-Claude, established the Theater Row–area restaurant Chez Josephine in New York City in tribute to Baker's life. Baker fell onto hard financial times and eventually moved, with some of her children, from her adopted nation of France to a home in Monaco, provided by her friend and patron Princess Grace. Baker occasionally returned to the United States to perform, but maintained her commitment to never perform in a segregated venue.

At fifty-seven years old, Baker stood before more than a quarter-million people in Washington, DC, in the summer of 1963. Although civil rights activist Bayard Rustin had helped to plan the March on Washington for Jobs and Freedom, his criminalized sexuality was an issue for some of his heteronormative contemporaries, such that it disqualified him from a more visible and vocal position at the podium. Baker did not make any explicit reference to her sexuality in her speech. Meanwhile, some of Baker's artistic contemporaries, most notably Gladys Bentley, publicly disavowed their queer sexuality and married men. Bentley's marriage, as it was covered in the Black press, included images of the masculine performer in feminine clothes, performing a normative gender role.

The rise of McCarthyism in the 1940s and '50s squelched the furtive queer social possibilities of the 1920s, and yet even then, for Black LGBTQ people, the threat of criminalization and social stigma contributed to how queer networks were established, maintained, or destroyed. For Baker, the March on Washington was the largest audience of her career, and she was the only woman to speak, and she did so before the official start of the program.[20] Dressed in a French military uniform, Baker began with a childhood story of displacement.

> When I was a child and they burned me out of my home, I was frightened and I ran away. Eventually I ran far away. It was to a place called France. Many of you have been there, and many have not. But I must tell you, ladies and gentlemen, in that country I never feared. It was like a fairyland place.
>
> I am not a young woman now, friends. My life is behind me. There is not too much fire burning inside me. And before it goes out, I want you to use what is left to light that fire in you. So that you can carry on, and so that you can do those things that I have done. Then, when my fires have burned out, and I go where we all go someday, I can be happy.

You know I have always taken the rocky path. I never took the easy one, but as I get older, and as I knew I had the power and the strength, I took that rocky path, and I tried to smooth it out a little. I wanted to make it easier for you. I want you to have a chance at what I had. But I do not want you to have to run away to get it. And mothers and fathers, if it is too late for you, think of your children. Make it safe here so they do not have to run away, for I want for you and your children what I had.[21]

Between fugitivity and fire, Baker names the material conditions and emotional toll that contributed to her decision to move to Paris as a young artist. The fire that burned her childhood home is turned into an expression of passion or personal energy—a yearning to remove oneself from a scene of racial terror. Europe again, like with the Crafts, is referenced as a place that alleviates fear for its Black (fugitive) inhabitants. This claim serves a rhetorical function in addition to being a statement of opinion. The rocky path references Baker's personal trajectory and a more collective sense of the political stakes of making the path smoother and "easier" for future generations. Although her speech suggests that she saw herself at the twilight of her life, Baker lived until April 12, 1975, passing just days after performing in Paris in a celebration of the fiftieth anniversary of her famous revue. At her funeral, the French government honored her with a twenty-one-gun salute, making her the first American woman to receive military honors.

Known worldwide, Baker may have very well been a model for Black queer creatives who escaped the racist, sexist, and homophobic constraints of the US. In a commissioned but never printed *Time* magazine interview between Baker and James Baldwin, with Henry Louis Gates Jr. in 1973, she described the pros and cons of her expatriation over dinner at Baldwin's then home in St. Paul de Vence. The two Black queer expats reflected on the distinction between being seen in France and being surveilled by a Jim and Jane Crow apparatus in the states. One wonders if the conversation ever turned to Jimmy's dear friend, "Sweet Lorraine," who had died eight years prior of pancreatic cancer.

Baldwin called her "Sweet Lorraine," and Lorraine simply called him, "Jimmy." Lorraine Hansberry also made use of pen names, often initials, to write about her feminist commitments, romantic and sexual involvements with men and women, lesbian identity, and politics. Born into a well-to-do family in Chicago in 1930, she was described by Kevin Mumford as "a rebellious young woman from the city's African American elite."[22] She earned international acclaim for her first play, *A Raisin in the Sun*, which debuted on Broadway in 1959. As Imani Perry explains, while Hansberry was married to Robert (Bobby) Nemiroff from 1953 to 1964, Lorraine took female lovers throughout her adult life:

> Both Molly [Malone Cook] and Bobby [Nemiroff] were part of Lorraine's life as she wrote *Raisin*. But only one is known publicly. As the story goes, one evening in the summer of 1957, Lorraine shared the play she was working on with Philip Rose. She and Bobby hosted him in their apartment at 337 Bleecker Street. . . . After he had returned home, Rose called Lorraine and said he wanted to get the play to Broadway. It was a life-changing moment, and like many, one she shared with Bobby. The entanglement and intimacy, the way Bobby was a lifeline to her work, was unceasing, even as she was finding her way with lovers, including with Molly, who was her kindred spirit.[23]

With letters signed "L.H.N." [Lorraine Hansberry Nemiroff] and "L.N." [Lorraine Nemiroff], Hansberry also engaged in an exchange about the politics of her gender and sexual desires with a broader lesbian public. Using the initials L.N. in a letter addressed to the staff and fellow readers of *The Ladder*, a publication established by the lesbian rights organization Daughters of Bilitis—perhaps written within days of her fateful meeting with Rose—Hansberry wrote:

> I think it is about time that equipped women began to take on some of the ethical questions which a male-dominated culture has produced and dissect and analyze them quite to pieces in a serious fashion. It is time that "half the human race" had something to say about the nature of its existence. Otherwise—without revised basic thinking—the woman intellectual is likely to find herself trying to draw conclusions—moral conclusions—based on acceptance of a social moral superstructure which has never admitted to the

equality of women and is therefore immoral itself. As per marriage, as per sexual practices, as per the rearing of children, etc. in this kind of work there may be women to emerge who will be able to formulate a new and possible concept that homosexual persecution and condemnation has at its roots not only social ignorance, but a philosophically active anti-feminist dogma. But that is but a kernel of a speculative embryonic idea improperly introduced here.[24]

This was not Hansberry's first letter to *The Ladder*. She had begun writing months earlier, at about the time she separated from her husband, Robert Nemiroff, using the initials "L.H.N." In these letters, she expressed her gratitude for the publication's existence and asked what differences exist between the lesbian scenes in San Francisco, where the organization was based, and New York where, according to Hansberry, "a vigorous and active gay set almost bump one another off the streets."[25] Across her published letters in *The Ladder*, Hansberry weaves an analysis informed by both feminist and homophile movements and often references the Civil Rights Movement, drawing comparisons with their strategies, aims, and concerns.

Perhaps the use of initials was a strategy for opacity, or a way of shielding oneself from a regulatory gaze, but one could also speculate about other possible explanations. Was it an indication of the presumed audience for her writing? Perhaps it was an opportunity for her to express ambivalence about her multiple identities. In a list of people and things she liked and people and things she hated, dated April 1, 1960, Hansberry writes "my homosexuality" in both columns. Her list of likes also includes several references to Dorothy Secules, an executive at Loft Candy Company, with whom she maintained a romantic connection until her death. In addition to giving Secules's name, Hansberry mentions her eyes and the way she talks. Her embargoed diaries include more reflections on her loves, providing more texture to the lesbian social world Hansberry inhabited.[26] According to Perry, Hansberry's queer musings in her diaries accessed an emotional register not as present in her public-facing writings or even in her reflections on other aspects of her life.[27] And while one may see this as further evidence of a closeted life, the different registers of Hansberry's writing practices also indicate an irrepressible plurality of identities and a willingness to experiment with literary forms in articulating the nature of her existence.

### CONCLUSION

History is not the past but a way of narrating a given figure or event's relationship to time. Throughout this chapter, we sought to highlight how Black queer history is shaped by what is available and permissible—in the normative prose of William Craft, in the embargoed archive of Hansberry's queer musings, in the inscrutability of the variously named Cathay Williams. In some instances, an alias might open the door to a more narrowly defined queer world for a public figure. In others, new identities are forged to express a shifting sense of gender or sexuality over time. In the absence of present-day language, blackness and queerness shape these stories—often partial and conflicting, and testifying to Black and queer strategies of survival. The frequency with which Black queer people used new names and donned new identities to navigate the hostile world they faced also names the various ways Black queer people have found alternate geographies of freedom through formal experimentation at the level of personhood.

This chapter has focused on the fugitive practices of certain Black historical figures, presenting the context and implications of cross-gender performances of freedom. In the twentieth century, while their acts were no less fugitive, Black queer artists and their naming practices also indicated finding a mode of expression amid limitations. In most instances, a person's proliferation of names is related to a desire for opacity. In the next chapter, we discuss how the closet is a racial paradigm and attend to how, for Black people, the process of coming out has been more a collective action than a personal activity.

### CHAPTER THREE

# ON THE OUTS

The Harlem Renaissance, or New Negro Movement, was an African American arts movement anchored in the Harlem neighborhood of New York City. It peaked in the interwar years between 1923 and 1938 and was national and international in scope, encompassing literature, visual art, music, and theater. Though there was no clear theme unifying the diverse cultural works of the period, the movement was centrally concerned with the creation, meaning, and political ramifications of Black art. Racial politics were the primary focus of artists and intellectuals, but gender and sexual politics were also central to this movement. As literary scholar Henry Louis Gates Jr. famously claimed, the Harlem Renaissance was "surely as gay as it was black." Writer Richard Bruce Nugent was openly gay and included explicit themes of homosexuality and bisexuality in his fiction and visual art. Many artists who were not out or did not identify as gay, lesbian, or bisexual encoded homoeroticism in their works. Poet, novelist, playwright, and children's book author Countee Cullen was among the latter group of artists.

Cullen was a leading figure in the Harlem Renaissance. Though his birthplace is unknown, Cullen was born on May 30, 1903. Loss shaped his childhood. Cullen lost his parents and sibling at a young age and is believed to have been raised by his paternal grandmother in the years before her death. Reverend Franklin A. Cullen and his wife, Carolyn Belle, subsequently took him in. The pastor of the historic Salem Methodist Episcopal Church in Harlem, the Reverend Cullen gained notoriety within the African American community for his local mission work with Black youth and his support of civil rights activism. Raised among Harlem's elite, Cullen gained notoriety at a young age for his poetry, winning a citywide poetry competition while still in high school. He graduated Phi Beta Kappa from New York University in 1925, the same year he published his lauded collection, *Color.* He went on to obtain a master's degree at Harvard University in 1926. Subsequently, he joined the staff of the National Urban League's journal *Opportunity*, a platform that elevated Black literary voices like Langston Hughes, Zora Neale Hurston, Arna Bontemps, and Sterling A. Brown.

Because of his accomplishments and visibility, Cullen was counted among the "talented tenth" that W. E. B. Du Bois tasked with reforming the race. In his 1903 book, *The Negro Problem*, Du Bois popularized the concept of the talented tenth, coined by Henry Lyman Morehouse seven years earlier. Du Bois used the term to describe the "exceptional men" that would save the Negro race. The "Best of his race" would guide the Black masses "away from the contamination and death of the Worst."[1] Instead of the vocational-industrial education for newly freed African Americans proposed by public intellectual Booker T. Washington, Du Bois championed a classical arts education led by the most high-achieving 10 percent of the Black population. In his famous 1905 "Atlanta Compromise" speech, Booker T. Washington advocated for vocational-industrial education to improve the socioeconomic conditions of Southern Blacks and Southern race relations. Washington sought to mitigate racial violence by promising that Black people would not agitate for social equality. He stated in the speech that both races could "be as separate as the fingers, yet one as the hand in all things essential to mutual progress."[2] Du Bois's talented tenth would cultivate African American social and economic progress beyond the second-class citizenship reinforced by the Southern segregationists who viewed them as an exploitable labor class.

Du Bois linked his ideas of racial progress and educational attainment to normative notions of gender and sexuality. Du Bois viewed the Black masses as defined by death, crime, and disease, but he viewed their pathology as formed through histories of racial, sexual, social, and economic subjugation. While noting the resilience of Black people in the face of adversity, his evidence of this resilience was their ability to hang on to "manhood and chastity and aspiration."[3] Du Bois's emphasis on a concept of manhood and chastity linked his ideals of racial progress and the leadership of the talented tenth to normative masculinity and women's sexual purity. The talented tenth was supposed to cultivate this "saving remnant" of "manhood and chastity and aspiration." While these character traits did not explicitly link to homosexuality, they implicitly discouraged or disregarded it.

Cullen had attained the classical liberal arts education necessary for him to be grouped among the talented tenth. He was among the "exceptional men" who would guide the Black masses from the "contamination and death of the Worst," and his talents gained him the respect and admiration of Du Bois.[4] In a 1926 address at the National Association for the Advancement of Colored People (NAACP) conference in Chicago, Du Bois recounted the story of a University of Chicago professor who recited a verse of poetry to his class and asked them to name its author. The students thought the author was the English Romantic poet Percy Bysshe Shelley or one of the Victorian poets, Alfred, Lord Tennyson or Robert Browning. But the verse belonged to Countee Cullen. Du Bois proudly recounted this story of Cullen's poem being thought about in the company of such great (white) writers and famous British poets. Du Bois used this example of Cullen to prove his theory that African Americans were equal to their white counterparts and that stereotypes of Black (intellectual) inferiority were rooted in white supremacist beliefs. This story would become a touchstone of one of Du Bois's most famous essays, "The Criteria of Negro Art," published in the NAACP's *The Crisis* magazine.[5] This essay would guide Harlem Renaissance debates about the role of the arts in Black racial progress.

Du Bois valued Cullen for what his literary achievements could prove to white people about African Americans' fitness for citizenship, but Cullen's "manhood and chastity" did not align with Du Bois's vision of the talented tenth. This conflict mounted when Du Bois, out of his profound regard for the poet, encouraged Cullen to marry his daughter. In 1928, Cullen married Du Bois's daughter, Yolande, which further cemented his status among Harlem's elite. Du Bois's fondness for Cullen was indisputable, and he helped plan the wedding. Countee and Yolande's elaborate wedding was the social event of the year and was widely remarked on by the Black press. According to poet and cultural critic Major Jackson, the wedding "represented a symbolic passing of the torch from the old guard of Black political leaders to the new crop of young Black artists and writers in attendance, the force and energy behind much of the fervor and excitement of the Harlem Renaissance."[6] Du Bois pushed the marriage to wed his vision of racial reform to Euro-American norms of heterosexual marriage and family.

Though rumors about Cullen's sexuality circulated before the wedding, they resurfaced when he went off to Paris with his best man, Harold Jackman, two months later. One year into their marriage, Yolande wrote to her father about her plans to leave Cullen. She had heard the rumors about his same-sex desire, but they were confirmed when he confessed to her that, as she put it, "he'd always known he was abnormal sexually."[7] In the letter, Yolande conveyed her feelings of "horror and disgust" about the "abnormality of it."[8] She had never loved Cullen, and the "enormous amount of respect" she had for him was lost after his confession.[9]

Just two years after their marriage, Countee and Yolande divorced—an event the media covered as it had their wedding. When Du Bois issued a statement announcing the couple's divorce, he failed to mention the reason, emphasizing instead that Cullen remained in Paris to do "literary work."[10] Arguably, this omission was first and foremost to protect his family (and Cullen). Mentioning Cullen's continued literary work calls into question whether the omission was also meant to ensure that the linkages Du Bois made between racial reform and gender and sexual norms remained intact.

Regardless of Du Bois's intent, Cullen remained closeted throughout his life. Though scholars have subsequently uncovered his underground sexual activities and the homoerotic themes in his poetry, the queer desires of the Harlem Renaissance's "poet laureate" remained in the racial closet. Cullen's sexual identity was tied to the identity of the Negro race—which was still fighting to show its moral worthiness for full citizenship. Cullen's story demonstrates how coming out of the closet—the dominant model of queer liberation in the post-Stonewall era—has remained elusive for some Black queer people because their identities have been linked to the public image of the race. White politicians and public figures used gender and sexual stereotypes about

Black people to maintain the racial and economic status quo. African American elites and reformers promoted middle- and upper-class norms of gender and sexuality to counter these stereotypes, which impacted prominent Black queer Americans like Cullen. They were forced to remain in the closet, removed from public-facing roles, or ignored as political constituents during key moments in the US Black freedom struggle.

Cullen's story relates to several concerns in this chapter. First, it demonstrates how racial politics have been tightly intertwined with gender and sexual politics. Du Bois's concept of the talented tenth relies on heteronormative ideas of marriage and family and the regulation and omission of sexual behaviors that deviated from these norms. Relatedly, Cullen's story demonstrates how political ideas espoused by Black elites reproduced dominant rhetoric about the individual sexual behaviors of Black people as reflections on the race as a whole. Public expressions of homosexuality—like Cullen's sexual liaison with another man after the wedding—threatened to taint the image of the race. These political perspectives created a Black racial closet from which gender and sexual minorities could come out and risk marginalization or remain in for the furtherance of racial equality.

Black elites and everyday citizens alike helped preserve the image of the race by regulating or distancing themselves from expressions of gender and sexuality that did not conform to Euro-American norms. In so doing, they often failed to take up the political concerns of the community's most marginal citizens. We explore these concerns by looking at key moments in the Black freedom movement when prominent Black queer intellectuals and activists have been marginalized, conditionally accepted, and asked or decided themselves to step away. These include Cullen, sociologist and Du Bois protégé Augustus Granville Dill, legal scholar and activist Pauli Murray, civil rights activist Bayard Rustin, and lesbian feminist poet Audre Lorde.

Cullen would die in the mid-1940s, still closeted, as US policymakers and politicians maligned Black people for their deviation from white middle-class norms of marriage and family. Though these policymakers and politicians were interested in extending rights to African Americans, their studies concluded that Black people responded to racial prejudice in pathological ways, especially in their nonnormative

family structures. In this chapter, we also examine how US policymakers have scapegoated nonnormative expressions of Black gender and
sexuality, both heterosexual and nonheterosexual, to advance national
narratives of social, political, and scientific progress.

We discuss writer and civil rights activist James Baldwin because
he maintained that white, heterosexual people reviled and brutalized
Blacks and gays because they needed scapegoats on which to project
their own deviant desires. We examine the media's marginalization of
Black trans women in the '60s that left them in the shadows of history
and the public shaming of "welfare queen" Linda Taylor that ushered
in the right turn in US governance in the 1970s. Political scientist
Cathy J. Cohen noted that the sexual choices of welfare queens, who
may not be lesbian or bisexual, are regardless not perceived as normal,
moral, or worthy of state support. Given welfare queens' sexually
marginal and stigmatized status, Cohen included them among the
list of queers "who stand on the outside of the dominant constructed
norm of state-sanctioned white middle- and upper-class heterosexuality."[11] Cohen extended queerness to include poor, heterosexual women
because they were among the populations most affected by the AIDS
epidemic. We take this into account as we consider how Black leaders
and their constituents viewed the Black poor and Black gender and
sexual minorities as being outside the "boundaries of blackness" after
the appearance of AIDS in the 1980s.[12]

### GAY PUBLIC SEX AND THE PROBLEM OF THE COLOR LINE

In 1903, W. E. B. Du Bois famously stated that the problem of the
twentieth century was the problem of the color line.[13] Given that
Du Bois linked his ideals of racial progress and the leadership of the
talented tenth to gender and sexual norms, that problem was also
about the line between heterosexual and nonheterosexual identities.
Debates in the early twentieth century hinged on how African American citizens should be included in the nation. Should they be led
by the most talented among them in ways that challenged the color
line—the racial order of white America that had subordinated Black
people—or should they be led by its workers who would pursue their
economic interests without threatening this racial order? This debate

has centered on the ostensibly heterosexual Black male leaders W. E. B. Du Bois and Booker T. Washington, and related discussions have often focused on race without interrogating the unspoken gender and sexual norms required to be representatives of the race. Leaving these norms uninterrogated has marginalized those whose genders and sexualities transgressed them.

The 1896 *Plessy v. Ferguson* decision, which challenged Louisiana's Separate Car Act, upheld the idea that there were white and Black races and enforced the differences between them. Homer Plessy, who was seven-eighths white, challenged the act by sitting in a whites-only train car. Plessy was arrested and convicted by the court for violating the 1890 law. Backed by the railroad company that sought to alleviate the expense of buying additional train cars, lawyers pleaded his case to the Supreme Court. Plessy's lawyers argued that the act violated the equal protection clause of the Fourteenth Amendment. On May 18, 1896, the Supreme Court ruled that the separate but equal law was constitutional. The court's decision was based on what they viewed as a fallacy of the plaintiff's argument: that segregation deemed the Black race as inferior. The *Plessy* case further enforced the idea of distinct races, which Du Bois called "the color line." Undergirding this enforced division were stereotypes about Black sexuality, in particular the sexual threat that Black men posed to white women.

Myths of predatory Black male sexuality and licentious Black female sexuality—holdovers from chattel slavery—were at the heart of mob violence in the South. Notions of Black female sexuality also obscured the prevalence of rape and sexual harassment of Black women. Ida B. Wells, a founder of the NAACP, exposed this myth in her reporting on lynching. She found that its overwhelming attribution to cases of Black male rape of white women concealed the more common occurrence of interracial sexual relationships. Attributing lynching to rape also overshadowed the most prominent cause of this violence and murder: Black economic mobility and the threat it posed to the racial and economic order. The post-Reconstruction era stereotype of the Black male rapist was a scapegoat used by Southern segregationists to reinforce the color line through mob violence and rape. Though the court ruled that the enforcement of Southern segregation through Jim Crow law did not rest on presumptions of Black inferiority, the extralegal policing of the color line through sexual violence, including lynching violence, enforced those presumptions.

White leaders pathologized the social and economic aspirations of African Americans through racial and sexual stereotypes that deemed them criminal and immoral. While rejecting the pervasive stereotypes attributed to the race, African American leaders simultaneously projected these stereotypes onto working-class people, many of whom were Southern migrants. During the first Great Migration, African Americans moved to Northern cities to escape violence, discrimination, and economic hardship in the South. They were met by vice inspectors, ministers, police officers, doctors, and reformers expressing concern about them being primarily young, single men and women who often lived together in boardinghouses. Among the many concerns expressed about these young men and women was their deviation from gender and sexual norms. For example, the increased public visibility of Black "lady lovers" and "bulldaggers" fostered anxieties among elite African Americans because their divergence from Victorian ideals of gender and heterosexuality might impact the image of the race.[14]

W. E. B. Du Bois focused on Southern migrants to assess the effectiveness of his vision of racial progress. As the Cullen example showed, Du Bois participated in regulating the gender and sexual expressions of the Black working class, embedding Victorian ideals of gender and sexuality in his vision of racial progress. Central to Du Bois's talented tenth was the role of education in the reform of the Black masses that were given to "lewdness" and to salvage the remnants of "manhood and character" that could not be "crushed" by three centuries of economic exploitation, cultural deprivation, rape, and torture. Du Bois linked the rape of Black women to their "dar[ing] to be virtuous." Du Bois wanted the talented tenth to cultivate the manhood, character, and virtue they had managed to maintain among the masses who had abandoned these principles under the weight of centuries of oppression. Du Bois's connection between the rape of Black women and their "dar[ing] to be virtuous" demonstrated how his attempts to regulate the sexuality of the Black masses were based on his conception of dignity as an act of resistance and sovereignty. It also demonstrated how attempts to be virtuous could not alleviate the threat of racial, gender, and sexual violence.

Moreover, attempts to police Black sexuality inadvertently limited Black sexual agency. Black elites viewed the sexual expression of the Black masses as evidence of the lewdness that resulted from years of racial oppression. Mandates from reformers and within Black working-class communities to conform to Victorian notions of virtue left little room for sexual exploration outside of these norms. This included the same-sex practices and public sexual encounters of Black elites. Examining the life and work of Augustus Granville Dill, a friend and colleague of Du Bois, exposes the limits of these mandates. Du Bois asked for Dill's resignation as business manager of *The Crisis* immediately after his arrest for public sex with another man. While Du Bois denied that this request was linked to the arrest, the timing of the request merits an exploration of how the problem of homosexuality intersected with the problem of the color line.

Augustus Granville Dill was born in Portsmouth, Ohio, in 1881. After earning a teaching certificate at fifteen, he enrolled as a student in Atlanta University's Department of Sociology, under the direction of Du Bois. He earned a second bachelor's degree at Harvard in 1908, and a master's degree from Atlanta University in 1909. After finishing his master's degree, Dill became the institution's Northern secretary, tasked with public relations outside the South, in hopes of raising money for the cash-strapped school. He subsequently took Du Bois's position as head of the Department of Sociology. In 1913, he resigned from Atlanta University and took a job offer from Du Bois as business manager of *The Crisis*, the official magazine of the NAACP. He held this position until 1927 when Du Bois asked for his resignation.

While multiple factors may have influenced Du Bois's decision to let Dill go—mental health issues and poor performance as measured by the decline in subscriptions—Dill's recent arrest in a gay sex sting surely contributed to the timing of Du Bois's request.[15] Du Bois denied that the arrest was the reason for firing Dill, but given Du Bois's promotion of the talented tenth as the primary means of "advancing" the race, the arrest was surely a factor. The taint of homosexuality and an arrest for public sex might have stalled racial advancement because it affirmed stereotypical depictions of African Americans as criminal and immoral. While we do not know what caused the mental health issues that Du Bois cited as a reason for asking Dill to resign, mental anguish associated with Dill's queer sexuality in a world of Black respectability, white stereotypes, and heteronormative ideals of gender and family may have played a role.

Black reformers' policing of working- and middle-class Black sexuality spoke to the ways that sexual stereotypes affected representations of "the race" rather than just individuals like Dill. As the Northern secretary of Atlanta University, Dill played a crucial role in disseminating information about the university's activities. Dill took a group of Black students who performed as a quartet on tour. He was aware of the ubiquitous racial and sexual stereotypes that pervaded American society and cautioned his students before their performance "to bear themselves through the whole with special dignity" to counter these stereotypes.[16] Pervasive stereotypes about African Americans prompted ideas from outside and inside the race that individuals should be mindful of how they represented the collective—their behaviors could either confirm stereotypes or dispel them. Given his instruction to the quartet members, Dill knew that the criminalized act of gay sex he was accused of could damage the public image of the race.

Dill continued to work for racial progress after his resignation. The Intercollegiate Association elected him president in 1929, bringing together intellectuals from both inside and outside the academy to tackle social issues. In 1932, he opened the Harlem Personal Services Shop—a bookstore, lending library, post office, and event space for public intellectuals and artists.[17] He continued his work as a public intellectual through speaking engagements at churches and in radio and newspaper interviews. However, the intellectual contributions Dill made after he left Atlanta University are marginalized in the history of the New Negro Movement, attesting to how his arrest detracted attention from his long-term political contributions.

## PAULI MURRAY, THE MAVERICK

The Reverend Dr. Pauli Murray is arguably one of the most important historical figures of the civil rights era. Yet, their contributions to twentieth-century US history have been the subject of historical scholarship only since the early 2000s, first in the field of women's history and later in queer and trans historical scholarship. Scholars of women's history have been central to establishing Murray's historical significance to the Civil Rights Movement, women's movement, and movements for gender and sexual freedom.

Murray's impact spanned a wide range of twentieth-century social movements, including the labor movement, leftist movement, peace movement, and the decolonization movement in Africa. They were an accomplished legal scholar and creative writer. Their research on constitutional law was used in arguments for *Brown v. Board*, and with Leslie Rubin, they authored *The Constitution and Government in Ghana* in 1961, which served as a legal reference book for a constitution still in formation. They published in a range of genres, including poetry, memoir, autobiography, and family history. Murray practiced law in the mid-1950s at Paul, Weiss, Rifkin, Wharton, and Garrison, a prestigious firm in New York, and taught American studies at Brandeis University in the late 1960s and early 1970s. They broke many barriers, including rising to the top of their class at the male-dominated Howard Law School and becoming the first Black person perceived as a woman in the United States to be ordained as an Episcopal priest.

Our description of Murray as a person perceived as a woman— taken from the Pauli Murray Center for History and Social Justice— raises the issue of how to reclaim Murray's historical contributions due to their complex gender identity. Murray wanted to transition genders in their early life. They pursued medical treatment for "gender dysphoria" while on the frontlines of the fight for racial integration. On both fronts they faced roadblocks at every turn. Historians have used various pronouns—she, he, s/he, he/she—whether to place them within the binary terms of historical scholarship or to respect the complexity of their gender.

Scholarly debates about how to sex Murray are not only about Murray's identity; they also regard the nature of Murray's social contributions. Murray is credited with coining the term *Jane Crow* to describe the racism and sexism they faced in various institutions of higher education. Scholars have attributed Murray's criticism of Jim Crow racism as a male-centered construction to Murray's multiply marginal status as a Black woman. Black women historians have used she/her pronouns to refer to Murray because Murray used she/her in their later life after giving up on gender transition.

Trans historians have argued that Murray, as a mixed-race, gender-nonconforming person, formed their conception of Jane Crow from the prejudice they experienced because of their location outside binary constructions of race and gender.[18] Murray also had relationships with women amid the increasing homophobia of the Cold War era, making them an important figure in lesbian history. After all, it was the death of their longtime partner, Irene Barlow, that prompted them to leave the academy to pursue the office of priesthood. They did not fit neatly into the category of lesbian, however. An important benchmark in their conflicts with binary constructions of gender was their rejection by a female lover who ascribed to normative male-female social roles in the relationship.

These debates reveal how various subfields of history—Black, women's, Black women's, trans, and even Black queer history—cannot fully encompass a complex figure like Murray. We use they/them pronouns to account for all the raced and gendered possibilities and impossibilities that made up Murray's complex personhood. We want to acknowledge the aspects of their existence that remain elusive to the project of historical recovery. To elaborate on these concerns, we put Murray—a symbol for the intertwined causes of racial, gender, and sexual justice—at the center of the NAACP's legal battles for school integration. Centering Murray in these legal battles shows how aspects of their identity are alternately foregrounded and deemphasized when historicizing their contributions to the Civil Rights Movement.

Among the goals of civil rights organizations like the NAACP was desegregating public schools, including institutions of higher education. These battles began much earlier than the *Brown v. Board of Education* decision in 1954, a significant benchmark of the Civil Rights Movement. In 1938, Murray joined the fight for school integration when they applied to the master of arts program in public welfare social work at the University of North Carolina–Chapel Hill. With deep roots in North Carolina, Murray decided to apply to UNC partly because they wanted to be closer to their aging aunts, Pauline—who had raised them and whom they referred to as mother—and Sally. Murray had completed their bachelor of arts degree in English at Hunter College in New York City in 1933. They began publishing poetry while working the evening switchboard at Hunter College, and their poetry reflected the revolutionary political fervor among youth. Murray noted a "sense of identification with the whole class of youth, the world of black, white, international communist youth, European whatever" and "the protest literature being written" that was "so heavily weighed with the protest of being a black person in America at this time."[19]

Murray's political radicalization occurred between their graduation from Hunter and their application to UNC. The year after graduation, they worked as the special field secretary for *Opportunity: A Journal of Negro Life* and then for the Works Progress Administration (WPA). Murray first taught remedial reading and later served in the federally funded Workers Education Project, where they were further influenced by future civil rights leader Ella Baker and other young, radical intellectuals involved with the project. They joined the Communist Party Opposition (CPO) in 1936. That same year, Murray attended Brookwood Labor College in Katona, New York, a school started by the American Federation of Labor for members of trade unions who could not afford college but showed leadership potential. The school offered courses in labor journalism, labor economics, and history, among other topics. While a student, Murray volunteered to help organize striking workers in Tarrytown, New York. These experiences impacted their racial consciousness and mobilized them to test a recent Supreme Court decision that granted equal protection to African Americans in higher education.

In November 1938, Murray wrote a letter to the University of North Carolina's president, Dr. Frank Graham, requesting an application, and received an application that included written questions about their race and religion. After Murray applied, they received a response from Graham, stating, "I'm sorry, but the constitution and the laws of the state of North Carolina prohibit me from admitting one of your race to the law school."[20]

Murray was empowered to contest this rejection because the Supreme Court had handed down the *Missouri ex rel. Gaines v. Canada* (1938) decision one day after Murray received the letter from the North Carolina school. The Supreme Court held that the state of Missouri had a duty to provide Lloyd Gaines, a graduate of historically Black Lincoln University, access to legal education at the University of Missouri Law School. Gaines was refused admission because of his race. He argued before the circuit court and the state supreme court that denying his admission violated his Fourteenth Amendment rights. Under the separate but equal doctrine of *Plessy v. Ferguson*, states had a duty to provide equal educational opportunities to Black students. Since Lincoln University did not have a law school, Gaines applied to the University of Missouri Law School. Though the state promised to create a law school at Lincoln eventually, the state supreme court ruled that Missouri needed to do more to immediately satisfy its responsibility to provide equal protection under the law. Murray swiftly replied to Graham's letter, saying, "Ah, but here is the Lloyd Gaines case."[21]

Murray's application ignited a media frenzy. Graham sent Murray's application to the state legislature, and it leaked to the radio and print media, with one outlet calling Murray an "unidentified Negress." Murray's family feared that the media exposure would put them in danger, as some of the editorials advocated for lynching violence as a response to Murray's attempt to integrate the college. Murray wrote to President Franklin D. Roosevelt, hoping to hold him accountable for a speech he gave at UNC the previous year. In his honorary doctorate acceptance speech, Roosevelt had spoken about the relationship between racial tolerance in the US South and US democratic leadership on the world stage. He challenged the youth in the audience to take up the cause of liberalism, despite the setbacks caused by racial intolerance.

Murray sent a copy of the Roosevelt letter to First Lady Eleanor Roosevelt, noting that they had participated in Camp TERA (Temporary Emergency Relief Administration), a residential work camp for women founded by the First Lady. They also wrote to local Black leaders for support. Most notably, Murray wrote asking Walter White, the leader of the NAACP, to take their case. They included all the correspondence between them and the university president, the president and First Lady, and local Black leaders, as well as the press coverage of their admission attempt. Murray thought their academic standing and previous education at Hunter College would give the NAACP the legal standing they lacked in *Hocutt v. Wilson*. In that case, the NAACP challenged the UNC College of Pharmacy's discriminatory admission's policy. The North Carolina College of Negroes refused to release the plaintiff Thomas R. Hocutt's transcript, however, resulting in the case's dismissal.

Despite Murray's academic standing, the NAACP neglected to take their case. Murray learned that the NAACP conducted careful background checks before selecting its cases, and that Murray was considered "not quite Simon-pure enough" and "too Maverick."[22] Thurgood Marshall—a lawyer for the NAACP and eventually a US Supreme Court justice—told Murray that their case was too risky because they were not a legal resident of North Carolina. Shortly after declining Murray's case, the NAACP attempted to recruit another out-of-state graduate school applicant. It was revealed later that Roy Wilkins, editor of *The Crisis*, vehemently opposed taking Murray's case. According to historian Glenda Gilmore, Wilkins thought Murray's correspondence with university officials and the press was not "diplomatic."[23] He feared the court would use the correspondence to argue that Murray did not want to study social work but instead wished to integrate North Carolina higher education institutions.

Gilmore contended that labeling Murray as too "Maverick" may have been a reference to their Communist affiliation and, perhaps, "something far more personal": "That the NAACP could not represent her because she did not conform to feminine standards."[24] Murray often dressed like a man and had lived with women. When they worked for the WPA, a self-reported gender identity crisis led to their hospitalization. Murray thought they were a "pseudo-hermaphrodite" and asked for an operation to find their male sex organs. Though they faced continued rejection from medical practitioners in their quest to transition genders, they pursued testosterone therapy until at least 1944. The court could have used Murray's seemingly private struggles with gender identity to discredit Murray's case for racial integration.

Gilmore ultimately considered the NAACP's refusal to take Murray's case as a major loss because it pushed the desegregation crisis into the late 1950s and made it easier for white Southerners to launch a massive resistance campaign against integration. The NAACP's politics of liberalism and gradualism did not allow them to represent a suspected communist—a maverick—and the argument that integrationists were communists held sway in the 1950s. The NAACP's decision to reject Murray's case was significant for another reason.

Murray was also a maverick in terms of their unorthodox gender presentation. Taking on Murray's case as a gender-nonconforming person in the late 1930s may have wedded the cause of racial justice to gender and sexual justice. These possibilities were curtailed because of perceptions that Murray's gender nonconformity might reflect negatively on the race. As with Countee Cullen, whom Murray knew while they were living in New York, the possible exposure of Murray's gender and sexual nonconformity might impede the movement for Black civil rights.

While we do not know if Marshall's suggestion that Murray was not "Simon-pure enough" was a direct reference to their gender and sexual difference, scholars have demonstrated how integral Murray's gender and sexual difference was to their ideas about racial justice, especially their formulation of the term *Jane Crow*. In response to a later rejection by Harvard Law School based on their perceived sex, Murray famously stated, "Gentlemen, I would gladly change my sex to meet your requirements, but since the way to such change has not been revealed to me, I have no recourse but to appeal to you to change your minds on this subject. Are you to tell me that one is as difficult as the other?" Had Murray's case been accepted by the NAACP, it would have been a test case not only for the cause of integration but also for queer and trans rights in Jane Crow America.

## BAYARD RUSTIN, THE CIVIL RIGHTS MOVEMENT, AND THE DOUBLE STANDARD OF BLACK SEXUALITY

Like Augustus Granville Dill, civil rights activist Bayard Rustin was forced to resign from his role as a civil rights strategist after he, too, was arrested for public sex with two white men in 1953. Rustin's career as an activist began while a student at the City College of New York. He joined the Young Communist League in the 1930s due to its commitment to racial justice. Based on the Quaker influences of his youth and as a leader in America's leading pacifist group, the Fellowship of Reconciliation (FOR), he helped usher in the nonviolent stance of the Civil Rights Movement. Rustin exercised the principles of nonviolent direct action in the face of Jim Crow–era segregation. In 1942, ten years before Rosa Parks, Rustin was forcibly removed from a bus for refusing to move to the "Negro" section. Though the police were characteristically brutal in their response, Rustin did not concede to police taunts and fear tactics, stating, "I am fortified by truth, justice, and Christ. There's no need for me to fear."[25]

Rustin's experience as a veteran activist prepared him for the Journey of Reconciliation in 1947. Organized by FOR and the Congress of Racial Equality (CORE), thirteen activists—Black and white—traveled by bus to fifteen Southern cities in order to challenge segregation there following the Supreme Court decision *Morgan v. Virginia* (1946), which ruled that segregation on interstate buses was unconstitutional. White activists sat in the back of the bus while Black activists sat in the front in the whites-only section. Twelve of the "Freedom Riders" were arrested over the two-week journey, including Rustin, who was sentenced to thirty days on the chain gang for breaking Jim Crow laws.

Bayard continued his peace movement work in the 1950s, representing FOR in South Africa as the organization launched a civil disobedience campaign against apartheid and in support of West African independence struggles. The delegation received him as a leading voice of the movement for nonviolent direct action in the United States. In addition to his peace movement activism, Bayard's experience on the Journey of Reconciliation led him to greater involvement in the Civil Rights Movement. A speaking engagement in Pasadena, California, would impact his involvement in the movement for years to come.

In 1953, Bayard went to California to organize protests against racial discrimination in theaters, hotels, and restaurants. While there he gave a public lecture to the Association of University Women, part of a series of speaking events to fund his return to Africa. Two white men invited him to a party after the lecture. The three of them had sex in a car in front of Rustin's hotel. After numerous arrests for civil disobedience in his two decades as an activist, including a twenty-six-month stint in federal prison for resisting the draft during World War II, Rustin was now arrested on a morals charge. His notoriety as a leading activist and public speaker made the arrest newsworthy. Rustin's homosexuality was already public knowledge by this time. In 1946, the Black press queried whether homosexuality was becoming acceptable after Rustin appeared in the US media alongside leaders of Indian anti-colonial movements. It was his participation in the Southern Civil

Rights Movement that would pose the most pressing challenges to his political involvement.

With Ella Baker and Stanley Levison, Rustin cofounded In Friendship, an organization established to raise funds from Northerners sympathetic to the cause of civil rights. In Friendship created the blueprint for the Southern Christian Leadership Conference (SCLC), a delegation of activist ministers that Martin Luther King Jr. would eventually lead. As an emissary for Northern civil rights organizations, Rustin was asked to go to Montgomery, Alabama, in 1956 to advocate for a coalition between Black Northerners and Southerners in the civil rights struggle. Northern civil rights leaders debated whether Rustin could represent them in the South given his reputation as an "out" homosexual who was "outed" due to his arrest. Civil rights leaders characterized racial discrimination as a moral crisis and appealed to America's consciousness on that basis. Rustin's arrest on a morals charge could jeopardize their moral standing if they made such an appeal. Leading Northern civil rights activist A. Philip Randolph helped to alleviate the leaders' apprehensions about Rustin's reputation, clearing the way for his trip to the South.

While in Montgomery, Rustin quickly developed a close working relationship with King, the newly minted PhD. Rustin raised King's profile through his Northern contacts and became a key advisor to him because of his vast knowledge of political strategy. Rustin told King about his sexuality, and King felt at the time that Rustin's advice as a political strategist outweighed the risk his sexual indiscretions posed to the Civil Rights Movement. Rustin was ultimately removed from Montgomery because of his visibility as a "Northern agitator." He maintained close contact with King and continued fundraising for the movement through In Friendship. Before the 1960 Democratic Convention, Rustin would be pushed out of the SCLC that he helped create. Wanting to keep civil rights at the forefront of national politics, Randolph planned a march at the convention. Harlem congressman Adam Clayton Powell Jr. vowed to tell the press that Rustin and King were sexually involved if the march was not called off. Though Powell's motivations for calling off the march were unclear, his ultimatum revealed the tensions between grassroots political approaches and

Powell's goal of advancing the rights of African Americans through the American political system.

Then, in 1960, King became involved with the primarily student-led sit-in movement in the South. Growing interest in this style of protest was due, in part, to its success in desegregating local establishments. News of the campaign's success spread widely, and tens of thousands of students participated in sit-ins in college towns across the South. King was invited by a group of student organizers to participate in a sit-in in Atlanta, where he was arrested and sentenced to six months of hard labor. Robert Kennedy, the brother of presidential candidate John F. Kennedy and eventual attorney general in the Kennedy administration, pressured Georgia governor Ernest Vandiver to release King. King's decision about whether to keep Rustin in the role of his trusted advisor had to be weighed against the damage that Rustin's reputation could cause to the growing momentum of student activism in the South and, perhaps, to John F. Kennedy's political campaign.

Rustin saved King the trouble of deciding by voluntarily stepping down from the SCLC, coupling his feelings of betrayal with an understanding of King's position. In an interview, Rustin described the "sexual double standard" regarding King's extramarital affairs and his own engagement in same-sex sex, which implied that sexual indiscretion was not a problem for the movement as long as it was between a man and a woman.[26]

It is this "double standard" that makes Rustin's decision to step down remarkable. The legacy of slavery had deemed Black sexuality as nonnormative, and Black people's purported sexual deviance was used to justify and uphold Jim Crow segregation. This instance of maligning Black sexuality presented an occasion to reject Victorian ideals of gender and sexuality as a requirement for Black politics and American citizenship. King's decision not to speak on behalf of Rustin reaffirmed white supremacist control of Black sexuality by ceding to its demand for sexual morality. In other words, whether a person was engaged in an extramarital affair or a public gay sexual encounter, the fear of exposure rested on assumptions that Black sexuality was immoral. Taking into account the fates of the millions of African Americans whose freedom was at stake, King and other civil rights leaders chose a path that would extend citizenship rights to Negroes without challenging the gender and sexual norms that undermined them. What remained unchallenged was the enduring white suprem-acist belief that individual sexual behaviors stood in for the gender and sexual deviance of the race. What's more, one of the architects of the movement was forced to minimize his oppression as a gay man in order to advance the rights of the race.

Though Rustin stepped away from the movement, the SCLC called on him again to help plan the historic March on Washington for Jobs and Freedom in 1963. The SCLC leadership knew that Rustin's expe-rience made him an ideal candidate to organize such a complex event, but dissension arose again about how Rustin's history might impact the march. The leadership reached a compromise by naming Rustin the deputy to march director A. Philip Randolph. Demoting Rustin did not prevent Southern Democrat Strom Thurmond from publicly disparaging Rustin as a homosexual, draft dodger, and communist on the US Senate floor. The press widely covered Thurmond's speech, though journalists did not follow Thurmond's lead in discrediting the march. Rustin supposed that the press respected the march's grassroots origins and saw through Thurmond's rhetoric. By that time, Rustin's sexual identity was widely known. The SCLC, though initially split about Rustin's involvement in the march, stood behind Rustin after Thurmond labeled him a "sexual pervert." Whether Black leaders rejected or accepted Rustin's sexuality, his public identity as an "out" gay man was not viewed as an individual expression of sexual freedom but as intimately tied to the African American struggle for civil rights.

## JAMES BALDWIN'S LESSON FOR BLACK GAY RIGHTS ACTIVISTS

Race relations in the United States underwent a transformation as a re-sult of the Second World War, a fight against racism and for democracy abroad. The war created a boom in urban industry, fueling the second Great Migration of Southern Black people to the urban North and West. African American migrants often faced racial discrimination and violence when trying to secure a federal job. In June 1941, A. Philip Randolph, then president of the Brotherhood of Sleeping Car Porters, a predominantly Black labor union, met with Eleanor Roosevelt and members of the Roosevelt administration about racial discrimination against African Americans. Randolph and other Black leaders pledged to bring tens of thousands of Blacks to the White House to protest if the president did not do something to end it.

Shortly after this meeting, President Franklin D. Roosevelt issued Executive Order 8802 prohibiting discrimination in the defense industry. Black service members who fought for their country during WWII still faced racial segregation and discrimination in the military and back in the US after they returned home. The treatment they received at home after serving in a war against white supremacy highlighted the nation's contradictory ideals. In 1948, President Truman addressed the ongoing civil rights concerns of Blacks by issuing Executive Order 9981, desegregating the US Armed Forces. These executive orders paved the way for a more expansive civil rights agenda led by everyday African Americans, especially those who faced Jim Crow segregation in the South.

Several significant events brought the plight of African American Southerners to the national and international spotlight. In 1954, the US Supreme Court ordered the desegregation of public schools in *Brown v. Board of Education*. State and local law-enforcement officials refused to adhere to the law. The Little Rock Nine in Arkansas faced a white mob and the National Guard when they tried to attend Central High School in 1957. President Dwight D. Eisenhower had to send federal troops to escort the students to and from school.

In 1955, white men lynched fourteen-year-old Emmett Till while he was visiting his relatives in Mississippi. The Chicago-born teenager's death brought attention to the violence of anti-black racism. His mother, Mamie Till-Mobley, insisted on an open casket funeral and published the photograph of his mangled body in nationally distributed newspapers and magazines. That same year, the arrest of Rosa Parks launched the Montgomery Bus Boycott, a yearlong mass, nonviolent protest against segregation on public transportation. Organized by the Montgomery Improvement Association and its president, Martin Luther King Jr., the boycott paved the way for other mass protests in the South. Eventually, it led to the Supreme Court ruling that segregated seating on buses was unconstitutional.

In 1960, four college students staged a sit-in at Woolworth's lunch counter in Greensboro, North Carolina. Hundreds joined their peaceful resistance, compelling Woolworth to desegregate its lunch counter after six months of protest. Widespread media coverage of the event brought increased national attention to the Civil Rights Movement. In 1961, thirteen Black and white Freedom Riders brought international attention to the movement when they embarked on a tour of the South to protest segregated bus terminals. Met with police and mob violence at every turn and facing arrest, the protesters eventually received federal support from President John F. Kennedy's administration. The Kennedy administration pressured the Interstate Commerce Commission to desegregate interstate transit terminals.

The most monumental event of the movement was the August 1963 March on Washington for Jobs and Freedom. The march brought an estimated 250,000 people to the National Mall to advance the cause of civil rights, during which the Reverend Dr. Martin Luther King Jr. gave his famous "I Have a Dream" speech. In 1964, activists won a significant victory in the passing of the Civil Rights Act, which prohibited the application of Jim Crow laws—outlawing segregation in businesses and public places, barring discrimination in employment and federally funded programs, and strengthening voting rights.

Queer intellectuals were at the forefront of the struggle for civil rights. In May 1963, just months before the march, James Baldwin, Lorraine Hansberry, and Bayard Rustin, among others, met with then attorney general Robert Kennedy at his home in New York City. According to historian Kevin Mumford, the meeting was partly prompted by Baldwin's essay "Letter from a Region in My Mind," published in the *New Yorker*.[27] The essay asked the impossible of white Americans: to acknowledge that the "color" of Du Bois's color line was a cultural invention used to maintain their dominance. Racial ideology had so infused US cultural institutions that "color" now appeared to be a human reality rather than a political one. Once white Americans had let go of this political reality—and ultimately their power—they finally would be able to face the horrors committed under their dominance and fully realize their humanity. Until then, Black Americans had no choice but to do everything in their power to change their fate, regardless of the risk of violence.[28]

After reading the piece, Attorney General Kennedy invited Baldwin and others to a meeting in order to get new ideas about how to deal with the issues facing Black Americans. Young civil rights activist and Freedom Rider Jerome Smith attended the meeting. Having faced harsh police brutality during the Freedom Ride, Smith embodied the need for stronger federal protections for civil rights demonstrators. Smith's harsh words to the attorney general served as a strong indictment of the federal government for its failure to protect African American citizens, and they received the support of Baldwin and Hansberry. Because of Baldwin, Hansberry, and Rustin's presence at the meeting, historian Kevin Mumford designated this moment as the beginning of modern Black gay activism.[29]

Mumford's claim permits us to speculate about James Baldwin's role in early Black gay rights activism, though Baldwin did not identify as gay. Born in 1924 in Harlem, Baldwin has been taken up as a Black gay historical icon because he was "out" as same-sex desiring in the 1950s, because of the queer subtext of his first novel, *Go Tell It on the Mountain* (1953), and because of the overt homoerotic themes of his second novel, *Giovanni's Room* (1956), which received backlash after its publication. His later fiction also explored queer themes. However, Baldwin was clear that he did not identify as gay or as a member of the gay community. Even as *Giovanni's Room* is widely hailed as a gay novel, Baldwin viewed the homosexual themes of the novel as merely a vehicle through which to address more profound questions about the human condition. Baldwin considered sexual preference to be an intensely private matter and regarded himself as "remote" from the "phenomenon" of gay identity and rights. When asked by interviewer Richard Goldstein in 1984 about the political import of coming out of the closet, Baldwin did not initially know what this phrase meant. After Goldstein explained it to him, Baldwin expressed his belief that one day the term *homosexual* would no longer be relevant.[30] Gay rights activists identified themselves as a sexual minority group to which rights should be extended. Baldwin thought embracing gay identity as a minority status meant confirming the majority's view of homosexuality as inferior.

Though Baldwin did not identify as a Black gay man, he did see race and sexuality as intertwined. He viewed the overlapping systems of racism and homophobia as negatively affecting society as a whole. This view was evident in his thinking about both the "nigger" and "faggot" as cultural "inventions." He reasoned that white, heterosexual men created these terms to secure their sense of selfhood and dominance. These slurs referenced a convenient other on which white, straight men could project their fantasies of deviance. In the interview with Goldstein, Baldwin stated, "I know from my own experience that the macho men—truck drivers, cops, football players—these people are far more complex than they want to realize. That's why I call them infantile. They have needs which, for them, are literally inexpressible. They don't dare look into the mirror. And that is why they need faggots. They've created faggots in order to act out a sexual fantasy on the body of another man and not take any responsibility for it."

Baldwin also spoke at a hearing before a New York State commission on teaching African American history in public schools. He discussed how teaching African American history was bound up with the way American history was taught. "Anyone who is black is taught, as my generation was taught, that Negroes are not a civilization or culture, and that we came out of the jungle and were saved by the missionary." Baldwin thought such racist pedagogy left Black children without a sense of identity. "If he sees in fact on the one hand no past and really no present and certainly no future, then you have created what the American public likes to think of, in the younger generation, as the nigger we invent and the nigger they invent. What has happened is that you destroy the child from the cradle."

Taken together, Baldwin's primary lesson for the modern Black gay rights activist was one of caution: It was not the Black gay community that was the social problem, nor was it their responsibility to change American hearts and minds about racism and heterosexism. The problem was American society's need for a scapegoat to avoid a broader interrogation of its own history and values. For Baldwin, "coming out" did not resonate because American history had been written such that Black people were forced to perpetually "[come] out of the jungle" and serve their role as the "nigger" with no civilization or culture and in need of white men's salvation.

Baldwin's statement about Black people being perpetually forced to "come out of the jungle" speaks to the issue of outing that we have identified as a problem facing African Americans throughout the twentieth century. White segregationists and liberals have outed Black people as deviant to maintain their claims to normalcy and socioeconomic dominance. Black elites and everyday citizens have projected deviance onto the bodies of gender and sexual minorities and the poor as scapegoats for broader cultural anxieties about Black folks' moral worthiness for citizenship. Baldwin refused to play this role for white, heterosexual society and instead turned his critical gaze back on white heterosexuals, forcing them to look in the mirror.

Forcing people out of the closet is not exclusive to those who seek to enforce Euro-American norms of gender and sexuality. The Black queer historian, striving to combat a history of marginalization, also faces this problem. As discussed in the second chapter, one principal issue in doing Black queer history is that we must place identity labels on historical figures who understood gender and sexuality differently from how it is presently defined. We also categorize these figures as LGBTQ and gender nonconforming when they did not self-identify as such. James Baldwin offers an example of this. Despite his rejection of gay identity, many have hailed him as a hero for the cause of gay rights. Baldwin turned the mirror toward white and straight men because he did not want to be the body on which they projected their fantasies of racial deviance and sexual immorality. We should also turn Baldwin's mirror toward us, for bestowing on him an identity he refused to claim.

### POSTWAR RACIAL LIBERALISM, THE PATHOLOGICAL BLACK FAMILY, AND BLACK TRANS REPRESENTATION

World War II, considered a war against oppressive racial ideologies, brought global attention to the experiences of African Americans in the US. Millions of African Americans enlisted and served in the war against fascism but still faced segregation and second-class status in the military and on the domestic front. The *Pittsburgh Courier*, the most widely read Black newspaper at the time, launched the Double Victory campaign, also known as the Double V campaign, in 1942 to bring attention to this contradiction. The Double Victory campaign stood for victory over enemies abroad and at home. James G. Thompson, whose letter to the editor sparked the campaign, captured this sentiment: "For surely those who perpetuate these ugly prejudices here are seeking to destroy our democratic form of government just as surely as the Axis forces."[31] The increasing attention to race relations in the US forced the country to assess its role as a protector of democracy abroad if its Black citizens were treated as racially inferior at home.

Under the increasing influence of psychology on American culture in the post–World War II period, racial liberal social scientists, who supported the dismantling of segregation and the extension of civil rights to African Americans, used imagery that conveyed Black psychological damage "in hopes of demonstrating that segregation was immoral because of the damage they believed it inflicted on personalities of Black folk."[32] The psyches of Black people became the sites on which contestations over US global leadership played out. The foundational text of the racial liberal project was Swedish economist Gunnar Myrdal's study *An American Dilemma: The Negro Problem and Modern Democracy* (1944). In this massive document, Myrdal framed the "Negro problem" as a "moral dilemma" that conflicted with the "American Creed," which he defined as its "high national or Christian precepts." Myrdal implied that the ideal US citizen is white by describing the "Negro problem" as "a problem in the heart of the American."[33] This language created a dichotomy between the un-American "Negro" and the (white) American citizen.

Though Myrdal considered the "Negro problem" to be a problem of perception on behalf of white Americans, in his analysis of Black communities he asserted, "In practically all its divergences, American Negro culture is not something independent of general American culture. It is a distorted development, or a pathological condition, of the general American culture."[34] Although he attributed their pathology to "caste pressures," Myrdal labeled Black culture as unassimilable because of its deviance from normative American culture. In his study of the stereotypes of criminality that have persistently attached to blackness, historian Khalil Gibran Muhammad said of Myrdal's study: "Myrdal's work signaled a renewed emphasis on culture defined as pathology."[35] He added, "Myrdal pointed to Blacks' psychological deviance and maladjustment to racial inequality," exemplifying how "post-WWII liberal discourse would shift its primary explanation for African American criminality back onto Blacks themselves."[36]

Myrdal's study disseminated the idea held among racial liberal social scientists that Black cultural deviance produced personality disorders and psychological damage in the "Negro." Myrdal's study was heavily influenced by culture-and-personality theorists of previous decades, many of whom relied upon separating "normal" from "pathological" cultures. This division did not stop at the level of the culture but was also mapped onto the Black psyche. Historian Joanne Meyerowitz surmised, "On issues of race, sexuality, and more, the culture-and-personality scholars often translated social and economic injustice into issues of mental health."[37]

Abram Kardiner, one of the foremost theorists of the culture-and-personality school, argued that the American "caste system" and its "built-in racial discrimination" damaged the psyches of African Americans, causing them to be self-hating and to have "low self-esteem and dangerous levels of repressed rage and aggression."[38] Many of these theorists blamed matrifocal childrearing for Black psychological damage, arguing that it caused varied symptoms of rage, low self-esteem, self-hatred, sexual confusion, and emasculation. As the last two symptoms explicitly point out, the damaging psychological effects of structural racism were seen to have a direct impact on gender and sexuality. Black people's dysfunctional genders, sexualities, and families became the subject of postwar liberal social science inquiries.

In 1964, social psychologist Thomas Pettigrew published *A Profile of the Negro American*, another influential study of the culture-and-personality school. He argued that father-absent Black families produced male effeminacy. Pettigrew cited psychological studies linking the female socialization of boys to weak ego development and a lack of a masculine self-image. He contended that Black male effeminacy did not only develop from family disorganization but also from the social roles many Black men were forced to play in the public sphere. Pettigrew maintained that Black men's relegation to low-paying service occupations generally labeled as "women's work" hampered their achievement of a masculine self-image. In his studies, he found that Black males often opted for "feminine" choices like wanting to be singers or expressing more intense emotion than other males. Pettigrew's study influenced the most infamous social policy report of the mid-twentieth century, future New York senator Daniel Patrick Moynihan's 1965 report, *The Negro Family: The Case for National Action.*

A sociologist and an assistant secretary of labor in the administrations of John F. Kennedy and Lyndon B. Johnson, Moynihan was charged with developing national policy to guide Johnson's War on Poverty. Moynihan sought to address Black people's outsized economic dependency on the state. In the preface of his report, Moynihan provided an overview of his findings: "The fundamental problem, in which this is most clearly the case, is that of the family structure. The evidence—not final but powerfully persuasive—is that the Negro family in the urban ghettos is crumbling. A middle-class group has managed to save itself, but for the vast number of the unskilled, poorly educated city working class the fabric of conventional social relationships has all but disintegrated."[39] For Moynihan, Black communities could not be lifted out of poverty through economic investment because their poverty was cultural, a cycle reproduced by the "Black matriarchy" who "seriously retard[ed] the progress of the group as a whole and impose[d] a crushing burden on the Negro male and, in consequence, on a great many Negro women as well."[40] Moynihan's focus on the "Black matriarchy" as emasculating the Negro male resonated with the liberal social science research that blamed Black people for their poverty and viewed Black gender abnormality, homosexuality, and Black familial dysfunction as psychological effects of racism and poverty.

With the rise of the Black Power movement in the mid-1960s, Black intellectuals heavily criticized the Moynihan Report and studies like it for purporting that racism damaged the Black psyche. Historian Ellen Herman noted, "Black Power was understood by critics and supporters alike as a bid for self-worth and psychological independence."[41] The "Black Liberation School" of psychiatry, a group that brought their activist involvement in the Black Power movement to bear on their research, concerned itself with the construction of "positive, healthy self-definitions of Afro-American identity." Though they continued to see racism as a mental health problem, these social scientists focused on resilience and resistance to racism to construct a positive self-image in Black communities. One of the reported members of this "Black Liberation School" was psychiatrist and Harvard medical school professor Alvin F. Poussaint. Poussaint had been involved in the early Civil Rights

Movement and was often called on by the popular press to address the psychological dimensions of Black Power and Black sexual politics.

In a special issue on "The Black Male" in the August 1972 issue of *Ebony* magazine, Poussaint wrote an article titled "Sex and the Black Male." Though he set out to challenge popular stereotypes of Black male sexuality, he rekindled racial-damage discourse, evidence of which could be found in expressions of Black male homosexuality: "Nonetheless our society's abuse of Black males' psyches has given them their share of sexual problems. Testifying to the fact that not all Black men are super-studs are data showing the significant incidence of homosexuality, impotence and premature ejaculation among Black men."[42] Homosexuality is named as one more sexual dysfunction associated with racial damage. Even though Poussaint focused on the sexual liberation of Black men who were "changing their self-image" and no longer "fe[lt] a need to suppress their sexuality," the Black male homosexual's psyche continued to be a site of racial damage.[43]

Mid-twentieth-century racial liberalism also impacted the lives of those who identified as trans. Delisa Newton, a Black trans woman, confronted racial liberal discourses of psychic damage when she spoke to doctors about her desire to be a woman. Newton was born in New Orleans in 1934 to a Haitian Creole mother and a Baptist minister father whom she didn't know well. Physicians viewed Delisa's claim to "ha[ve] the mind and soul of a girl and the body of a boy" as symptomatic of family disorganization. In her article, "From Man to Woman" published in the Black magazine *Sepia* in 1966, Newton recalled, "The doctors say I had no father figure to pattern myself after, so I identified with my stern, no-nonsense mother. Maybe." Newton's description aligned with Pettigrew's arguments that father-absent Black families produced male effeminacy, while descriptions of her mother as "stern" and "no-nonsense" invoke the emasculating "Black matriarchy." Newton's ambivalent response to these doctors indicates their impact on the lived experiences of Black trans people.

The appearance of Newton's story in the Black press reflected the increased media attention to transsexuality in the mid-twentieth century. Yet, aside from a few sensational stories in the tabloids, her story did not spark mainstream public interest. Newton's account was among several media representations of trans women of color that appeared after the rise to fame of trans "blond beauty" Christine Jorgensen. Jorgensen became a celebrity in the 1950s, with numerous articles written about her life, and published her autobiography in 1967. Her conventional (read as white, feminine, and middle-class) beauty gave her star quality, while her quest for "sex-change" surgery and success in getting it resonated with postwar American, liberal ideals of individualism and self-determination. She represented the societal advancements ushered in by science and technology in the Atomic Age.

Her very public transition also stoked existing cultural anxieties about the role of women and men due to women's unprecedented entry into the labor force during wartime. As Meyerowitz explained, the headline "Ex-GI Turns Blond Beauty" did not solely announce Jorgensen's transition but "suggested a larger cultural leap, from 'ex-GI,' the quintessential postwar masculine representation to 'blond beauty,' the hallmark of 1950s white feminine glamour."[44] Those following her story wondered whether Jorgensen was indeed a woman. She endured intense media scrutiny about her sex life, but her embodiment of "1950s white feminine glamour" helped make her story universal. Other transsexuals, unable to fully embody this ideal, did not enjoy this universality.

Delisa Newton was also an ex-GI, and her first love affair occurred in the military. Her sexual coming of age in the military reflected the ways that enlistment provided an escape from the heterosexual mandates of home to sex-segregated environments where queer people could express their desires. Newton had the opportunity to explore her sexuality, but her femininity led to constant harassment from fellow soldiers. Sexed as a male in an all-male environment, she was unable to flourish as a woman. Newton's first long-term relationship was with her white sergeant, but her squadron was racially segregated. Newton's racial identity prevented her from moving from "ex-GI" to the American ideal of (white) femininity like Jorgensen.

As historian Emily Skidmore has argued, racial stereotypes about Black men as hypermasculine and threatening to white women meant that "African American men would have been poor candidates for 'passable' women." Jorgensen's embodiment of white femininity and her pursuit of individual freedom became a universal ideal, while Newton's story was ignored by the mainstream press. Liberals and white supremacists alike would have viewed Newton's trans identity as symptomatic of Black cultural deviance.

### AUDRE LORDE, LESBIAN LOVE, AND THE BLACK ARTS MOVEMENT

Black Americans grew impatient with the lack of social change in their communities after the passing of the Civil Rights Act of 1964. More radical factions of the Black liberation movement contended that "the long history of African Americans being denied citizenship protections even in the midst of social and legislative change meant that Black-controlled organizations and spaces were vital to African Americans surviving in the U.S. environment."[45] This growing emphasis on Black nationalism and revolution among the Black masses came to be known as the Black Power movement. The artistic arm of this movement was the Black Arts movement. Artists of this movement sought to incorporate and disseminate revolutionary Black nationalist politics through arts and culture.

The Black Arts movement has been widely criticized for its homophobia and sexism. One notable example was Black Panther Eldridge Cleaver's characterization of James Baldwin's homosexuality as a "racial death-wish" in his seminal *Soul on Ice* (1968). Cleaver's rhetoric confirmed Baldwin's claim that straight men projected their fantasies of racial deviance and sexual immorality onto the queer body. The familial rhetoric of the Black Arts movement and its emphasis on idealized manhood equated revolutionary nationalism with masculinity and heterosexuality, marginalizing women and non-heterosexuals.[46] Despite the heterosexism of the movement, some Black LGBTQ artists and activists saw in this movement the seeds of their own liberation. Among those radicalized by the Black Power movement was the poet Audre Lorde. Born in 1934 in New York City to West Indian parents, Lorde dedicated her life to the arts and education. Educated at Hunter College and Columbia University, Lorde became a public librarian in the 1960s. She began publishing poetry in the late 1960s at the height of the Black Power movement and amid the growing call for Black studies in US institutions of higher education.

Historically, Black colleges and universities in the South hired up-and-coming radical Black artists to lead the way for Black studies programs. In 1968, Lorde received an invitation to be a short-term artist in residence at Tougaloo College in Jackson, Mississippi, where she encountered and taught many militant Black students. This invitation demonstrated Lorde's growing impact on the Black Arts movement and its impact on her work. Lorde's early works aligned with many of the revolutionary ideals of the era, and she published her early poetry collections with Broadside Press, one of the most important publishers of Black Arts movement writers. Her time at Tougaloo and her involvement in the Black Arts movement helped her develop her groundbreaking theories of race, class, gender, and sexual oppression as inseparable. Yet, the ideas espoused by revolutionary Black nationalists could not fully encompass Lorde's identity as a "Black, lesbian, mother, warrior, poet."

At the request of her editor, Dudley Randall, at Broadside Press, Lorde deleted "Love Poem" from her third poetry collection, *From a Land Where Other People Live* (1973), because it contained homoerotic themes. According to Lorde's biographer Alexis De Veaux, Randall believed that using the feminine pronoun *her* in the line "When I entered her" might confuse the reader. Broadside Press marketed Lorde as a mother, a teacher, and an African-identified woman. Seemingly, the inclusion of queer-themed poetry in the volume might jeopardize her authenticity as an "African-identified woman" presumed to be heterosexual. Lorde's literary representation of female same-sex desire ran counter to the heteronormative familial rhetoric espoused by Black revolutionary nationalists. Though her reputation was growing among Black nationalists, she became increasingly uncomfortable with publishing poetry that celebrated only part of her identity. At a public reading in 1973, Lorde read "Love Poem." The poem was eventually published in her fourth collection at Broadside, but her subsequent decision to end her relationship with the press served as a bold affirmation of her identity as Black lesbian poet. It also served as a powerful indictment of the heterosexism of the Black Arts movement.

## WELFARE QUEENS, DOWN LOW MEN, AND THE HIV/AIDS EPIDEMIC

As the Black Power movement waned, partially due to the counterinsurgency campaigns waged by the Federal Bureau of Investigation, another figure became the target of the state's vitriol. In 1974, the *Chicago Tribune* published an article about Linda Taylor, who had been dubbed a "welfare queen" because "she is alleged to have bilked Illinois and 13 other states out of hundreds of thousands of dollars in false welfare claims."[47] The media reported that she had used "80 different names, 30 addresses and 15 telephone numbers on behalf of three dead husbands and 27 children" to collect welfare and Social Security checks.[48] On the campaign trail, presidential hopeful Ronald Reagan repeated these media accounts to bolster his welfare reform–focused political platform. Media accounts of Taylor's case exaggerated the charges. James Piper, the assistant state's attorney prosecuting Taylor, charged her with using four aliases instead of eighty, and $8,000 in fraud rather than $150,000.[49]

Journalists' and politicians' sensational accounts of Taylor's story reflected the growing frustration among state officials about the growing welfare rolls. It also reflected the opinion among citizens that unwed and divorced mothers should enter the labor sphere. Public scrutiny of the "welfare queen" extended and fueled the state crackdown on the "undeserving" poor who were dependent on state aid. In the 1940s and '50s, cities like New York, Detroit, and Baltimore used anti-fraud efforts to curb the use of state aid by African American urban migrants. That city officials targeted welfare recipients rather than other recipients of state aid, such as the elderly and the disabled, highlighted how Black gender and sexual deviance figured in the increasingly harsh response to welfare fraud.[50] As discussed in the introduction, the sexual choices of the "welfare queen" are not perceived as normal, moral, or worthy of state support.

African American leaders did not support poor, single Black mothers, despite the welfare queen stereotype's roots in racial discrimination. Civil rights leaders such as Martin Luther King Jr., Roy Wilkins, and Whitney Young echoed the liberal sentiment that the overabundance of female-headed households was the source of the Black family's pathology. They encouraged Black men to take their rightful places as heads of households.[51] In the 1960s and '70s, mainstream Black politics, rooted in heteropatriarchal church doctrine, left Black, poor, single mothers struggling for welfare rights to fend for themselves. Again, Black leaders' political efforts to prove they were worthy of citizenship depended on following norms of heteropatriarchal and middle-class gender, sexuality, and family. Because of this, they reinforced the notion that single Black women on welfare were immoral and criminal.

Existing socioeconomic divisions within the Black community positioned those most vulnerable to AIDS—poor Black women, injection drug users, gay and bisexual men, and sex workers—on the margins of the Black community's political agenda. Historian of science Evelynn Hammonds noted, "Black women with AIDS are largely poor and working-class; many are single mothers; they are constantly represented with regard to their drug use and abuse and uncontrolled sexuality." Because Black, poor women were stereotyped within dominant AIDS discourse, they were not "embraced by the public as people in need of support and care."[52] Black leaders who rose to prominence in the wake of the Civil Rights Movement did little to advocate for people living with AIDS, even as they were elected in areas with large Black populations that were disproportionately affected. Because homosexuality, injection drug use, and single motherhood were stigmatized, the deadly disease took hold within Black communities. People living with HIV and AIDS were confined to the Black racial closet. Their stigmatized practices and desires might have negatively affected the upward mobility of the race.

Another queer figure emerged during the third decade of the AIDS epidemic as the scapegoat for the disproportionate impact of HIV in Black communities. Between the years 2000 and 2005, HIV infection was the leading cause of death for African American women ages twenty-five to thirty-four.[53] The disease prevalence among Black women ushered in the figure of the "down low" Black man or the "DL." *Down low* is a term used to describe self-identified straight men who have sex with men. The figure of the DL man appeared in the media in the first decade of the twenty-first century as an explanation for the disproportionate impact of HIV on Black women.

In 2004, Oprah Winfrey hosted a show titled "A Secret Sex World: Living on the Down Low." She cited the statistics mentioned above and claimed that one of the "big reasons" women were getting HIV was men on the DL: "Their husbands and their boyfriends are having secret sex with other men."[54] J. L. King, one of the guests on the show who self-identified as a DL man, had recently released a best-selling book, *On the Down Low: A Journey into the Lives of "Straight" Men.* When King and those featured in the book came out as DL, they were perceived as closeted gay men who threatened to infect each other and the heterosexual Black community. Rather than an individual coming out, a DL man provided "a body upon which we can inscribe blame."[55] Again, some African Americans subscribed to the discourse of blame rather than confront the structural causes of the epidemic in Black communities. These structural issues included the homophobic blame placed on DL men and the class divisions that made poor Black women unworthy of support from the state and Black communities.

### CONCLUSION: OUTING AS PROCESS

Queer scholars have encouraged us to think of coming out as processual, meaning that it is not a one-time event. Rather, it recurs over time in various contexts.[56] This also means that queer people sometimes choose to remain closeted in certain contexts for a range of reasons. In the context of the twentieth- and twenty-first-century United States, where racial and sexual stereotypes have been and remain pervasive, Black Americans have not always been afforded the choice to remain closeted. Segregationists, right-wing conservatives, and liberals have maligned Black familial organization, gender expressions, and sexual behaviors to naturalize whiteness as heterosexual and gender normative and to maintain the racial and economic status quo. To overcome these stereotypes, Black Americans have strived to present themselves as adhering to the Euro-American norms of gender and sexuality. Though Black people have never been viewed as cis or straight in the United States, Black Americans have embraced a politics of sexual conservatism that has required the confinement of queer and trans people, including welfare queens, to the closet. Black leaders' predominant response to LGBTQ issues has been silence, not only regarding queer sexuality and gender nonconformity but also regarding Black sexuality in its entirety.

Conversely, since Black people have been "outed" as nonheterosexual and gender deviant throughout the twentieth century, those who have attempted to come out as queer or trans have had to articulate their gender and sexual identities against the backdrop of prevailing racial and sexual stereotypes of African Americans. Countee Cullen remained closeted for the rest of his life after his sexual proclivities disrupted Du Bois's vision of racial reform. After turning in his resignation to Du Bois, Augustus Granville Dill continued his important political work. Yet, history has marginalized his contributions. Bayard Rustin "chose" to step away from the SCLC so as not to impede the momentum of the Civil Rights Movement. Though marginalized in the mainstream media, Delisa Newton was able to tell her story in the Black press. Her sense of cross-gender identification was viewed as a pathological response to racial oppression rather than a legitimate narrative of transsexuality. Newton's failure to adhere to the standards of white beauty made her transition from ex-GI to womanhood less compelling.

Black communities stigmatized poor, single women, portraying them as the downfall of the Black race and perpetuating the cycle of poverty. Stereotypes of their "uncontrolled sexuality" and criminality made them scapegoats for the swelling welfare coffers in the US. Thus, their struggles with AIDS, and those of other queer people, went largely unremarked. The marginalization of people with AIDS within Black communities is the culmination of neglect of the needs and desires of LGBTQ people throughout the modern Black freedom movement.

Whether they have been in the closet or "out," LGBTQ people have been part of the Black freedom movement. Yet their needs have often been ignored due to the focus on the color line as "the problem" of the twentieth century. The pervasive gender and sexual stereotypes about African Americans highlight how race, gender, and sexuality are intertwined. These stereotypes also show how the color line was maintained by policing gender and sexuality and enforcing Euro-American norms of marriage and family.

Rather than embrace Black sexual stigma as central to the fight for racial justice, Black leaders often displaced this stigma onto the bodies of queer and trans people. Even those who advocated on behalf of these stigmatized populations or who fought for an intersectional approach to racial justice were viewed as a threat to Black political advancement. For example, Black lesbians who fought to put HIV/AIDS on the Black political agenda were viewed as traitors to the race.[57] Though the marginalization of LGBTQ people in the Black community and in US culture has impacted the material conditions of their lives, with the ongoing, deadly impact of HIV/AIDS being the most glaring example, Black LGBTQ people have continued to fight for justice for their communities and for those who would come after them.

### CHAPTER FOUR

# WERK!

By 1920, an estimated three hundred thousand Black Americans moved from the US South to the North to escape a system of discriminatory laws and social practices, referred to as Jim or Jane Crow, and to pursue better work opportunities and life chances in urban enclaves in cities like New York, Chicago, and St. Louis. Harlem was one of the most popular destinations for these migrants. In his essay "The Negro Artist and the Racial Mountain," Black bisexual poet Langston Hughes wrote, "Let the blare of Negro jazz bands and the bellowing voice of Bessie Smith singing Blues penetrate the closed ears of the colored near-intellectuals until they listen and perhaps understand."[1] Writing at the height of the Harlem Renaissance in 1926, or what he describes in the essay as "the present vogue in things Negro," Hughes condemned the social and financial pressures exerted on Black artists to create work that is palatable to white and Black middle-class audiences. For Hughes, listening and "perhaps" understanding Smith's "bellowing voice" was an invitation to "colored near-intellectuals" and the Black middle class, more generally, to find and embrace the genius and beauty of everyday Black life.[2]

Empress of the Blues Bessie Smith started as a street performer on Ninth Street in Chattanooga, Tennessee. Born in 1894 or 1895, Bessie was the last of eight children born to William and Laura Smith.[3] William, a day laborer and Baptist preacher, died in a work accident soon after Bessie was born. Laura Smith was a laundress who died in 1906, making Smith an orphan by the time she was twelve years old.

In 1912, Smith auditioned for the Moses Stokes company, a traveling performance troupe, and was hired as a dancer. Her eldest brother, Clarence, whom she looked up to, already worked as a comedian and master of ceremonies for the company. In just a few months, Smith started performing with another troupe alongside other ex-Stokes company members, Will and Gertrude "Ma" Rainey.

Smith became Ma Rainey's protégé, and the two traveled with a variety of companies, most notably the Rabbit Foot Minstrels and Silas Green shows. Using their contralto voices, they sang about the major tensions and contradictions of their time, sonically rendering the possibilities and limitations Black people faced under de jure and de facto segregation in the South, and the newly found difficulties Black people faced in terms of increased surveillance from political and social actors in the North and Midwest. Rainey and Smith may have seen themselves in one another. They were both born into poverty in the US South; Rainey's family hailed from Columbus, Georgia, and Smith's from Chattanooga. They were also both bisexual; their shared queerness caused many to speculate that they were lovers. Their relationship was also the subject of outlandish rumors—did Rainey kidnap Smith from her family to bring her on the road? Was Smith even talented, or just Rainey's mimic? Both performers found humor in speculations about the nature of their relationship.

By 1913, Smith became a regular headliner at Atlanta's 81 Theater, a key venue in the Black vaudeville circuit. Noted gospel composer and musician Thomas A. Dorsey used to sell soft drinks at the 81 before becoming Ma Rainey's accompanist. Of Smith, he said: "It was about 1913 or 1914 and Bessie was already a star in her own right, but she really got her start there at the '81'—I believe that's really where she made it—and I don't recall Ma Rainey ever having taken credit for helping her."[4]

Bessie Smith was a rising star on the Black vaudeville circuit during World War I, in which more than 380,000 Black Americans served in the United States military, often enduring discriminatory and substandard treatment during their service. Several factors, including financial interest and Germany's wartime strategies—such as its unrestricted submarine attacks on merchant and passenger ships—precipitated

President Woodrow Wilson's decision to commit US forces to the war in 1917.

Just months after the war's end in 1919, the Eighteenth Amendment, prohibiting the manufacture, sale, and transportation of alcohol in the United States, was ratified. For Smith, who was an avid drinker and preferred homemade liquor, Prohibition neither stifled her personal habit nor her ability to make a living as a blues singer. It was the eve of the Roaring Twenties, and blues would become the soundtrack of the decade. In 1923, Smith was signed to Columbia Records. Her first hit, a recording of Alberta Hunter's "Down Hearted Blues," sold 780,000 copies in less than six months.[5] Smith would record several hits for Columbia Records throughout the 1920s, including "St. Louis Blues," "Reckless Blues," and, just weeks before the stock market crash of 1929, "Nobody Knows You When You're Down and Out." Smith's "bellowing voice" was a prophetic sounding of the 1920s.

Before Smith's singing career was significantly impacted by the Great Depression, she found an opportunity, in 1925, to repay her mentor and friend Ma Rainey, bailing Rainey out of jail after she was arrested for hosting a "lesbian party" in her home in Chicago. Rainey would reference the moment in her 1928 hit "Prove It on Me Blues," singing:

> *Went out last night with a crowd of my friends*
> *They must have been women, 'cause I don't like no men.*
> *It's true I wear a collar and a tie,*
> *Makes the wind blow all the while*
> *Don't you say I do it, ain't nobody caught me*
> *You sure got to prove it on me.*

Rainey's lyrics offer a playful response to the rumors surrounding the incident and the public personas of her and her "crowd of friends," including former protégé, Smith. As K. Allison Hammer notes about both Rainey and Smith, their use of "B.D. style" in their performances allowed them to express rage alongside female sensuality and "outrageousness" in their music.[6] *B.D.*, an abbreviation of bulldagger or bulldyke, was a term popular in the 1920s and 1930s that typically referred to Black and brown women who displayed bravado and other attributes typically associated with masculinity. Hammer's emphasis on "B.D. style" to describe their performances is significant, as it does not collapse performance with performer but rather gestures to what Lucille Bogan sang: "B.D. Women . . . can lay their jive just like a natural man."[7] Rainey and Smith charted their own paths in a creative marketplace that worked differently for Black women, as their music discussed the difficulties and pleasures in doing so.

This chapter focuses on the creative and artistic contributions of Black queer and trans communities, with a specific emphasis on music and performance. Black music offers a portal for examining the significance of race, gender, and sexuality in national politics over time, as it can be read as a reflection of Black life or a critique of the dominant social order and interrogated as a site of labor exploitation, cultural appropriation, and theft. As we saw with Bessie Smith, her discography and performance became an archive of desire, of struggle and striving. Black queer and trans performance across the twentieth century found more ways to express a critique of the circumstances people were facing from the compounding gender and racial discrimination of Jane Crow to other modes of state and extramural violence, which shaped Black American life in the early and mid-twentieth century (and beyond). As such, this chapter shifts focus from dominant Black political visions of freedom in America and outlines how the labeling of Black communities as collective closets for gender and sexual deviance created the conditions for vibrant Black queer and trans cultures to emerge.

Following Bessie Smith's example, "Werk!" traces some of the significant forms of cultural expression that emerged out of these conditions, focusing on sexual cultures in Harlem, Chicago, and Los Angeles. We name these early- and mid-twentieth-century cultural formations as historical antecedents to contemporary queer and trans cultures like the ballroom communities represented in *Paris Is Burning*, the gender-bending performances of disco queen Sylvester, and the house music scene emerging out of Black queer subcultures in Chicago. This chapter celebrates the imaginative forms of queer and trans life created under conditions of Black subjugation and illuminates how Black queer and trans expressive cultures have fostered kinship, pleasure, and survival.

### WILLMER "LITTLE AXE" BROADNAX, PEACOCK RECORDS, AND THE GOLDEN AGE OF GOSPEL

The golden age of gospel (as well as rock and roll and rhythm and blues) emerged from and overlapped with the golden era of the blues, and Black queer and trans musicians contributed and performed across all musical genres. The Father of Gospel Music, Thomas Dorsey, who had previously accompanied Smith and Rainey on piano, said that aside from lyrics, there was little distinction between gospel music and the blues.[8] The establishment of a marketplace for Black sound, such as the creation of "race records," which included various musical genres, including blues, gospel, and rhythm and blues, created pathways for Black queer performers to circulate beyond the vaudeville stage, even as the majority of record profits remained with white label owners.

Gospel tenor Willmer M. "Little Axe" Broadnax was a member of at least five gospel groups between 1930 and 1970 and became a long-standing collaborator with the noted gospel quintet the Five Blind Boys of Mississippi beginning in 1960 and off and on through the 1970s and 1980s. Described as small in stature with a naturally high non-falsetto singing voice, Broadnax began his singing career in his hometown of Houston, Texas, in the 1930s.[9] With his brother William "Big Axe," Little Axe Broadnax was part of some of the major gospel groups of the 1940s, '50s, and '60s. As early as 1940, he became the lead of his own quartet, Little Axe and the Golden Echoes. After releasing a single of "When the Saints Go Marching In" for Specialty Records, and being dropped before they could record a follow-up, the Golden Echoes disbanded. During the 1950s, Little Axe joined the Spirit of Memphis Quartet and later the Fairfield Four, but in 1960 he replaced lead singer Archie Brownlee, signing on to sing with the Five Blind Boys of Mississippi as their second lead. As a "Blind Boy," he would record several singles with Peacock Records, including "Precious Memories," "Sending Up My Timber," and "Father I Stretch My Hand to Thee."

Named after founder Don Robey's Houston nightclub, the Bronze Peacock, Peacock Records focused on making Black music, with artists making hits across genres, including gospel and R&B. Broadnax's label mates would include singer-songwriters and queer icons Little Richard and Big Mama Thornton. The success of Peacock's recordings made

Don Robey the first African American record mogul in the United States, approximately one decade before Berry Gordy Jr. established Motown Records in Detroit. Although Little Richard was no longer a Peacock artist by the time Broadnax and the Five Blind Boys had started recording with the label, one wonders if the two ever crossed paths. In the early 1960s, and after the success of songs like "Tutti Frutti," Little Richard was on a temporary reprieve from secular music. With End Records and later Mercury Records, Richard put out several gospel songs that charted on the US and UK pop charts at that time. Big Mama Thornton's wildly popular hit "Hound Dog" charted almost ten years before Broadnax joined the Peacock pantheon of artists. A founder of rock and roll known for her way of playing the guitar, bravura performance, and booming voice, Big Mama Thornton's "B.D. style" places her in direct conversation with Rainey and Smith.

But Little Richard and Big Mama Thornton are queer icons, in part, because of what we imbue to their personal histories in the present. Even as we can read about how their genders and sexualities did not conform to cisheteronormativity, we must also appreciate that they were not "out" queer performers. It was not known that Willmer Broadnax was a man of trans experience until an autopsy was performed on his body as part of a criminal investigation. In 1992, following an altercation with his lover, Lavina Richardson, Broadnax was stabbed to death. News of his assigned gender circulated among the gospel community, precipitating an all-too-common response about trans people who are outed after death: more speculation and *suspicion*. In other words, the revelation of Broadnax's assigned gender was treated as an open secret, widely known but unspeakable.

Whether as an open secret or the result of disavowal, the repression of queer and trans presence in gospel music produces questions about whether artists who often found themselves performing for sexually conservative audiences felt that coming out was possible, desirable, or within their control. Take, for example, the gospel singer and Godmother of Rock and Roll Sister Rosetta Tharpe, who moved across musical genres throughout her multi-decade career. Her 1944 recording of "Strange Things Happening Every Day" was the first gospel song to find inclusion in *Billboard* magazine's Harlem Hit Parade. And according to Gayle Wald, Tharpe's biographer, this song was also the first rock and roll record in the United States.[10] As a highly skilled guitar player, Tharpe's performance persona was linked with masculinity due to the rarity of female guitarists at the time. Her nightclub performances, where she sometimes sang gospel songs in a lineup with blues and jazz musicians, dancers, and showgirls, caused her to be rejected by some in the gospel community. Tharpe married three times and was rumored to have had romantic relationships with women, including with R&B singer Marie Knight, with whom she recorded music and went on tour. Tharpe's reception in the '40s illustrates how open secrets function as an index of surveillance, as segregated cities and performance venues became glass closets for Black queer and trans performers working the performance circuit under America's Jim and Jane Crow regime.

Tyina Steptoe further explains that by the mid-1950s, the post–World War II political climate of anti-Communist propaganda and the linking of heteronormativity with American national values lead to an intensification of repressive social forces.[11] Black civil rights activists responded to national culture by espousing and practicing a politics of respectability, which made heterosexuality and normative gender part of a program for racial progress. Recognizing all of this, perhaps Broadnax didn't feel like his assigned gender was anyone's business. Perhaps he felt the need to create a gospel persona that continued to hold the carnal and the spiritual at arm's length. Speculation about Broadnax and his blues predecessors and contemporaries tells us as much about time and place as it does about the performers themselves.

### SIR LADY JAVA, TRANS STREET PERFORMANCE, AND RULE NUMBER 9

By 1965, the multitalented entertainer Sir Lady Java, also known simply as Lady Java, was a mainstay on the Los Angeles nightclub circuit. Born in New Orleans in 1943, Java transitioned in childhood with the support of her mother. Java began singing and dancing in local clubs in her hometown before moving to Los Angeles. There she became embedded in the Black entertainment scene, frequently featured in *Jet*, *Variety*, and *LA Advocate*. Citing Josephine Baker, Lena Horne, and Mae West as inspirations, Java included singing, dancing, impersonations, and comedy in her performances. In September 1967, after Java had finished a successful two-week engagement at the Redd Foxx Club, the Los Angeles Police Department (LAPD) began shutting down her performances, citing Rule Number 9, a city ordinance that made it illegal to "impersonate by means of costume or dress a person of the opposite sex" without a special permit from the LA Board of Police Commissioners.[12]

Los Angeles's Rule Number 9 was not unprecedented. St. Louis, Missouri, passed the first anti-cross-dressing ordinance in 1843. Often referred to as "masquerade laws," similar city ordinances emerged across the country in cities like Columbus, Ohio (1848), Nashville, Tennessee (1850), Chicago, Illinois (1851), and San Francisco, California (1863). The emergence of anti-cross-dressing laws in the nineteenth century highlights the interplay of social concerns about sexual and gender nonconformity with racial anxieties, as fugitives from enslavement often cross-dressed to evade their captors.

In Los Angeles, cross-dressing, or any form of public gender nonconformity, was criminalized in 1898 with the passage of Municipal Ordinance 5022. The ordinance was amended in 1922 to specify penalties of six months in jail and a $500 fine for those in violation. The Board of Police Commissioners, in 1940, developed what would later become Rule Number 9, requiring bar owners to get written permission from the commission to host cross-dressing performers. To avoid violating the ordinance, performers were required to wear at least three items of "properly gendered" clothing.

The LAPD threatened the club owner, the comedian Redd Foxx, with fines, arrest, and the revocation of the bar's liquor license. In October 1967, Foxx applied for a permit but was refused. Java picketed Redd Foxx's club and hired the American Civil Liberties Union to bring a lawsuit to contest the legality of the ordinance. In a front-page story of the *Los Angeles Advocate*, Java related, "The law is depriving me of my livelihood. I feel it's unconstitutional."[13] The courts eventually rejected Java's case, stipulating that only club owners could sue. Rule Number 9 was struck down after a separate dispute in 1969. As Treva Ellison explains, "Java's struggle against the LAPD elucidates the labor of 'werqing it,'" which Ellison describes in terms of the labor politics of working in the entertainment industry as a transfeminine performer and "the liminal labor of insisting on and inventing an undercommons for Black and queer social life through and under the oppressive forces of racial capitalism."[14] For the purposes of this chapter, *werk* and *werqing it* refer to the labor of Black queer and trans performers navigating the racial, gender, and sexual politics of working in the entertainment industry while also creating social environments for Black queer and trans pleasure, communion, and survival. Part of the labor of creating these social environments was activism against police harassment.

Lady Java's activism finds parallels with transfeminine Chicago-based dancer Ava Betty Brown. Although Brown was described as a dancer in the press, less is known about the venues in which she performed or if she was a solo or ensemble performer. Brown's activism and response to the Chicago police department adds another layer of significance to the lack of distinction cops made between the stage and street, between drag queens and trans people. In different ways, Java and Brown illustrate the creative labor of Black queer and trans people's resistance to police surveillance and violence. Targeted in the streets and onstage, Black drag queens and trans performers engaged in community building and protest to resist oppressive conditions and care for each other. Their werk exhibits a creative talent and politics of survival that has been integral to sustaining Black queer and trans life under compounding conditions of oppression.

Described by the *Chicago Daily Defender* as "a Chicago version of the Christine Jorgensen story," Ava Betty Brown's story appeared in the local Black press under the headline "'Double-Sexed' Defendant Makes No Hit with Jury." According to the article, "Brown was arrested on March 14 [1957] . . . [while] standing on the corner of Oakley and Madison waiting for her boyfriend."[15] Though minding her own business, Brown was arrested for wearing women's clothes on Chicago's West Side that day, taken to a police precinct and "undressed and found to be physically a man."[16] She was charged with female impersonation. Less than a month later, Ava Betty Brown testified in court that she was "double-sexed," announcing plans to go to Denmark for an operation to correct her condition. Brown's defense attorney, George C. Adams, described Brown's arrest as unconstitutional, citing that it infringed upon her rights as a private citizen. As with Java, police harassment and the selective enforcement of anti-gender-nonconforming laws were an all-too-common feature in her life.

As the article's headline indicates, the jury found Brown guilty of female impersonation, and she was fined one hundred dollars. More than twelve years later, Brown appeared again in the *Chicago Daily Defender*. On Monday, October 13, 1969, on the heels of the Stonewall rebellion, an old publicity photo of Brown appeared on the front page of the paper with the caption headline "Brutality 'Twist.'"[17] Readers of the *Daily Defender* would have been keyed into the ongoing struggles with police violence. The Division Street rebellion had happened just three years prior, in which Puerto Ricans on the West Side of Chicago took to the streets, overturning and setting fire to police cars in response to the police shooting of a young Puerto Rican man, Arceles Cruz. Police maintained racial divisions in what remains the most segregated city in the United States. Ava Betty Brown, now forty-four years old and a domestic worker, resurfaced in the news due to filing an official complaint with the Police Internal Inspections Division after being attacked by two Wabash District policemen three days prior. In the article, Brown describes being arrested twice that day and explains how her earlier protests of treatment while in lock-up likely spurned the second attack. She told the *Daily Defender* that she had been "arrested and convicted several times on various vice raps," even after she was able to legally change her name.[18] As we wonder what happened next for Ava Betty Brown, we also hope that the decline in media coverage following this article led to a life that was less burdened by public scrutiny.

### FRANKIE KNUCKLES BURNING DOWN THE HOUSE

As a teenager in the early 1970s, Francis Nicholls Jr. and his friend Larry Levan frequented disco clubs in New York City. While studying textile design at the Fashion Institute of Technology, Nicholls and Levan started working as DJs, playing R&B, disco, and soul in underground clubs, including at the Continental Baths, a gay bathhouse located below the Ansonia Hotel. Professionally known as Frankie Knuckles, Nicholls became the resident DJ at the Continental Baths until it closed in 1976. In 1977, Knuckles received an offer to become resident DJ at the Warehouse, a nightclub on the West Side of Chicago, which catered to a Black gay clientele. As disco faced significant backlash in the late 1970s, Knuckles began experimenting with reedits and remixes to keep the genre alive. Knuckles's experiments with sound became the blueprint and foundation of house music; its name is an abbreviation of the Warehouse, where Knuckles's experiments began.

Chicago was an epicenter of the backlash against disco and disco's reinvention. At the urging of local radio DJ Steve Dahl, and in partnership with White Sox promotion manager Mike Veeck, on July 12, 1979, at a home game in Chicago, thousands of audience members brought their vinyl for Disco Demolition Night. The event—which included the fireworks-laden destruction of more than fifty thousand disco records and a riot that destroyed the batting cages and set off several bonfires on the turf—was not an isolated incident. As Gillian Frank explains, "The backlash was directed not simply at a musical genre but at the identities linked to disco culture."[19] First identified with Black women like Donna Summer and Gloria Gaynor, and the image of the "disco diva," the musical genre was particularly popular in gay nightclubs. For many, Gaynor's "I Will Survive" (1978) is considered the disco anthem of the gay liberation movement. Although disco's Black sound was intrinsic to gay social worlds, its messages, often of overcoming racial and gender discrimination, were not central to mainstream gay politics.

Knuckles must have spun Sylvester's hits "You Make Me Feel (Mighty Real)" and "Dance (Disco Heat)" in his Warehouse sets. The androgynous singer Sylvester, nicknamed the Queen of Disco, began singing in a gospel choir at the Pentecostal church in his hometown of Los Angeles, but due to homophobia he found himself out of the church and on the streets. While in his teens on the streets of Los Angeles, he joined the Disquotays, a group of Black transwomen, cross-dressers, and gay men. In his early twenties, Sylvester moved to San Francisco and became a member of the avant-garde drag troupe the Cockettes before pursuing his music career and going solo. Sylvester worked across musical genres, with gospel, R&B, dance music, and disco represented across his multiple albums. He was most commercially successful with his disco singles, and Sylvester's success, alongside the visibly queer presence of disco audiences and other artists, such as the Village People, is seen as an impetus for a homophobic backlash against the genre. As Frank explains, "Disco's timeline ran parallel to the rise of and backlash against gay rights."[20]

Yet Sylvester embraced his iconicity even as he also understood that there were as many differences between himself, as a Black gender-nonconforming man, and his fans. In an interview with a journalist, he explained, "I realize that gay people have put me on a pedestal and I love it. After all, of all the oppressed minorities, they just have to be the most oppressed. They have all the hassles of finding something or someone to identify with—and they chose me. I like being around gay people and they've proven to be some of my closest friends and most loyal audiences."[21] Sylvester continued putting out music until 1986; in 1988, he died at age forty-one due to AIDS complications.

Knuckles, also known as the Godfather of House Music, continued DJing at the Warehouse until November 1982 before starting his own club, the Power Plant. Around 1983, Knuckles bought his first drum machine, its pulse becoming the backbone to the house sound. In the '80s, Knuckles would record, produce, and write music with Jamie Principle, the Pet Shop Boys, and Robert Owens of Chicago-based deep house group Fingers Inc. House music began as a Black queer subcultural sound; as it went mainstream, Knuckles and many of his protégés found new audiences. Internationally renowned, Knuckles did stints in London and New York. In 1991, he released his debut album *Beyond the Mix* on Virgin Records, which contained "The Whistle Song," the first of his songs to hit number one on the US dance charts. In the same year, Knuckles also released the album *Rain Falls* with Def Mix Productions. The album's track "Workout," featuring Roberta Gilliam, would return to the dance music charts in 2005 with international celebrity drag queen RuPaul's new cover release.

House music's use of remix and reedits, both in terms of musical genres and queer scenes, also speaks to Black queer reinvention in the post-Stonewall era. As the gay liberation movement made advancements for LGBTQ people, rights accrued to the more privileged in the queer and trans community. Put differently, white gay men were often the first to directly benefit from the gay rights movement. The iconicity of figures like Sylvester mirror and foreshadow the visibility politics that characterize contemporary trans liberation struggles, wherein Black transwomen represent the acute vulnerability of trans communities. But DJs like Knuckles, in his desire to preserve disco and to perform "disco's revenge," should be read not only as talented entertainers but also as educators who affirmed Black queer life through a musical archival praxis that continued to underscore the relevance of disparaged ideas and art forms. Among his many awards and honors, Knuckles was inducted into the Chicago LGBT Hall of Fame in 1996 and won the Grammy Award for Remixer of the Year, Non-Classical, in 1997. Knuckles died in 2014 due to complications from diabetes.

### AND WERK!

Born in Cincinnati, Ohio, and raised primarily in rural Arkansas, poet, activist, educator, and performer Tim'm T. West was the second born of nine children to Charles Edward, a storefront preacher, and Irma Pearl West, who worked alternatively as an administrative assistant and nurse. His childhood speech impediment informed the sounding of his name, as Timothy became Tim'm to family and friends before it became a more public name associated with his various political and creative projects. West was raised in a musical household, and from early on, he was a good student and a lover of music, identifying reggae, rap, and house music as some of his favorite genres to listen to when growing up: "I was this strange, eclectic, heady black boy who couldn't wait to escape. These forms of music for me represented a new space."[22]

West left rural Arkansas to attend Duke University, where he earned his BA, and in the late '90s began a PhD program in modern culture and media at Stanford University. In 1999, he learned he was HIV positive, which caused him to take a step back from his academic work, and in early 2000, West founded the gay hip-hop (or "homo-hop") group Deep Dickollective (D/DC) with Juba Kalamka, a Black bisexual artist and activist, and Phillip Atiba Goff, who at the time was a Stanford graduate student pursuing his PhD in psychology. The name Deep Dickollective was part of the group's strategy to signal their intent to trouble hip-hop's heteronormative and masculinist politics. With eleven albums and eleven queer men having recorded or performed as members of D/DC, Deep Dickollective, along with artists like Hanifah Walidah, Katastrophe, Rainbow Flava, and other artists and groups, took up queerness as a key aspect of their personas and performances in an underground hip-hop scene.

Despite the documented presence of Black LGBTQ rappers, the figuring of mainstream rap as hypermasculine and heterosexual by audiences and critics precipitated a redundant call for the first openly gay rapper at least until the early 2010s. In 2012, Azealia Banks, Syd, and Frank Ocean were each hailed as the "first" openly gay hip-hop artists. There are at least two reasons for cognitive dissonance here. In terms of genre, Frank Ocean is not a rapper, but also in terms of time, how can three people all be *first*? These contradictions show us something about the assumptive logic of the question itself. That is, "Who's out in hip-hop?" is symptomatic of a dominant framing of hip-hop as homophobic and presupposes a need for visible queers and mainstream representations to read alongside (and position against) perceptions of hip-hop as a site of Black misogyny and homophobia. It dismisses the queer sonics of hip-hop, as it also proposes the tokenization of queer musicians as an acceptable response to hip-hop's image problem and lyrical hostility.

Scott Poulson-Bryant, cofounder of the iconic '90s hip-hop media outlet *VIBE* magazine and Black performance studies scholar, describes having a related and familiar sense of wonder the first time he encountered vogue and listened to rap, writing:

> The first time I saw a pair of young men voguing, moving sinuously, rhythmically, across the dance floor of a nightclub called Tracks in 1987, I felt the same way I felt the first time I heard rap music, standing on the broken, weed-strewn running track at my suburban New York junior high school. Voguing looked, to my neophyte eyes—new to social, public "gayness," new to the rarified, hothouse intensity of gay club life—as brazen and candid as rap music had sounded. It registered as something defiant in presentation yet simple and declarative in tone; as self-making; as powerful.[23]

Voguing is a repertoire of dance techniques and styles that emerged from the ballroom scene, in which groups or "houses" of Black and brown queer and trans people compete in a variety of categories, from "realness" or the performance of "straightness" or "cisness" to voguing style (i.e., the old way vs. the new way). To read Poulson-Bryant's recollection, one might surmise that the defiant gestures and "public 'gayness'" of vogue shared much in common with the candid and declarative sound of hip-hop. Indeed, as Poulson-Bryant argues, "rap music, sonically and vocally birthed from a poly-cultural mix of influences, including the African griot tradition, Caribbean dub music, and loops of black American percussive funk breaks, is queer."[24] As he explains, both in its form and in the process by which it came into being, rap can be read as a queer art form.

Hip-hop, and particularly rap, have historically been coded through, and represented by, Black heteromasculinity, while disco, house, and voguing retain their Black queer cultural ties, even as they have all become more mainstream. The similarities and continuities between disco, house, and rap bear examination. They are all musical forms that emerged from working-class Black cultural producers, and have become, in different moments, the dance music of a given era. Dwelling in the decade of their shared beginnings, the 1980s, house and hip-hop seem to function as two sides of the same coin. On one hand, house performed "disco's revenge"—that is, it remixed a sound criticized for being too feminine and queer—to offer new generations of Black queer music lovers a soundtrack to dance to. House music, among all the places it circulates, continues to be the score to any ballroom event. On the other hand, rap might be figured as disco's (repressed) response. That is, to make Black sound more edgy (read: masculine), rap represses its ties to disco and its shared scene of reiteration(s) and reinvention(s): the DJ's booth and the nightclub. Rap's response to disco's feminine and queer representation produced hip-hop as a scene of racialized (hetero)normativity.

Imagining house and rap as twin musical genres, born of the same time and reflecting the times in which they emerged, means also considering how they work in tandem to offer a view of Black life in and after the 1980s, marked by key moments like Jesse Jackson's presidential race, the Free South Africa movement, the Cold War, and the LGBTQ march on Washington in 1987, to name a few. The 1980s were a time of economic austerity and conservative retrenchment—both of which contributed greatly to the figuring of HIV/AIDS as a gay and Black disease and a national political strategy to ignore or blame the structural realities that made AIDS particularly deadly for Black and queer people.

When almost twenty years later West learned of his status as HIV positive, an event that catalyzed the development of D/DC, he and his bandmates used their lyrics to remark on the multiple social structures that shaped their lives and life chances as Black queer men. In their single "Butchqueen" (2007), for example, D/DC sonically and lyrically demonstrate the fluidity of musical genres and masculinity, as the song opens with funk and disco grooves and a performance sketch of commonly used pejorative understandings of Black gay and bisexual men's sexuality and masculinity. West's verse reflects on ballroom culture's codes of masculinity and describes the social pressures of living with HIV.[25] In the same verse, West positions his outness in relation to US policy on queer participation in the military, rapping, "Never undercover, if you ask I tell." Adopted as the official federal policy on LGBTQ people in the US military in 1994, "Don't Ask, Don't Tell" required that in order to remain in service queer soldiers not disclose their sexuality. It was repealed in 2011.

D/DC's most recent album is a compilation of greatest hits, released in 2012. Kalamka continues to make and produce music, and Goff is a professor of psychology. West continues to engage Black queer youth as an educator and through his activism. He has been the managing director of the LGBTQ initiative with Teach for America, the director of youth services for Chicago-based LGBTQ community center, Center on Halstead, and in 2023, he became the executive director of the LGBTQ Institute at the National Center for Civil and Human Rights, headquartered in Atlanta, Georgia.

### CONCLUSION

In a 2011 interview with the *London Evening Standard*, singer, songwriter, rapper, and actor Janelle Monáe Robinson describes having gone from the "wonderground to the mainland" to explain their experience of the critical and commercial successes of their albums *Metropolis* (2007) and *The ArchAndroid* (2010). Born and raised in

Quindaro, a working-class community in Kansas City, Kansas, Monáe learned to sing in the local church while writing musicals as a child. After enrolling in New York's American Musical and Dramatic Academy to study musical theater, Monáe left to go to Atlanta and pursue their own sound. Their debut album, *Metropolis*, released when Monáe was twenty-one years old, also introduced audiences to Monáe's alter ego, Cindi Mayweather, "a time traveling android" clad in a tuxedo.[26] Monáe explains that the choice to wear a tuxedo is a nod to their working-class roots and the uniforms their parents wore as a janitor, hotel maid, truck driver, or postal worker. In a feature article in the *New York Times Magazine*, Monáe explains, "Cindi helps me talk more. . . . You can parallel the other in the android to being a black woman right now, to being a part of the L.G.B.T.Q. community."[27] As journalist Jenna Wortham summarizes, "Mayweather was a proxy for all the things about Monáe that made others uncomfortable, like her androgyny, her opaque sexual identity, her gender fluidity—her defiance of easy categorization."[28] Monáe continues to express all of these aspects on their own terms, sharing with audiences that they are nonbinary, polyamorous, and pansexual, and noting that their "pronouns are free-ass motherfucker—and they/them, her/she."[29]

As the visibility of Black queer performers in the entertainment industry continues to grow, it remains crucial to hear again poet Langston Hughes's caution to listen and perhaps understand. Even with the rise of Black queer and trans celebrity, we also know that commercial and social forces continue to repress and underplay the implications of the undeniable fact that working-class Black queer and trans creative expression is intrinsic to Black sound. While this chapter has endeavored to write about a range of lesser-known to more well-known Black queer and trans musicians, it is not to suggest that identifying Black queer presence is merely about listing creative contributions from out or outed performers. Our work (werk), as Hughes powerfully recommends in light of Bessie Smith, is to attempt to listen differently and perhaps understand the complex history of Black popular music and its relationship to Black and queer politics and life.

## PART II

# WE CANNOT LIVE
# WITHOUT OUR LIVES

### CHAPTER FIVE

# COMING TOGETHER

I n May 1959, the Los Angeles Police Department raided Cooper's Do-Nuts, a popular after-hours café for queer, trans, and gender-nonconforming communities who frequented the gay bars in the city's Skid Row district. When the police raided the bar and asked patrons for identification without any cause for suspicion, patrons of the café resisted in solidarity with those the police attempted to arrest. According to gay Latino writer John Rechy, who provided the only account of this event on record, patrons threw donuts, paper plates, coffee cups, and anything else they could get their hands on at the police.

The Cooper's Do-Nuts raid reflected the Cold War political climate of the late 1940s and 1950s. The US's Cold War with the Soviet Union ushered in a campaign against communism, both domestically and abroad. Right-wing politicians stoked fear that communist spies had infiltrated the federal government. The culture of fear regarding communist infiltration—often referred to as the Red Scare—spread throughout American politics, culture, and society. In 1947, President Harry S. Truman issued an executive order directing federal government departments to create loyalty boards to assess whether their employees were loyal to the government. As the Cold War escalated and pressure mounted to purge the government of subversives, President Dwight Eisenhower issued another executive order in 1953 expanding the power of sensitive agencies to dismiss any employee that posed a security risk. Among those risks was "sexual perversion." Federal authorities viewed homosexuals as exhibiting "character weaknesses" that made them more vulnerable to Soviet blackmail. At its peak, the Red Scare led to an estimated 2,700 dismissals and 12,000 resignations of federal workers.

This hostile political climate led to the intensification of policing and containment of queer public cultures. Policing had long been a focus of queer resistance struggles. Since the early twentieth century, cities and counties like Los Angeles have employed vice squads to entrap gay men for engaging in public sex.[1] Gay sex was illegal in both public and private spaces, and cross-dressing was prohibited in public areas.[2] The police often targeted gay bars and hangout spots patronized by homosexuals and cross-dressers. Officers arrested patrons for lewd vagrancy, sex perversion, and prostitution-related offenses. They frequently asked patrons for identification and arrested them if their documents did not match their gender presentation. Due to this undue scrutiny, gay bar owners often turned away gender-nonconforming people to prevent police targeting. Sandwiched between two gay bars, Cooper's Do-Nuts was exceptional because it welcomed gender-nonconforming people. So, when the police raided Cooper's, one of the few places where they could congregate, patrons aimed their donuts at a more extensive power structure that limited queer people's claims to social space and bodily autonomy.

The LAPD honed these tactics of violence, harassment, and abuse of gay men and cross-dressers by policing Black migrants who arrived in Los Angeles in large numbers in the late 1930s and the 1940s.[3] LAPD's shift toward statistical policing and crime prevention in the 1950s also meant that police enforcement was often heaviest in areas populated by racial and ethnic minorities like the Skid Row district. LAPD's vice squad increasingly targeted gay and lesbian people through these racialized structures of policing. Because Cooper's was located in downtown Los Angeles on a blighted stretch of Main Street, police cars regularly patrolled the area. Its location at the converging sites of outlaw genders and sexualities and urban poverty made Cooper's Do-nuts a target for policing and surveillance.

Designated by queer historians as one of the first acts of queer rebellion against police harassment, this act of collective resistance against the police, later known as the Cooper's riot, ran counter to the political strategies of more mainstream lesbian and gay organizations.

In the context of state repression, early homophile groups—as gays and lesbians called themselves in this period—viewed conformity to the norms of society as the best method for obtaining freedom and social equality. For example, the homophile organization Daughters of Bilitis described as part of its mission the integration of homosexuals into society through education and adopting socially acceptable modes of behavior and dress. Cooper's patrons' resistance to the state enforcement of binary gender norms and the racial and economic status quo signaled their exhaustion with the current social order. Rather than integrate and adapt to the norms of society, they sought to transform them.

This chapter focuses on queer collectivity as a driving force of social transformation. We trace the shifting identities and political strategies guiding queer and trans organizing from the homophile movement in the 1950s to AIDS activism in the 1980s. Throughout the latter half of the twentieth century, queer people came together to transform the conditions of their lives. People in queer communities navigate various forms of difference. Cooper's patrons who did not appear to transgress gender norms fought for the most vulnerable customers because they knew their fates were linked. Though drag queens may have been the most prominent targets of the police, male hustlers' participation in sexual commerce put them at risk of arrest. They recognized that the common occurrence of police raids on establishments frequented by racial minorities, cross-dressers, and hustlers was part of a broader system of inequality. The Cooper's riot demonstrated how building alliances across differences could combat social inequality.

The example of the Cooper's riot illustrates some of the central concerns of this chapter. First, it shows how a broader political climate of state repression can make already marginalized communities more susceptible to discrimination. The rising Cold War tensions fueling the US anti-communist campaigns led to increased scrutiny of homosexuals in the public and private sectors. These tensions also led to greater policing of gay and gender-nonconforming people in public spaces. Second, it shows the diverse and changing responses of non-heterosexual and gender-nonconforming people to this political repression. While some organizations, like the Daughters of Bilitis, advocated for social conformity as a response to marginalization, other groups chose more oppositional strategies bent on transforming society.

The Cooper's riot further illustrates how race and queerness are intertwined. The police honed its tactics of policing gender and sexual minorities from its discriminatory treatment of Black migrants, showing how racial discrimination buttressed gender and sexual discrimination. We can also see how race intersects with queerness in the way that anti-racist activism informed queer activism. Influenced by the Black liberation movement, queer and trans activists staged sit-ins, boycotts, riots, and other forms of public protest to combat discrimination. Yet, queer people did not always see their causes as intertwined with racial justice. Instead, they often compared queer oppression to that of racial minorities. This meant that the concerns of people negotiating prejudice based on both their race and their sexuality or gender were peripheral to early visions of queer liberation.

Providing historical context for the Black queer organizing that proliferated in the 1970s and 1980s requires examining the peripheral place of people of color in previous decades of queer rights organizing. Historical records of the rebellions in gay bars and restaurants that preceded the Stonewall rebellion in 1969 give little information about those who frequented the bars and restaurants and those included in the action. The queer organizations that are well documented, like the homophile organization Mattachine Society, founded in Los Angeles in 1950, included people of color or expressed solidarity with them. Their organizational records do not give much information about the experiences of racial minorities. With little evidence of who was there, it is helpful to reflect on how whiteness shaped the political vision of queer organizations.

We view whiteness as a structure of power that acts as an invisible marker of racial difference and a standard by which all other racial groups are compared. As a structure of power, whiteness grants access and privilege to white people. Instead of focusing on the racial inclusivity of each queer organization, protest, or movement, a focus on whiteness reveals how identity categories like "women," "gay," "lesbian," and "trans" are imbued with racial meaning. For example, the members of the Mattachine Society regarded themselves as an "oppressed minority" like their "fellow minorities—the Negro, Mexican, and Jewish people."[4] Implicit in this view is the assumption that racial minorities cannot also be gender and sexual minorities. When the constituents of homophile organizations focused exclusively on their rights as "oppressed minorities," the unspoken assumption was that those seeking rights were white.

Building on these concerns, we provide an overview of the local queer and trans protests in the 1960s that followed the Cooper's riot and culminated in the Stonewall rebellion. We show how racial politics intersected with queer politics in these protests, even as some of the organizers reinforced a mono-racial notion of queer politics. We also see this interrelationship in the multiracial alliances forged within queer movements and between queer and anti-racist groups. The prominence of people of color in the Stonewall rebellion underscores their leadership in the queer liberation movement, and the significance of multiracial alliances in the movement.

Despite these historical alliances, Black feminists and queer folks founded separate organizations because of the racial, gender, sexual, and class divisions embedded within the civil, women's, and LGBTQ rights movements. The effects of these social divisions are witnessed in Black lesbian feminist organizations, which started as offshoots of organizations like the Gay Activist Alliance and the National Black Feminist Organization. Black lesbian feminists created intersectional political analyses to understand how racial, gender, sexual, and class oppression intersected to create the conditions of their lives. Their intersectional analysis paved the way for a national Black queer movement focused on the community's specific needs.

In addition to political organizing, Black queer people created a vibrant and visible cultural life. The 1970s and 1980s saw the flourishing of Black queer public culture that included bars, literary and performing arts groups and spaces, and LGBTQ-affirming churches. These spaces became sites of community formation, pleasure, spiritual fulfillment, acceptance, and a rich cultural arts tradition. The appearance of AIDS in 1981 shifted the political commitments of Black queer activists and artists and interrupted the burgeoning Black queer public culture. AIDS was stigmatized because of its association with gay men and poor Black people, leaving Black feminists and queer activists to address the disproportionate impact of the epidemic in Black communities. We briefly examine how the grassroots AIDS organizations formed in the early to mid-1980s provided the foundation for the national campaign against AIDS in Black communities.

## POWER AND PROTEST IN THE 1960S

Five years after four Black students staged a sit-in at a Woolworth's lunch counter in Greensboro, North Carolina, to protest discrimination against Black patrons, another restaurant became a site of protest against discrimination in Philadelphia. Dewey's, a family-owned chain of diners, had become a popular after-hours hangout spot for sex workers, drag queens, gay men, and "nonconformist" youth in the 1960s, giving the restaurant the reputation as "fag Dewey's." The management of Dewey's often refused to serve queer youth, whom they deemed rowdy and spent little money. On April 25, 1965, management asked three teenage patrons to leave and called the police after they refused. Clark Polak, head of the homophile organization Janus Society and publisher of the LGBTQ-themed *Drum* magazine, was called to the scene and began advising the teens of their rights. While the events that transpired after Polak's arrival are unclear, the police arrested Polak and the three teenagers. After the arrests, Polak organized a boycott and picketed the restaurant for five days. One week later, a group of teenagers staged a second sit-in. The police were called, but they mediated between the restaurant management and the youth this time, and the restaurant began serving youth again shortly after.

In the 1960s, Center City Philadelphia, where two of Dewey's franchises most popular with queer people were located, became increasingly segregated. According to historian Marc Stein, Black people who patronized lesbian and gay bars in Center City frequented the predominantly Black commercial establishments north and south of Market Street, where the two Dewey's franchises were located. Others avoided Center City altogether because of racial and sex discrimination. They attended predominantly Black bars, nightclubs, and restaurants outside of Center City and in predominantly Black neighborhoods. Others who feared backlash from their employers, their families, and their communities preferred socializing with other

Black gays and lesbians, and often congregated at house parties in West and North Philadelphia. Black people did patronize Dewey's, but the murky details of the protests provide no evidence of whether Black patrons were turned away and how often or if they participated in or witnessed the sit-in. Black queer attendance at predominantly Black bars, nightclubs, restaurants, and house parties, Black queer concerns about the stakes of their visibility, and the infrequent participation of Black people in homophile organizations cast doubt about whether the Dewey's protest resonated with the broader Black queer community, which was already facing racial and class discrimination in public spaces.

In San Francisco, another rebellion took place at a restaurant that discriminated against gender-nonconforming patrons. In 1965, the queer and trans youth activist organization Vanguard formed to address the discrimination and increased policing and surveillance they experienced in the Tenderloin. Deemed the first queer youth organization in the United States, Vanguard described itself as an "organization for the youth in the Tenderloin attempting to get for its citizens a sense of dignity and responsibility long denied."[5] One of the group's first actions was to confront the managers at Compton's Cafeteria, a twenty-four-hour cafeteria in the blighted Tenderloin District that attracted drag queens, hustlers, cruisers, and locals in the 1960s. Vanguard held its meetings at Compton's, though Compton's management mistreated its gender-nonconforming patrons. The group complained about the "service charge" used to make up the money they did not spend at the restaurant and to hire security guards to keep the youth out. Vanguard formed a coalition with the LGBTQ-inclusive Glide Memorial Church and local homophile activists to picket the restaurant. Though the picket received media attention, it did not change the managers' discriminatory treatment of its queer and trans patrons.

Management's continued mistreatment of local residents sparked the Compton's Cafeteria riot, which involved some of Vanguard's members. On a busy weekend night in August of 1966, the cafeteria managers became frustrated with a lively group of drag queens because they were taking up space and causing a disruption without spending much money. As at Dewey's, the managers called the police. The police often targeted drag queens because of their presence in the Tenderloin

District, primarily occupied by poor people and known as a hub for sex work and other illicit activities. The police were particularly harsh to "street queens"—drag queens engaged in street prostitution—many of whom frequented Compton's. On this particular night, when the police attempted to remove one of the young queens, they reportedly threw coffee in a policeman's face. Around fifty restaurant patrons joined in, prompting the police officer to call for backup. The customers vandalized the restaurant before the police came to round them up. They continued their fight by beating the police with purses, kicking them with high-heeled shoes, vandalizing patrol cars, and burning a newspaper stand to the ground.

Historian Susan Stryker deems the Compton's riot the beginning of the most militant phase of the transgender rights movement, and she locates this militancy within the broader social upheavals brought on by the Civil Rights Movement and the radicalism of Black Power, among other movements for racial justice. Still, Vanguard defined its guiding political concept of "street power" against "Black Power": "WE HAVE HEARD TO [SIC] MUCH ABOUT 'WHITE POWER' AND 'BLACK POWER' SO GET READY TO HEAR ABOUT 'STREET POWER.'"[6] Vanguard's emphasis on economic justice and forging a coalition with the "street queens" who patronized Compton's marked a turning point in the queer movement. Yet, it defined "street power" as distinct from, rather than intersecting with, racial politics.

Even queer organizations that expressed solidarity with people of color maintained a distinction between racial and queer politics. In 1967, protesters at Black Cat Tavern in Los Angeles used a more peaceful strategy to fight against police raids and brutality. After the clock struck midnight on January 1, undercover police officers witnessed the predominantly white patrons of the Black Cat Tavern and neighboring gay bar New Faces kissing. The police began beating the patrons, severely injuring several people and arresting sixteen. Those arrested were charged with lewd conduct and drunkenness, and one person was charged with assaulting a police officer. On February 11, around two hundred people gathered on Sunset Boulevard in front of the Black Cat Tavern to protest police harassment of queer people. Historians have deemed this event the first gay protest in Los Angeles. Like other queer and trans protests in the 1960s, the Black Cat action is significant because it represents the shifting political terrain of the modern LGBTQ rights movement from the single-issue, predominantly white homophile movement to the leftist, multi-issue platform of gay liberation.

The organizer of the Black Cat protest, Personal Rights in Defense and Education (PRIDE), defined itself as more militant than the homophile organizations founded in previous decades. PRIDE staged the protest a month after the initial incident to align with the leftist organization Right of Assembly and Movement Committee (RAMCOM), which designated February 11 a day of protest. PRIDE linked the targeting, surveillance, and policing of LGBTQ people in the Silver Lake neighborhood to similar treatment of other vulnerable groups and neighborhoods: hippies in Venice and the Sunset Strip, Black people in Watts, and Chicanos in Pacoima and East LA. But according to historian Emily K. Hobson, PRIDE did not have a relationship with Black and Chicano leaders, and the Watts, Pacoima, and East LA protests did not end up occurring. PRIDE's imagined solidarity with racial minority groups inadvertently reaffirmed the assumption that all gay people are white. The group's stated support for communities of color manifested more in words than actions. It implied that these communities' issues were separate from their own and existed elsewhere. PRIDE overlooked the possibility that racial minorities within their own ranks might have resided in these areas or might have been singled out because of their race. Archival images of the Black Cat protest show at least one Black man on the picket line. Despite his presence at the protest, PRIDE shared with homophile groups a tacit mono-racial vision of gay liberation.

Queer and trans protests throughout the 1960s paved the way for the Stonewall rebellion, the most widely recognized protest in the modern LGBTQ rights movement. The Stonewall Inn was located in the Greenwich Village neighborhood of Lower Manhattan. It initially catered to gay men and, like other gay bars, frequently faced police raids. Later, the bar began admitting women and sex workers and holding after-hours parties, bringing increased police scrutiny. In the early hours of Saturday, June 28, 1969, police raided the bar. Believing it was going to be a routine bust, only a few officers were present. Patrons ran to the bathroom to get rid of their drugs and began pairing with those of the opposite sex to look straight. The police asked for proof of gender identity under the three-article rule and arrested thirteen people for violating it.[7] After finding illegal alcohol, the police closed the bar and asked patrons to leave. The patrons left the bar but did not disperse. Tired of police raids, patrons and residents who congregated around the bar began rioting in the streets, fighting and throwing objects at the police and turning over cars. Police officers barricaded themselves inside the bar, which patrons breached, attempting to set the Stonewall Inn on fire.

The Stonewall rebellion brought the issues of racial and trans inclusion to the forefront of the movement. Popular accounts of it often center on Black drag queen performer, trans sex worker, and gay activist Marsha P. Johnson. Marsha "Pay It No Mind" Johnson was born in 1945 in Elizabeth, New Jersey. Rejected by her family, Johnson moved to New York City after graduating high school in the 1960s and became a sex worker, primarily in the Times Square area, along with women and drag queens from Harlem, the Bronx, and New Jersey. The police often targeted her and jailed her numerous times. It was her history of arrests as a trans sex worker that initially drew her to the Stonewall Inn. Though it was primarily a white gay men's bar, Stonewall had developed a reputation as a space where drag queen prostitutes could work without the fear of arrest.[8] Johnson stated in an interview, "I was one of the first drag queens to go to that place. 'Cause when we first heard about this . . . and then they had these drag queens workin' there. They didn't never arrested anybody at the Stonewall. All they did was line us up and tell us to get out."[9] The bar's changing reputation as an after-hours space of cross-gender affiliation and sexual commerce exposed patrons to increasingly violent and invasive forms of policing. According to Johnson, the night before the riots, "every single body" was searched by the police "because the place was supposed to be closed, and they opened anyway."[10]

Johnson recalled being at a party uptown and arriving at the Stonewall Inn at 2 a.m., after the raid had already begun: "I was uptown and I didn't get downtown until about two o'clock, because when I got downtown the place was already on fire. And it was a raid already. The riots had already started. And they said the police went in there and set the place on fire. They said the police set it on fire because they originally wanted the Stonewall to close, so they had several raids."[11] The fire department and riot squad eventually arrived, successfully putting out the fire and dispersing the protesters. Riots involving thousands of people ensued in the area for six days. Johnson described the police's violent response to these protesters: "They were hurt on the streets outside of the Stonewall 'cause people were throwing bottles and the police were out there with those clubs and things and their helmets on, the riot helmets."[12]

Though the queer and trans riots throughout the 1960s preceded those at Stonewall, it was the emergence of an array of LGBTQ activist organizations, most notably the Gay Liberation Front, the Gay Activist Alliance, and Radicalesbians, that made the event so remarkable. These organizations, among others, carried forward the militancy that had fomented across the decade and announced a decisive break from the more conformist and discreet politics of homophile organizations.

At least two other Black gender-nonconforming people were present for the riot: cross-dressing, Black butch lesbian performer and community activist Stormé DeLarverie, and Black trans performer and activist Miss Major Griffin-Gracy. Miss Major was in her mid- to late twenties at the time of the rebellion. She had experienced police raids as part of New York City's drag scene, as a bar patron, and as a sex worker. Stormé DeLarverie was in her mid- to late forties at that time and had experienced her share of police violence because of her gender presentation and racial identity. She recalled being uptown performing with the drag performance group Jewel Box Revue when the riots started.[13] DeLarverie arrived after midnight to check on her friends. After she came, she remembered a police officer telling her to "Move on, faggot!" What happened after that is less clear. DeLarverie sometimes claimed that the officer hit her on the back of the head, and that she turned around and knocked him out. At other times, she claimed that she was not the rumored "cross-dressing Black dyke" who threw the punch that started the riot.

Despite these conflicting accounts, DeLarverie has continually been identified as the person who threw the first punch that started the Stonewall riot. And though Johnson remembered arriving late to the riot, she has been named in popular accounts as the person who threw the first brick at the police. These persisting narratives demonstrate a shift in how the story of the modern LGBTQ rights movement is told. That people of color have been falsely remembered as being on the frontline of the Stonewall rebellion speaks to cultural anxieties about a movement that has historically centered white gay men and, less so, white lesbians in ways that have left racial minorities, trans, and gender nonconforming people in the margins.

An often-cited moment in the years following Stonewall speaks to the marginal presence of racial and gender minorities within the post-war LGBTQ rights movement. Sylvia Rivera, a Latina trans activist, was also present at the Stonewall rebellion, but it was her 1973 speech that raised awareness about racism and the lack of trans inclusion within the movement. Born in 1951 in New York City, Rivera met Johnson in 1963 as a young "street queen." Rivera described Johnson as playing a motherly role in her life at that time. The mainstream gay rights movement marginalized underhoused sex workers and drag queens of color. An activist in the peace and Black freedom movements, Rivera brought her revolutionary spirit to Stonewall.

Rivera has refuted the claim that she threw the Molotov cocktail that sparked the riot. Rivera did not throw a Molotov cocktail or the first punch at Stonewall, but she did claim her place on the front lines of the LGBTQ movement. In 1973, Rivera interrupted the Christopher Street Day Liberation Rally—held yearly to commemorate Stonewall—to tell those at the rally that trans sex workers like her had paved the way for their liberation. She spoke of the violence she had experienced as a trans woman of color and sex worker. The reception to her speech was mixed. This moment has been taken up as a challenge to the white gay male–centered vision of the movement that had, before the Stonewall rebellion, included some people of color and trans people but marginalized them in their vision of liberation.

Three years prior to interrupting the rally, Rivera and Johnson had founded Street Transvestite Action Revolutionaries (STAR), an organization for trans youth of color living on the street and engaged in sex work. The group's political platform included "free gender expression, an end to prison injustice and homelessness, and the creation of an inclusive community that rejected binding definitions of gender and sexual identity."[14] Catering to the needs of trans youth of color who often fell between the gaps of social services, Johnson and Rivera created the short-lived STAR residence in the East Village, which housed as many as two dozen "street queens." The organization's multi-issue platform and intersectional focus led the way for the Black lesbian feminist and queer organizations of the post-Stonewall era.

### SECOND-WAVE FEMINISM AND THE POLITICS OF DIFFERENCE

As in previous decades, queer activists debated whether the movement should be broad-based and coalitional or focused exclusively on securing the rights of gays and lesbians. The break between the leftist, multi-issue Gay Liberation Front (GLF) and its offshoot, the Gay Activist Alliance (GAA), exemplifies this tension. Gay and lesbian activists organized GLF in the weeks after Stonewall. The group embraced coalitional politics and gay identity as a form of resistance. It viewed itself as revolutionary, believing that existing social institutions that imposed sexual roles and rigid identity categories must be abolished to achieve complete sexual liberation. The group quickly spread to cities across the nation and internationally. Then, a small group of GLF members became disaffected by the organization's emphasis on broad-based coalitions. Partly due to GLF's alliance with the Black Panthers, which some members deemed homophobic, the GAA developed with an exclusive focus on gay and lesbian rights issues. Both groups were more confrontational in their political demonstrations than homophile organizations of previous decades. Both organizations quickly developed branches across the country.

GLF created a space for trans people of color with its view of gender and sexual experimentation as a form of self-determination and the inclusion of racial and economic justice in its platform.[15] Marsha P. Johnson became active in the GLF's women's caucus, which aimed to disrupt male-centered visions of queer liberation. The creation of the GLF women's caucus confirmed the impact of the women's movement on queer activism. The 1963 publication of Betty Friedan's *Feminine Mystique* was a seminal moment in the women's movement. The book mobilized women to reject the post–World War II return to rigid gender roles that confined women to the home. In 1966, a racially diverse group of women who wanted to end sex discrimination founded the National Organization for Women (NOW) and appointed Friedan as its president. While organizations like NOW concentrated on the rights of women as a unified group, the 1970s gave rise to debates about the differences between women, including between heterosexual and lesbian women.

Lesbian struggles within the women's movement continued earlier queer activism against the heterosexism of society. Lesbian feminist activism was unique in its battles against an already marginal group that held viewpoints challenging gender and sexual oppression. Though the disparagement of lesbianism more often came from conservative voices outside the women's movement, lesbian feminists called attention to the homophobia within feminist organizations. While some feminists viewed lesbianism as a challenge to rigid gender and sexual roles, Betty Friedan worried that the issues raised by lesbians might jeopardize the credibility of the women's movement. The movement's challenges to patriarchy often gained participants the label "man-hating lesbians."

Faced with lesbian feminist direct-action campaigns at women's conferences across the nation, Friedan publicly derided lesbian dissenters as "the lavender menace." The rifts in the women's movement regarding lesbianism came to a head when a group of lesbian activists led by Gay Liberation Front women and Radicalesbians protested the second Congress to Unite Women in New York City in May 1970. The group arrived wearing Lavender Menace T-shirts and held the stage for two hours, discussing the heterosexism of society and challenging feminist views of sexuality as a public issue, not just a private one. The action was effective, resulting in several resolutions affirming lesbian difference and acknowledging the significance of lesbian issues to the feminist movement.

The growing visibility of Black feminism in the late 1960s and 1970s posed further challenges to monolithic conceptions of women as an oppressed minority. When Black women joined the women's movement, the focus on women as a unified group did not fully account for Black women's specific struggles. For instance, *The Feminine Mystique* targeted white heterosexual, middle-class women while neglecting the specific needs of working-class women and women of color. In her call for women to reject the post–World War II return to rigid gender roles that confined women to the home, Friedan did not consider Black women's historic participation in the labor force, including the domestic work on which white middle-class housewives depended. In part, Black women came together as consciousness-raising groups in response to such oversights in the women's movement.

Black women also came together because the prominence of male leaders often overshadowed women's leadership and participation in the Civil Rights Movement. Some women also experienced discrimination and harassment by men in the movement. Historian Kimberly Springer points out, "Far from contemplating formal organization, Black feminists reached out to one another to confirm that they were not alone in seeing disparities between the rhetoric of the civil rights movement and the treatment of women within the movement."[16] Black feminist consciousness developed through these burgeoning political and personal networks, eventually leading Black women to create formal organizations like the Third World Women's Alliance (TWWA) and the National Black Feminist Organization (NBFO), which centered Black women's personal and political concerns.

In 1968, former NAACP youth leader and Student Nonviolent Coordinating Committee (SNCC) member Frances Beal cofounded the Black Women's Liberation Caucus in an effort to formally examine how racism and sexism were affecting SNCC's constituency.[17] The caucus split with SNCC the following year, renamed itself Black Women's Alliance, and expanded its membership to include other women of color and poor women. Later that year, the group changed its name again, this time to the Third World Women's Alliance, reflecting its anti-imperialist stance and solidarity with Third World women in the US and abroad. Despite its broad political platform and focus on differences between women, this group, too, struggled to address heterosexist oppression. While the East Coast branch of the group included LGBTQ rights as part of its political platform, the Bay Area branch of the organization lost several members due to internal struggles over differences in sexuality.[18]

Another East Coast organization, the Combahee River Collective (CRC), foregrounded heterosexual oppression as a Black feminist issue. Founded in Boston in 1974, the CRC developed out of the members' disillusionment with the NBFO, which had formed a year earlier as an offshoot of NOW. The NBFO declared its mission as contesting male-dominated media images that represented the women's liberation movement as a movement for white women and a threat to the patri-archal social order pervasive in communities of color. These images prevented Third World women from perceiving the women's liberation movement as instrumental to their freedom. It rejected claims by Black male leaders that Black women involved in the women's movement were "selling out" or "dividing the race." NBFO leaders focused on how anti-racist struggles often centered on the suffering of Black men under white supremacy at the expense of Black women's experiences of racial and sexual domination since slavery. NBFO wanted to cre-ate positive self-images for Black women while holding the women's and Black liberation movements accountable for their needs. Despite its call for the Black community to "stop falling into the trap of the white male Left, utilizing women only in terms of domestic and servile needs," the group still fell into the trap of privileging normative gender and sexual roles through its investment in heterosexism.[19]

Black feminists first formed the CRC as a consciousness-raising group. To its credit, NBFO carved out a space for CRC cofounders Barbara Smith and Beverly Smith to call themselves feminists. A for-mer civil rights and anti-war activist, Barbara had previously viewed feminists as a group of privileged white women. Her attendance at the Eastern Regional Conference of NBFO changed her perspective. With her sister, Beverly, and the Black Power, anti-war, and feminist activist Demita Frazier, she reached out to other Boston-based con-ference attendees to start an NBFO branch in Boston. At its initial meeting, attendees devised a socialist critique of NBFO, arguing that it leaned too heavily into NOW's liberal agenda and that an integrated analysis of racial, economic, and sexist oppression was necessary to liberate Black women.

Dissatisfied with the NBFO, the new branch split off and formed its own group, naming itself the Combahee River Collective after an action led by the revolutionary abolitionist Harriet Tubman. Only after its initial meetings as an autonomous group did the CRC incorporate heterosexist oppression into its agenda. In its groundbreaking mission statement, the group stated, "A combined anti-racist and anti-sexist position drew us together initially, and as we developed politically we addressed ourselves to heterosexism and economic oppression under capitalism."[20] The group rejected a lesbian separatist stance in favor of a collective struggle with other Black and Third World people. Members' lack of racial, gender, economic, and heterosexual privilege compelled them to organize themselves autonomously.

In 1974, in New York, another Black lesbian feminist organization, Salsa Soul Sisters, was formed to address the marginalization of Black lesbians and lesbians of color in queer political organizations and the discrimination against Black women in social spaces like bars and restaurants. The group started as the Black Lesbian Caucus of the Gay Activists Alliance. The GAA's push for housing and workplace protections for sexual minorities, militant action against homophobic policies and police brutality, and backing of gay-friendly candidates made the group attractive to its Black lesbian members. But Black lesbians faced racism and sexism within the organization and created the caucus to provide lesbians of color a safe space to discuss their experiences. Led by the Reverend Dolores Jackson, a minister at the queer-inclusive Metropolitan Community Church and a women's prison, the group then broke off from the GAA and organized itself as a womanist organization: a culturally specific, Black women–centered ideology created by bisexual writer Alice Walker to acknowledge the multiple forms of oppression Black women faced.

Black lesbian feminists gained their ideological footing in the cultural expression of Black feminist writers and social critics in the 1970s. Toni Cade Bambara edited *The Black Women: An Anthology* (1970), one of the seminal texts of the Black women's literary renaissance. The collection featured contemporary queer Black women writers like Nikki Giovanni, Alice Walker, Paule Marshall, and Audre Lorde. The volume included TWWA cofounder Frances Beal's seminal essay "Double Jeopardy: To Be Black and Female," which was one of the first to directly connect Black women's experiences to feminism.[21]

Indeed, 1970 marked a watershed year in Black feminist cultural production, as Black women writers published political analysis and literary texts that could encompass the complexities of their lives. For example, Audre Lorde's second volume of poetry, *Cables to Rage*, included the long poem "Martha," considered one of her first published works to explore homoerotic themes.[22] The poem interweaves meditations on love, loss, and longing with a broader social and political analysis of racial, gender, and national politics. Lorde's example and her direct involvement in the CRC empowered its members to take on heterosexism in a time of intense homophobia in the country and within feminist and Black revolutionary nationalist organizations.

Though most Black feminist organizations dissolved by 1980, Black lesbian and lesbian-of-color feminist writers and publishers continued the literary and critical traditions of the previous decade. One crucial development in this vein was the founding of Kitchen Table: Women of Color Press, which included in its ranks Barbara Smith, Audre Lorde, Hattie Gossett, and Cherríe Moraga. Kitchen Table defined itself as "the only press in North America committed to publishing and distributing the writing of Third World women of all racial/cultural heritages, sexualities, and classes."[23] The press understood its work as cultural and political and designed it to create a communication network for women in the United States and worldwide. Two anthologies would become touchstones of Black lesbian and lesbian-of-color feminism: *This Bridge Called My Back: Writings By Radical Women of Color* (1981) and *Home Girls: A Black Feminist Anthology* (1983).

Persephone Press, a white women's press in Watertown, Massachusetts, first published *This Bridge Called My Back* in 1981. After Persephone Press shut down, co-editors Cherríe Moraga and Gloria E. Anzaldúa gained control and republished the volume through Kitchen Table. The editors began working on the book after experiencing racism and elitism at a women's retreat. Eventually, they shifted the book's focus to affirming the commitment of women of color to feminism. The editors encouraged their contributors to focus on their differences and envisioned the volume as creating a stronger solidarity between women of color in the US. The press viewed its work as connected to the worldwide freedom struggles of people of color. It used the term *radical* to put "revolution in the hands of women."[24] The volume included a section called "On Culture, Class, and Homophobia."

*Home Girls*, edited by Barbara Smith and published in 1983, used "home" as a metaphor to claim a space for Black (lesbian) feminists within the Black community and affirm that Black feminist consciousness emerged from the Black experience. The volume centered on the voices of Black lesbians and dispelled myths about the discussion of gender and sexual issues as a distraction from the real struggle of racism. It ultimately affirmed a home truth: there was a vital Black feminist movement in the US, and lesbians were central to the movement.

The publication of *This Bridge Called My Back* and *Home Girls* demonstrated how the growing emphasis on difference in the women's movement was shaping Black and women of color feminist politics. Black lesbian feminists incorporated their intertwined personal experience and political consciousness into their writings, thereby establishing the significance of lesbians in Black feminism and in the broader Black and women's liberation movements. These publications also showed the importance of cultural expression and community formation to these politics. Like the feminist consciousness-raising and network building of early Black feminist organizations, these volumes used culture to build communication networks and solidarity across differences.

Black lesbian feminists established a visible cultural presence on the East Coast that would also influence the development of Black gay male literary production and activism in the 1980s. Their emphasis on the arts and culture as a site of community building and political organizing anticipated the increasingly visible arts and urban nightlife scene that would sustain Black queer communities amid the rise of right-wing conservatism and racial, gender, and heterosexual discrimination in the public sphere.

## IDENTITY, VISIBILITY, AND PUBLIC CULTURE

In the late 1970s, Black queer people attained greater political visibility in municipal politics and fought to secure increased protections for their communities in law and policy. Black queer activist groups formed to resist the racial and sexual discrimination they experienced in the public sphere. Local Black queer organizations sprang up in metropolitan areas across the country. These gains took place against the backdrop of intensified homophobia, political conservatism, and racism under the Reagan administration and the rise of the New Right and Christian right. Black queer activists joined in the fight against the rising tide of conservatism while facing racial discrimination within lesbian and gay communities and sexual discrimination within Black communities.

The rise of American conservative politics in the 1970s presented one of the most significant obstacles to the women's and gay and lesbian movements. Conservative activist Phyllis Schlafly's ten-year fight against the Equal Rights Amendment to guarantee equal protections for all Americans regardless of sex provides one of the most notable examples. The success of Schlafly's anti-feminist campaign stemmed in part from the way she portrayed the advancement of women's rights as an opening for gay and lesbian rights. Schlafly's work to defeat the ERA provided scaffolding for the Christian right's campaign against lesbian and gay liberation in the late '70s and into the '80s. It also contextualized and confirmed Betty Friedan's fear that a focus on lesbian issues would jeopardize the success of the women's movement.

The coalition of religious and social conservatives known as the second New Right organized against the advancement of women's rights and gay and lesbian rights in the 1970s. One of their most notable efforts was the fight to overturn a gay rights ordinance in Dade County, Florida. The ordinance protected against housing and workplace discrimination based on sexual orientation and granted protections to teachers at private Christian schools. In 1977, celebrity singer and evangelical Christian activist Anita Bryant launched the "Save Our Children" campaign to repeal it. In her view, the ordinance allowed gays and lesbians to promote an alternative, immoral lifestyle among children and deprived parents of the right to teach their children biblical morality. Her campaign led to a special election and overwhelming popular support in favor of overturning it. The repeal of the gay rights ordinance in Dade County led to further repeals and gay rights defeats in Oklahoma, Kansas, and Minnesota.

Anita Bryant's "Save Our Children" campaign drew national media attention and incited a wave of conservative backlash against gay rights. It also empowered lesbian and gay activists to fight back and regain their rights. For example, in 1977, Dade County gay activists launched a nationwide boycott of orange juice after the Florida Citrus Commission, for whom Bryant had previously served as a spokeswoman, began supporting her campaign. In 1978, gay and lesbian activists in California organized against the Briggs Initiative. Sponsored by state senator John Briggs, Proposition 6 was a ballot measure to ban lesbians and gays and their supporters from teaching in California public schools. Lesbian and gay activists, including San Francisco Board of Supervisors member Harvey Milk, organized a statewide grassroots campaign against the measure. Californians voted down the measure, pronouncing the "No on Six" campaign as a decisive victory against a powerful conservative movement.

One can trace the emergence of self-identified Black gay organizations to the mid-1970s, as evidenced by the formation of the Association of Black Gays in Los Angeles in 1975. The beginnings of a national Black lesbian and gay rights movement came three years later in the mid-Atlantic region. In 1978, ABilly S. Jones-Hennin of the DC Coalition of Black Gays and Louis Hughes and the Reverend Delores Barry of the Baltimore Coalition of Black Gays joined forces to "pursu[e] power . . . as Black lesbians and gay men."[25] Out of the coalition between the Washington, DC, and Baltimore branches came the National Coalition of Black Gays (NCBG), the first national organization of lesbians and gays of African descent in the United States.

The NCBG had as its motto "As proud of our gayness as we are of our blackness." Under the umbrella of the NCBG, branches formed in major metropolitan areas across the country, including Philadelphia, New York, Norfolk, Minneapolis, New Orleans, Atlanta, Chicago, Portland, St. Louis, San Francisco, Washington, DC, Boston, and Richmond, Virginia, among others. The organization formally changed its name to the National Coalition of Black Lesbians and Gays (NCBLG) in 1985 "in an effort to raise its feminist consciousness and outreach to Black Lesbians."[26] NCBLG's board of directors included veteran Black lesbian feminist activists Audre Lorde and Barbara Smith. The group held a yearly national conference for Black and Third World gays. It published a news magazine, *Black/Out*, edited by the Philadelphia-based Black creative writer and journalist Joseph Beam, one of the leading figures of the 1980s Black gay cultural-arts movement. The magazine covered issues as diverse as anti-gay violence, Black queer arts and culture, and the trial of the anti-apartheid, gay rights, and AIDS activist Simon Nkoli in South Africa. NCBLG dissolved in 1990, reportedly due to staff burnout.

In 1979, the National Coalition of Black Gays and the National Gay Task Force—founded in 1973 as the first national gay nonprofit in the United States—sponsored the historic Third World Lesbian and Gay Conference, held at the Harambee House hotel in northwest Washington, DC. The organizers planned the conference to coincide with the National March on Washington for Lesbian and Gay Rights, being held in commemoration of the tenth anniversary of the Stonewall rebellion. For the first time, "gay Asians, Indians, Chicanos, Latinos, and Blacks . . . assemble[d] as a unified body" for the conference. The main goals were to create a nationwide network and address the intertwined problems of racism, sexism, and homophobia that Third World gays face.

Beyond its significance as an act of solidarity among Third World gays and lesbians, the conference held significance because it addressed stigma within Black and gay communities. The historic meeting ended with Third World gays marching down Georgia Avenue through a predominantly Black neighborhood. Led by the Salsa Soul Sisters, conference attendees arrived at the national march together to represent a visible Third World lesbian and gay contingent. Audre Lorde spoke at the Third World conference and was among the few people of color to take the stage as a speaker at the national march. Building on the political ideals espoused at the Third World conference, and by the CRC two years earlier, Lorde reminded national march participants, "Not one of us will be free until all of us are free." The conference and march announced a multi-issue agenda and moved toward increasing the visibility of queer people of color, which would guide activists in the 1980s.

This newfound visibility was also forged by the growth of Black queer public cultures, represented by the increasing number of bars and cultural spaces catering to Black lesbians and gays. The 1960s and '70s saw the proliferation of bars with predominantly Black queer clientele: In Chicago, there was the Warehouse, Jeffery Pub, and Club Escape. In New York City, there was Blues Bar, the Nickel Bar, the Warehouse, the Hideaway, Chi-Chi's, Paradise Garage, and Tracks. In Atlanta, there was Bulldogs, Foster's Lounge, Loretta's, and Marquette. In Washington, DC, there was Delta Elite, Brass Rail, and La Zambra. Many Black lesbians and gays preferred to socialize at house parties because they offered discretion and safety, since attendance was often limited to established networks.

Black lesbians often met at house parties because there were limited public spaces for women and because of the discrimination they faced in existing ones. Bar discrimination often occurred through carding. Gay-owned bars and restaurants frequently asked Blacks and women to present multiple forms of identification while not asking the same of white patrons. Dress codes or claims of bars being closed for a private event were also common forms of racial discrimination against Black gays and lesbians. In the early 1980s, Black lesbian activist Marlene Colburn, one of the founders of the New York City Dyke March, experienced carding at the lesbian bar party Shescape, held in various venues around New York City. Colburn sued the owners of the bar in 1985 for discrimination against Black and brown people. The flourishing public culture of bars and venues catering to predominantly Black queer people provided refuge from an otherwise hostile public sphere.

While bars often provided an escape from an otherwise racist, heterosexist, and transphobic society, Black queer people experienced police harassment at bars long after Stonewall. In September 1982, New York City police officers raided Blues Bar, a working-class Black queer bar in the Times Square area, after repeated police harassment of patrons in previous weeks. Following reports that two nearby police officers had been beaten by some of the patrons during the raid, despite no evidence to support these claims, forty police officers stormed into the bar, hurled homophobic slurs, and brutally beat bar patrons, primarily Black men and some trans women. The police officers were especially ruthless toward these women. Some patrons had to be hospitalized, and the officers caused thousands of dollars' worth of damage to the bar.

The Blues Bar raid sparked a multiracial coalition of 1,500 people to protest this police brutality and an investigation of the officers involved. While the police officers were not held accountable, the demonstrations evidenced solidarity among queer people across differences. Journalist Lionel Mitchell reported in the *New York Amsterdam News*, a Black newspaper, that "many white gays were asserting that the police would not have dared brutalize white people in the same way."[27] De facto segregation still stratified the queer bar scene. White queer people recognized through the example of the Blues Bar raid how interlocking systems of racial, gender, sexual, and class oppression made the bar's patrons more vulnerable to police violence.

After its opening in 1975, the ClubHouse in Washington, DC, became the central focus of Black queer nightlife in the District, serving as an important community space for Black lesbian and gay Washingtonians. In 1979, the ClubHouse held a "Rally Ball" to help fund the National Third World Gay Conference. It also held several campaign rallies and fundraisers in the early 1980s for Mayor Marion Barry and to support local Black queer activists' mission in taking a more forceful role in municipal politics. The ClubHouse would continue to serve as a multipurpose space throughout the decade.[28]

Nightclubs were not the only spaces where Black queer people congregated; a rich culture of the arts developed at this moment. In New York City, the Blackheart Collective and Other Countries, a writers' collective, served as spaces of artistic expression, community building, and social activism for Black gay men. In 1980, Harlem-born Isaac Jackson founded Blackheart Collective, a group of fellow New York City–based Black gay artists who channeled their creative energies into producing several issues of its literary journal, *Blackheart*: "Yemonja" (1982), "Blackheart 2: The Prison Issue" (1984), and "The Telling of Us" (1985). Due to disagreements among the leadership and the devastating impact of HIV/AIDS on Black gay communities, Blackheart disbanded in 1985, and another Black gay writing group formed in its wake.

In 1986, former Blackheart member Daniel Garrett called for forming Other Countries, a writers' workshop based at the Lesbian and Gay Community Services Center in New York City. Its mission was to develop, disseminate, and preserve the diverse cultural expressions of Black gay men. Other Countries believed that creativity was "an indispensable element of organizing people politically" and dedicated itself to the "creative empowerment" of Black gay communities through poetry workshops, public performances, and journal publications.[29] It published three edited volumes, *Other Countries: Black Gay Voices* (1988), the book-length *Sojourner: Black Gay Voices in the Age of AIDS* (1993), and *Voices Rising: Celebrating 20 Years of Black Lesbian, Gay, Bisexual, and Trans Writing* (2007).

Another space of Black queer creative expression and collectivity was the ENIKAlley Coffeehouse in Washington, DC. A converted carriage house in an alley between E, N, I, and K Streets, the coffeehouse provided a central hub for the burgeoning Black queer arts movement in Washington, DC, serving as a rehearsal, performance, and community gathering space for Black queer Washingtonians. In 1982, Black gay activist Ray Melrose, who eventually served as president of the DC Coalition of Black Lesbians and Gays, opened the space to cater to local queer artists. Audre Lorde, Barbara Smith, and DC-based Black gay poet, essayist, performer, and cultural critic Essex Hemphill, a prominent figure of the 1980s Black gay arts movement, graced the stage. Black lesbian filmmaker and performance artist Michelle Parkerson also performed there with artists' collective Station-to-Station. Visual artist and musician Wayson Jones performed there with Hemphill and Larry Duckette as the performance trio Cinque. The space also functioned as a meeting space for the DC-Baltimore Coalition of Black Gays and the Sapphire Sapphos. Amid the AIDS and crack epidemics and racist, sexist, and heterosexist backlash against civil rights gains in previous decades, ENIKAlley Coffeehouse offered a space of joy, creation, and reprieve for DC's Black queer community.

Churches also became important spaces for Black queer community formation and spiritual affirmation in the 1980s. Religious institutions and organizations had long been essential sites and sources of social connection, political mobilization, economic support, and community ethics in Black communities. But Black religious institutions had not often espoused a religious doctrine that is inclusive of queer people. Religious oppression took on greater resonance in this period, given the outsized role of evangelicals as lobbyists for anti-queer laws and policies in the United States. Black churches frequently adhered to this doctrine, advocating for marriage as a right reserved for heterosexuals. Many churches deemed homosexuality a sin and one of the worst one could commit. The "fire and brimstone" messages from ministers, including Black political leaders, caused emotional pain for and, sometimes, serious harm to queer people.

In the 1980s, when homophobia routed through the country's Judeo-Christian foundations intensified during the AIDS crisis, Black queer clergy created their own institutions for spiritual fulfillment. Notable among these is the Black, gender-nonconforming Archbishop Carl Bean's Unity Fellowship Church, founded in 1982 in Los Angeles. Unity Fellowship Church attracted many Black queer and trans congregants who could not find a home among Black churches that preached damnation to queer people and were inhospitable to drug-dependent and HIV-positive people. The church provided a sense of community and familiar church rituals that helped heal histories of neglect, pain, and marginalization among its predominantly Black, poor, and LGBTQ members. Unity Fellowship is often considered the first Black church for queer people in the United States, and today it has seventeen affiliate churches in the United States and the Caribbean. The affirming church movement that Bean pioneered has increased in subsequent decades.

### COMING TOGETHER IN A TIME OF CRISIS

Black queer community formation in the 1980s took place against the backdrop of, and sometimes in response to, the global AIDS pandemic. Though it had been present in the US since 1969, what we now call the HIV/AIDS was first recognized in the US in June 1981, when University of California, Los Angeles, physicians found cases of Kaposi sarcoma, a rare cancer that sometimes manifests in people with HIV, in five homosexual men. The race of the five men was not mentioned in the Centers for Disease Control and Prevention's (CDC) *Morbidity and Mortality Weekly Report*.[30] An additional two cases, one a gay Black man and the other a presumably heterosexual Haitian man, were not included in the report. Doctors in major cities around the country reported similar cases. AIDS became a national health crisis when the *New York Times* reported on the "rare cancer" seen in forty-one homosexual men in New York and California.[31]

The disease was also early on referred to as gay compromise syndrome and gay related immune disorder (GRID), among a range of other identity-inflected monikers, until in 1982 the CDC convened and renamed it acquired immune deficiency syndrome (AIDS). The following year, the CDC began tracking the disease by race and found cases among Black and Hispanic women and male prisoners.[32] Of particular note was the prevalence of the disease among Black children, who made up 50 percent of the caseload. In 1984, scientists isolated the human immuno-deficiency virus (HIV) as the cause of AIDS. President Ronald Reagan didn't bring up the AIDS crisis until a press conference in September 1985, assuring citizens that AIDS research was a high priority for his administration. His constituents were concerned that school-age children and medical personnel would be at risk for the virus. From 1981 to the 1995 invention of highly active antiretroviral therapy (HAART), AIDS claimed the lives of 501,310 people in the United States.[33]

Despite the disproportionate impact of AIDS on US racial minorities since its appearance, dominant AIDS discourses from scientific and queer activist communities focused on white gay men in the pre-HAART era. Black communities also failed to mobilize around the issue due to the stigma attached to homosexuality and HIV/AIDS. Though AIDS, like other viruses, does not discriminate, it primarily affects poor women, queer people, immigrants, sex workers, and drug users. Reagan's belated and limited response to the AIDS epidemic because of the stigmatized communities it impacted further exacerbated its effects. As late as 1986, five years into the epidemic, a National Academy of Science report called for presidential leadership to bring together all elements of society to deal with the problem.[34]

The Reagan administration's economic policies also factored into the failed AIDS response in Black communities. These policies produced divisions within Black communities because they benefited middle-class Blacks while entrenching poverty among Black poor and working-class people. The Reagan administration also cut social welfare programs that could have increased health access and social services for economically vulnerable people affected by the illness. The virus's initial neglect by scientists, politicians, including Black politicians, and Black institutions created the conditions for the virus to take hold in Black communities. From 1981 to 2019, more than 290,000 Black Americans died of AIDS.[35]

Facing the neglect of politicians, scientific institutions, and Black heterosexual communities, Black queer activists and advocates responded to the epidemic from the beginning. The early effects of AIDS on Black communities pushed activists like Miss Major Macy-Griffin and Stormé DeLarverie to shift their focus to caring for friends and community members affected by disease. The Washington, DC-based

Black queer–themed news magazine *Blacklight* cosponsored a forum at the ClubHouse and ran ads targeting Black gay men to raise awareness of the prevalence of AIDS in the Black queer community. After noticing that club members were going missing, ClubHouse manager Rainey Cheeks organized fundraisers, date auctions, nightclub events, and pajama parties to raise money for those who were unable to pay their rent. He also organized people into buddy systems to help ill members with everyday tasks.

Jewel Thais-Williams, owner of the Jewel's Catch One disco in Los Angeles, established Rue's House, the nation's first housing facility for AIDS-affected women and their children. Along with Archbishop Carl Bean, Thais-Williams founded the Minority AIDS Project. She also joined the board of directors of AIDS Project Los Angeles to "bring the services they provided down to the hood." The ClubHouse and Jewel's Catch One closed in 1990, with AIDS and the deaths of nightclub attendees playing a significant role.[36]

In 1984, Washington, DC-based Black lesbian activist Colevia Carter organized the first DC conference on women and HIV/AIDS. In the early 1980s, Carter served on the DC Human Rights Commission and helped form the Hughes/Roosevelt Democratic Club. This group sought to give Black lesbians and gays more representation in DC politics. Carter also acted as the Sapphire Sapphos' political action committee chair and did a stint on the executive board of the DC and National Coalition of Black Lesbians and Gays. Like other activists whose initial focus was on the broader struggle for Black queer liberation, Carter became an AIDS activist after witnessing its impact on her communities, dedicating her career to AIDS advocacy. When the NCBLG received a grant from the DC Commission of Public Health on "minorities and AIDS" in 1987, Carter helped develop the training program to organize Black volunteers for AIDS education in the community. At the same time, she worked full-time as a community resource development specialist for the DC Department of Corrections, where she also promoted AIDS education. In the mid- to late 1980s, Carter volunteered as chair of the Education/Outreach Committee at Whitman-Walker Clinic. In 1992, she became the DC Department of Health's state adolescent health coordinator, directing a program focused on HIV programs for children, adolescents, and women.

In 1985, the Chicago chapter of the National Coalition of Black Gays began educating Black gay Chicagoans on the South Side about AIDS. Executive board member Chris Cothran, who also ran the group's magazine, *Habari-Daftari*, had already been struggling to grow the chapter because many Black gay Chicagoans were closeted. Cothran believed it was harder to be open about one's sexual preference on the South Side as opposed to the North.[37] These conditions made it difficult for him to educate Black gay men on the South Side about the epidemic. In an interview in *GayLife* newspaper that year, Cothran relayed that, although the white community was discussing risk reduction, the Black community did not know about the epidemic.

One of NCBG-Chicago's first actions was a meeting at a South Side church, which Cothran described as "more positive than expected."[38] Cothran deemed the meeting a success because those in attendance not only recognized the epidemic was affecting Black and gay communities but also expressed a need to further educate the community about it. Despite the heterosexism that produced their secrecy and the racial and class stratification that left the South Side's Black gay community underinformed, NCBG-Chicago leaders risked stigma in the face of the urgent need to educate Black gay men and the broader Black community.

The deaths of Black bar attendees sparked early AIDS activism in Philadelphia, as they had in Washington, DC, at the ClubHouse. According to historian J. T. Roane, by 1986, at least five patrons of the Smart Place, a bar in the Chinatown section of the city that was popular among Black queer people, had died of AIDS. Noticing the neglect of social spaces where Black people congregated, including the Smart Place, community activists Rashidah Hassan (now Rashidah Abdul-Khasser) and Wesley Anderson cofounded Blacks Educating Blacks About Sexual Health Issues. BEBASHI launched a sexual health education campaign targeting public housing residents, Black religious organizations, and youth in foster care systems. BEBASHI went beyond the state's behavioral model, which did not account for the structural conditions that make disease possible, by promoting culturally specific AIDS education materials. Its AIDS campaign exposed how interlocking systems of oppression, especially poverty and de facto racial segregation, made Black communities more vulnerable to the disease. A critical aspect of its campaign was a series of films targeting Black heterosexual women. The videos emphasized how gender hierarchies shaped women's vulnerabilities to AIDS. They also made visible the reality of AIDS: that despite the dominant images of white gay men in state and media discourses on the virus, Black women were susceptible to it and dying from it. BEBASHI's intersectional approach to AIDS education and advocacy paved the way for current public health approaches that consider structural determinants of health as factors in HIV transmission.

In 1987, the AIDS Coalition to Unleash Power (ACT UP), the most noted AIDS activist group in the United States, began its direct action campaigns to get "drugs into bodies." Several local branches of the organization understandably received widespread critical and popular attention for ACT UP actions' scope, scale, and spectacular nature. Black feminists, queer activists, and other advocates began organizing against AIDS in the early 1980s, albeit on a much smaller scale; two years prior to the establishment of ACT UP, organizations such as Sisterlove, Inc., in Atlanta, Black and White Men Together in San Francisco, and the South Carolina AIDS Education Network developed safer-sex campaigns, culturally tailored education programs, and community care structures in the absence of community support and state protection. These regional initiatives contributed to raising awareness of the effects of AIDS in Black communities across the country. The US Public Health Service awarded the NCBLG a grant in July 1986 so it could host the first-ever National Conference on AIDS in Black Communities, in Washington, DC. Gil Gerald, former executive director of the NCBLG and director of the DC chapter, claims that Black feminists' and lesbian and gay activists' grassroots efforts created the model of cultural specificity and cultural competence.[39]

## CONCLUSION

Black lesbian feminist politics challenges us to juxtapose the state's narratives of progress with the realities on the ground. Robert Lomax, president of the Best of Washington, a social club for Black queer men, did just that. Though Washington, DC, was one of the first major cities to provide human rights protections for gay, lesbian, and bisexual people, Lomax believed that the majority of DC's Black queer population would remain closeted for quite some time. In an interview in the Washington, DC–based, queer-themed newspaper *Washington Blade*, he stated, "Most of them come from a religious background that is not compatible with the Gay lifestyle. The law does not protect them from their families, their colleagues, and their peers."[40] Lomax's point demonstrated why it was so crucial for Black queer people to come together in these decades. Though some were fighting for further legal protections from racial and sexual-orientation discrimination, they understood that these protections would not eliminate the intersecting forms of oppression they were experiencing on the ground.

Human rights protections and pleas for acceptance did not protect Black lesbians, gays, bisexuals, and trans people from racism, sexism, homophobia, transphobia, poverty, and AIDS phobia in the 1960s, '70s, and '80s. Black queer people banded together in the face of the ongoing structural inequalities that narratives of progress concealed. They established consciousness-raising groups, grassroots movements, and formal organizations, all rooted in the lived experiences of Black queer people.

Black queer collectivity extended beyond political activism. The public cultures that increased in the 1970s and '80s also emerged as spaces for community building; intellectual stimulation and sharing home truths; artistic creation and the dissemination of knowledge; joy, pleasure, and sex; and pride and celebration. These groups formed based on their experiences of discrimination on multiple fronts. Out of these experiences came cultural expression, political analysis, and activism that could encompass the intersecting forms of racial, class, gender, and sexual oppression they faced.

### CHAPTER SIX

# SURVIVAL IS NOT A LUXURY

On October 11, 1987, an estimated 250,000 people descended on the nation's capital for the second National March for Lesbian and Gay Rights.[1] The first had occurred in 1979, sparked by the assassination of San Francisco board supervisor Harvey Milk a year earlier. Milk, the first openly gay elected official in California, took charge of march planning after it had been stalled for years. His assassination by a political rival on the Board of Supervisors pushed community members nationwide to finish what Milk had started.

Organized by diverse groups of lesbian and gay activists across the country, the second march was largely a reaction to the federal government's slow response to the AIDS crisis and to the 1986 *Bowers v. Hardwick* Supreme Court decision, which upheld a Georgia law that criminalized private sexual contact between same-sex couples. The event brought together the various branches of the radical AIDS activist group ACT UP, and it was the first time the NAMES Project's AIDS Memorial Quilt was publicly displayed. More than one thousand elected officials and civic, labor, and religious leaders attended the march.[2] Presidential nominee Jesse Jackson pledged his support for gay rights and called for increased federal spending on AIDS research and education. The event ended with an act of protest against the *Bowers* decision held in front of the Supreme Court building, where an estimated eight hundred activists were arrested.

March leaders created a list of demands focused on recognition of lesbian and gay domestic partnerships, social services and sex education for gay and lesbian youth, a repeal of *Bowers*, and that "the term 'sexual orientation' be added to the Federal Civil Rights Act to prohibit discrimination against lesbians and gay men in employment."[3] They also called for a number of executive orders to "eliminate all discrimination based on sexual orientation in all aspects of executive branch employment, programs and policies."[4] Their demands included ending discrimination against people with AIDS (PWAs) and redistributing federal money from the military budget to health and social services for PWAs and AIDS research, education, and prevention programs. John E. Bush, cofounder of Men of All Colors Together Boston and cochair of the National Association of Black and White Men Together, was quoted in the *New York Times* as saying about the march, "All men are created equal. And we have to stand up and say, 'We're gay and we're here.' It is particularly acute for those of us of color. We've paid our dues and it's been painful. It's time we stop paying and start collecting."[5]

Bush's statement addresses two central concerns of the chapter. First, it demonstrates how, in the latter decades of the twentieth century and the first decade of the twenty-first, gays and lesbians viewed the fight for federal recognition and civil rights protection as the primary means to "stop paying and start collecting." The convergence of AIDS and civil rights activism at the second march shows how gays and lesbians sought to turn their pain into political grievance. Second, it shows recognition of the distinct needs and concerns of lesbians and gays of color within the broader fight for lesbian and gay rights.

Eight years later, on October 16, 1995, an estimated seven hundred thousand attended the Million Man March/Day of Absence to publicly express unity among African American men.[6] The event was organized by Louis Farrakhan, head of the Nation of Islam, and the Reverend Dr. Benjamin F. Chavis Jr., a veteran civil rights activist and ordained minister in the United Church of Christ. The primary emphasis of the march was on restoring Black men's place as leaders of their families and communities, as well as on enacting spiritual renewal in the face of the ongoing marginalization of the Black poor, especially Black men and boys, in the United States. The demonstration also served as a space of healing amid the pervasive stereotypes of Black men, the violence associated with the War on Drugs, police brutality (most notably the case of Rodney King), and gang warfare.

The leaders of the Million Man March called for Black men to atone for failing to take responsibility for assisting the community in realizing its full potential, and for their mistreatment of Black women. They also placed a strong emphasis on mending their differences with one another and with their inner spiritual beings.[7] In line with the march's emphasis on atonement, its mission statement called on the government to atone for the historical and current wrongs it had committed against Black people. It called for reparations, universal health care, affordable housing, rebuilding cities, and preserving and protecting the environment, among other calls for the government to right past wrongs.[8] However, these calls for government accountability and atonement came after the challenges march leaders posed to the community; their emphasis was on turning inward to stress personal and community responsibility for the problems in Black communities and to repair the broken bonds that emerged in response to the political, economic, cultural, and social changes of the post–civil rights era.

In his reflection on the twentieth anniversary of the Million Man March, published in the LGBTQ newspaper *Washington Blade*, former cochair of the DC Coalition of Black Lesbians and Gays, Courtney Williams, recalled fondly marching with a contingent of around 150 Black gays and a few lesbians to the Million Man March.[9] The marchers received support from passersby and by the time they reached the mall, the group had doubled. Williams remarked on how "the mass of brothers opened like the parting of the Red Sea to allow us to enter among the many hundreds of thousands already on the Mall." Williams and his fellow marchers saw their pre-rally march as an opportunity: "for their peers to see Black gay men as an important part of the community and that we are here to stay" and "to see us believing in ourselves enough to come out of the closet and be open about who we are as Black gay men—and to respect us more."[10] Williams's participation in the march shows how Black gay and lesbian desires for belonging, protection, and recognition were not only directed at the state but also at African American communities.

In this chapter, we show how legal reform efforts led by white gays and lesbians and mass mobilizations led by Black civic leaders, clergy, and grassroots activists impacted Black LGBTQ people in the late twentieth and early twenty-first centuries. We examine LGBTQ leaders' increasing emphasis on marriage equality and preventing hate crimes, and how Black queer people responded to and were marginalized by these efforts. Calling attention to racism's embeddedness within the law and its adjudication and enforcement, we show the limits of rights-based activism for alleviating the multiple forms of harm faced by Black queer and trans people. We then shift to a focus on how the broader African American community responded to the mainstreaming of gay and lesbian issues in US politics. For example, marriage equality became a key issue among the African American electorate through public support of California's Proposition 8 ballot initiative to ban same-sex marriage in 2008, and later in response to the Obama administration's announcement that it would no longer defend the Defense of Marriage Act in 2011.

To gain a broader perspective on African Americans' changing views of lesbian and gay issues, we look at how LGBTQ issues featured in mass mobilizations by African Americans: the Million Man (1995), Million Woman (1997), and Re-Ignite the Legacy (2004) marches. Though all these marches were focused on broader issues facing the Black community, either directly or indirectly they reinscribed heterosexual and gender norms by emphasizing the role of the family and the church as the most powerful Black institutions for affecting social change. We conclude with an analysis of the coterminous legalization of gay marriage in the US Supreme Court case *Obergefell v. Hodges* (2015) and the rise of the queer feminist–led Black Lives Matter movement. Black queer activists criticized mainstream LGBTQ activists for having a narrow political agenda that marginalized other pressing concerns faced by Black Americans, including anti-black state violence. Black queer and trans activists also pushed the Black Lives Matter campaign to be more inclusive of the distinct vulnerabilities of gender and sexual minorities. Centering Black queer and trans political issues in these coterminous movements shows how Black queer and trans people have been "squeezed between and invisible in" mainstream Black and LGBTQ movements and reveals the need for a broader political platform that can address the multiple forms of harm they face.

### RACE AND THE FIGHT FOR MARRIAGE EQUALITY

On September 17, 1998, the Harris County, Texas, sheriff's department received an anonymous call from a man reporting that "a Black male was going crazy in the apartment, and he was armed with a gun." The caller, Robert R. Eubanks, met the police when they arrived. The police asked Eubanks the location of the man with the gun, and he directed them to John Lawrence's apartment on the second floor. With guns drawn, four deputy sheriffs knocked on the door and entered after they found it unlocked. What happened next remains unclear due to conflicting accounts.

In his interview with legal historian Dale Carpenter, the lead officer, Joseph Quinn, claimed that they announced their presence. After receiving no response, the officers peeled off and began searching all the rooms in the apartment. During their search, they found a Hispanic male in his thirties on the telephone in the kitchen and arrested him. They noticed there was another bedroom behind the kitchen area. The four officers gathered to enter the dark room, and one of them, William Lilly, claimed to make out two naked men having anal sex—one on the bed, Tyron(e) Garner, a Black male; and the other, John Lawrence, a white male, standing behind him. The officers claimed that, even after yelling stop, the men continued to have sex "well in excess of a minute." Finally, the officers pulled Lawrence away from Garner. Lawrence and Garner were subsequently arrested and jailed for "homosexual conduct," which was illegal in Texas in private and public.[11]

Their arrest led to the landmark Supreme Court case, *Lawrence v. Texas* (2003), which decriminalized consensual same-sex intimate behavior on the basis that extending this right only to heterosexual couples violated homosexuals' Fourteenth Amendment right to equal protection of the law. The ruling overturned the *Bowers v. Hardwick* (1986) decision, which had found that the Fourteenth Amendment did not prevent a state from criminalizing private sexual conduct involving same-sex couples.

Although the case marked a significant victory for LGBTQ rights, the racial dynamics of the initial arrest have received less attention. After the two men were arrested, the initial witness, Eubanks, confessed to the police that he made up the story about a weapons disturbance because he was jealous that his current lover, Garner, was sleeping with his ex-lover, Lawrence.[12] Carpenter noted that it is likely that Eubanks used a racial slur rather than the descriptor "Black male" when phoning the police.[13] Eubanks spent two weeks in jail for filing a false police report. Eubanks's false report likely played a part in the sheriff's decision to take Lawrence and Garner to jail rather than issue them a citation, since the offense was a Class C misdemeanor. Carpenter believed that the officers may have taken the men to jail because of the potentially deadly situation for all parties involved. In Carpenter's interview with Quinn, the deputy sheriff stated, "It was a lover's triangle that could have got somebody hurt. I could have killed these guys over having sex. They were stupid enough to let it go that far."[14]

This major court victory for LGBTQ rights depended not only on the violation of a same-sex couple's right to privacy but also on long-standing stereotypes of Black men as violent criminals. Quinn's focus on a "lover's triangle" overlooks the stereotypes of Black criminality used by Eubanks. As Siobhan Somerville contends, "If we frame this incident in a way that does not detach the history of racism in the United States from that of sodomy and homosexuality, it is possible to see that the racialization of Garner may have played a significant factor in eliciting the police's scrutiny."[15]

Despite the intertwined nature of race and sexuality in this case, the racial identities of Garner and Lawrence are not included in the Supreme Court decision.[16] Yet, Garner's blackness—as figured by the haunting stereotype of the armed Black man "going crazy" in the apartment—did play a role. The extension of LGBTQ people's right to privacy was contingent on long-existing racial stereotypes that continue to erode Black people's right to privacy—especially in regard to warrant executions.

Though race is often unmarked in mainstream perceptions of LGBTQ people's fight for equality, it played a prominent role in the legal battles LGBTQ people faced in the first decade of the twenty-first century. This decade saw the rapid escalation of LGBTQ legal petitions for the right to marry. The Lambda Legal Defense Fund's major victory in the *Lawrence* case fostered this mobilization. Though not all courts citing Lawrence sided with the plaintiffs, the case played a significant role in LGBTQ people's legal fight for same-sex marriage rights: When the Massachusetts Supreme Court invalidated its same-sex marriage ban, they cited *Lawrence*. And when the California Supreme Court legalized same-sex marriage in the state, it also cited *Lawrence*. Only twelve years passed between the decriminalization of same-sex sex in *Lawrence* and the legalization of marriage in *Obergefell v. Hodges*.

Race or, more precisely, histories of racial discrimination also played a role in *Obergefell*. In *Obergefell*, the court identified marriage as a "keystone of the Nation's social order," stating that "states have contributed to the fundamental character of marriage by placing it at the center of many facets of the legal and social order."[17] The court also ruled that there is an abiding connection between marriage and liberty. This ruling rested on the *Loving v. Virginia* Supreme Court case, which invalidated interracial marriage bans under the law. In *Loving*, the court decided that Virginia's miscegenation statute banning interracial marriage violated the due process clause of the Fourteenth Amendment. The court declared that Virginia's miscegenation statute served no legitimate purpose other than "invidious racial discrimination." The court's finding that laws banning interracial marriage were intended to discriminate against racial minorities has made it a touchstone among LGBTQ rights advocates arguing that bans on gay marriage discriminate against sexual minorities.[18]

In *Baker v. Nelson* (1972), the Minnesota Supreme Court rejected a male same-sex couple's petition for a marriage license, unsuccessfully using *Loving* as an argument. The court found that there was a clear distinction between marital restriction based on difference in race and one based on difference in sex. Justice Anthony Kennedy cited *Loving* when the US Supreme Court struck down parts of the federal Defense of Marriage Act in *Windsor v. United States* (2013). Virginia federal district judge Arenda Wright Allen invoked *Loving* when she removed the state's constitutional amendment defining marriage as solely being between a man and a woman. The use of *Loving* by LGBTQ advocates and judges alike positions the landmark legal decision ending racial discrimination in marriage law as legal precedent for ending discrimination based on sexual orientation. Somerville calls this comparison the "miscegenation analogy" to show how it promotes a single-issue agenda that marginalizes communities who face discrimination based on both race and sexual orientation.[19]

The "miscegenation analogy" fails to capture the feelings of marginalization and invisibility of Black LGBTQ people within civil rights and LGBTQ rights movements. Sociologist Marcus Anthony Hunter found, in his interviews and informal conversations with Black lesbians and gays in Chicago, Philadelphia, and New York City over the course of the first decade of the twenty-first century, that they viewed marriage equality with skepticism because of their histories of un-belonging within the civil rights and gay rights movements. The researcher reported that Black lesbians and gays expressed "feelings of being simultaneously squeezed between and invisible within both the Black and gay communities," and thus marriage as the "ultimate attainment of cultural belonging" did not resonate with those who did not feel a sense of strong membership in Black and gay communities.[20] Hunter also found that the racial discrimination many Black lesbians and gays faced in their daily lives factored into their conceptions and considerations of the institution of marriage, its limitations, and the power dynamics within it. These examples show how the dominant discourse of gay marriage protection under the law as a necessary step to achieve liberty and justice for all sexual minorities marginalizes the views and experiences of Black queer people.

One aspect of the gay marriage debates that Hunter's interviewees considered was its historical legacy and foundations in ownership, particularly slavery. One interviewee, Kima, a twenty-five-year-old Black lesbian from Chicago, stated, "Gay marriage jumps over the simple fact that marriage as an institution is a problem. . . . I am worried that we may be forgetting the history of black people and marriage and slavery." Kima's response speaks to the gender and racial hierarchies inherent in marriage as an institution. As many feminist scholars have argued, the marriage contract has historically subordinated women and produced an unequal division of labor between women and men. It also has created a system of inequality in which women perform the work of social reproduction without remuneration.

This inequality has become entrenched due to the all-out assault that social conservatives have launched on social welfare since at least the 1970s. Conservative politicians and policymakers' attacks on social democracy discriminate against poor and unmarried people. Poor and unmarried people do not have the legal protections guaranteed to married couples. Nor do they have the economic wherewithal expected of married couples as private units that the state has deemed financially responsible for their own social well-being.

Histories of racial inequality exacerbate the gender inequality ingrained in the institution of marriage. The marriages of enslaved people were not legally recognized by the state, and the enslaved were deprived of the rights and privileges of marriage granted to free people. Slave masters also determined the validity of these marital unions and often did so only to pacify the enslaved. The sale of slaves as the property of masters often broke up these marital unions.[21] Even when tied to the emancipation of the enslaved, marriage became a means of social control.

Legal scholar Katherine Franke has discussed the dynamics of using marriage as a tool of recruitment for the Union during the Civil War. The Union Army began to enlist Black men enslaved in the state of Kentucky who were willing to run away from their masters and fight for the North. However, their family members often remained enslaved under the law. Some of those who enlisted were forced to leave their wives and children back on the plantations, which made these women and children more vulnerable to cruel treatment as retaliation. Even the family members who came along to the Union camp were not safe. The Union Army removed more than four hundred women and children from Camp Nelson, in Jessamine County, Kentucky, as recruitment numbers grew. In 1864, 102 women and children living in nearby encampments died in the freezing cold.[22] Even though the enslaved were freed by marriage through the act of enlistment, Franke says the right to legally marry created new vulnerabilities due to the racial and gender hierarchies already embedded in the institution of marriage.

Franke uses this case study to warn same-sex couples that being legally equal to marry does not necessarily change one's status as inferior within a broader system of racism and heterosexism and transphobia. Franke's findings have implications for the "miscegenation analogy," which leaves out an analysis of the history of marriage as a racist and patriarchal institution that historically has been exclusive and coercive. Even when some exclusivity was lifted in favor of extending to the enslaved the "freedom" to legally marry, this did little to guarantee the social welfare and bodily autonomy of Black women and children under the prevailing racist and sexist social order. Nor has it eliminated the gender and sexual stereotypes attributed to contemporary African American families. If we reassess the "abiding connection between marriage and liberty" from the perspective of African Americans, that connection becomes much more tenuous.

Beyond the question of whether the oppression faced by Black people and LGBTQ people can be compared, these examples reveal a more fundamental issue: the racism, sexism, and homophobia embedded in the nation's social order cannot be eliminated through the extension of rights. Many people view legal decisions like *Obergefell* as proof of social progress, but this hides the fact that racism, sexism, and heteronormativity still affect marriage and have done so for a long time. As historian Marc Stein has shown in his study of Supreme Court decisions and US legal constructions of sexuality, *Loving* reproduced social inequalities. Though *Loving* struck down cohabitation and marriage laws that included "race distinction," had the Lovings had sex or lived together outside the confines of marriage, they would have been vulnerable to prosecution under purportedly race-neutral fornication and cohabitation laws.[23]

Using *Loving* as precedent for LGBTQ freedom limits a broader analysis of the heteronormative ideals that undergirded the court decision. Moreover, it begs an analysis of how extending the right to marry as the ultimate form of national belonging and state protection holds up when considering the systemic inequalities faced by Black queer and trans people. Examining LGBTQ advocates' push for stronger hate crimes laws as a remedy to anti-queer and anti-trans violence further reveals these systemic inequalities. Centering Black trans women's experiences of racial and gender violence exposes the limitations of hate crime legislation that requires evidence of discrimination and uses carceral solutions as a preventative measure.

### HATE CRIMES AND THE LAW

On July 6, 1992, the body of a Black trans artist and activist was found floating face-down in the Hudson River with a head wound. The police ruled Marsha P. Johnson's death a suicide, but members of the gay and lesbian community, who considered Johnson a hero to the LGBTQ cause because of her involvement in the Stonewall rebellion, believed it was murder. In addition to hosting memorial celebrations of Johnson's life, members of the community started a campaign to demand a police investigation. "Justice for Marsha," a working group of the LGBTQ activist organization Queer Nation, issued flyers for a rally on Christopher Street near the Hudson. They demanded that the police reclassify the cause of her death from suicide to cause unknown and conduct a thorough on-site investigation of "transvestite hooking" from Christopher Street to Twenty-First Street. They also requested the arrest records and incident reports from that weekend and the days before, as well as demanding the continued availability of detectives to receive new information on a daily basis.[24]

The New York City Gay and Lesbian Anti-Violence Project posted a reward for any information in the "mysterious death of a famous transvestite."[25] They also suspected foul play given other such incidents in the area, "Because of a number of anti-gay incidents in the West Village around July 4, including one incident in which a person was pushed into the river by a gang of youths, the Project believes that foul play cannot be ruled out."[26] The ad hoc group Friends of Marsha also demanded justice for Johnson. They pressured the police to arrest and question the four males who, allegedly, were seen physically abusing her, spinning her around in the air, and calling her "faggot" and other names that night, just fifteen feet from where her body floated up from the bottom of the river. They also demanded that these young men be placed in a police lineup for identification by people mugged by men who matched their descriptions.[27] The group issued membership forms with a questionnaire asking potential members how they would like to participate in political demonstrations and if they had any documentation and interesting stories to archive to preserve Johnson's memory. Other groups called for gay men to unite in self-defense. In a flier calling for justice for Johnson, they instructed gay men to "PACK A PIECE IN YOUR PURSE BE A SISTER OF FEAR!"[28]

Queer Nation viewed Johnson's death as a sign of the failures of the Stonewall rebellion to improve the conditions of queer lives, especially since the Sixth Precinct that raided the Stonewall Inn was also the precinct called on to investigate her death. They viewed Stonewall and Johnson's participation in it as "putting queers on the map," yet the police scrutiny and abuse of queer communities had not stopped. The role of the state and its agents in policing and failing to protect queer life was especially poignant in the context of the AIDS epidemic. Police officers brutalized AIDS protesters and continued to neglect them when it came to their vulnerability to violence, especially sex workers like Johnson (who was HIV-positive and participated in AIDS activism). Queer Nation weighed ongoing police harassment against calling on the police to investigate the case.[29]

In 1993, New York Democratic congressman Charles H. Schumer reintroduced the Hate Crimes Enhancement Sentencing Act to the House of Representatives. The bill would amend the federal judicial code to require the US Sentencing Commission to put into effect or amend existing guidelines to provide for sentencing enhancement of no less than three levels if the court determines, beyond a reasonable doubt, that the crime was motivated by hate based on the actual or perceived race, color, religion, national origin, ethnicity, gender, or sexual orientation of any person. President Bill Clinton added the bill to the Violent Crime and Law Enforcement Act and signed it into law in September 1994. Commonly referred to as the "Crime Bill," the act remains controversial due to the Violent Offender Incarceration and Truth-in-Sentencing Incentive Formula Grant Program. The program authorized $10 billion in incentive grants to states to build or expand correctional facilities to incarcerate people convicted of violent crimes, and mandated that the incarcerated serve at least 85 percent of their sentences.[30]

According to the 2010 Congressional Research Service report *Economic Impact of Prison Growth*, the number of state and federal adult correctional facilities rose 43 percent between 1990 and 2005.[31] The nation's prison population more than doubled between 1980 and 1995. Though gender identity was not included as a protected category until the passing of the Hate Crimes Prevention Act in 2009, let's consider the Violent Crime Control and Law Enforcement Act as a response to the deaths of Black trans women like Johnson. Using carceral solutions to punish hate crimes helped expand the carceral state, which disproportionately impacts African Americans and sex workers. The rate of increase in the nation's prison population dropped steadily following the Crime Bill, indicating that the bill was not directly responsible for the increase. The point is that the Hate Crimes Enhancement Sentencing Act could not protect members of vulnerable populations like Johnson from the multiple forms of harm they experienced, like the racist, colorist, ableist, and anti-poor biases that factored into the overpopulation of African Americans, disabled people, and sex workers in jails and prisons.[32]

Civil rights protections require plaintiffs to prove that an act of discrimination has occurred—such as taking race, sexual orientation, or gender identity into account when hiring, firing, or leasing to someone. Legal scholars have shown how systemic forms of oppression such as racism, homophobia, and transphobia are embedded in the law and its adjudication and enforcement; because they often cannot be attributed to single actors, they often cannot be proven to be intentional acts.[33] Legal reform efforts focused on hate crimes legislation and punishing individual perpetrators of bias-related crimes leave intact the systemic oppression that makes marginalized communities vulnerable to hate crimes in the first place. Focusing on Black trans experience shows the limitations of using carceral solutions to prevent future hate crimes. The police were slow to investigate Johnson's death as a possible bias-related crime. During her life, Johnson claimed to have been arrested over one hundred times, undoubtedly due to her identity as a Black trans sex worker. Though the state professed its interest in protecting marginalized groups through "tough-on-crime" policies, these policies made Black trans women more vulnerable to incarceration and police harassment based on other markers of difference.

Hate crime violence moved to the forefront of the US public consciousness after the deaths of white trans man Brandon Teena in 1994 and white gay teenager Matthew Shepard in 1998. On December 24, 1994, John Lotter and Marvin Nissen kidnapped, raped, and assaulted Teena after he refused Lotter's advances at a gathering in Richardson County, Nebraska. Though the assailant warned him not to tell anyone, Teena reported the incident to the police the next day. One week later, Lotter and Nissen broke into the house where Teena was staying and fatally shot and stabbed Teena and his friends Phillip DeVine and Lisa Lambert. Devine was a twenty-two-year-old Job Corps student from Iowa who was in Falls City, Nebraska, visiting his girlfriend. Lambert was a twenty-four-year-old mother from Humboldt, Nebraska, who was renting the farmhouse where the three were murdered. News of the murders circulated in local, state, and some national media. The case became the subject of a true crime book, a documentary film, and a Hollywood feature film, *Boys Don't Cry* (1999), for which Hilary Swank won an Academy Award for Best Actress in a Leading Role. The story drew media attention primarily because of Teena's gender. The media constantly referred to Teena "posing as a man," making it a story of "deception."[34]

Teena's tragic murder received more media attention than the killings of Lambert, a white woman, and DeVine, a disabled Black man, especially after the release of *Boys Don't Cry*. Though the film brought unprecedented attention to hate crime violence directed toward trans people, Phillip DeVine's life and death were completely erased from the film. Critics have linked director Kimberly Peirce's omission of DeVine from the film to the history of racial stereotyping, where racial ideology can be dismissed under the guise of artistic license and the limitations of the genre.[35] The common description of DeVine's death as "wrong place, wrong time" disavowed the mutual constitution of anti-blackness and transphobia.[36] Including DeVine as a victim demonstrates how the crime was rooted in differences in race and class, as well as in gender and sexuality, and that whiteness played a role in making the victims' deaths a political rallying cry.

Despite the media's simplification and erasure of the differences that animated these murders, these differences have played a key role in gay rights activists' and LGBTQ advocacy organizations' lobbying for the government to enact federal hate crime legislation. For example, Lambda Legal wrote an amicus brief in support of *Brandon v. Richardson County* (2004), Teena's mother's lawsuit against the Richardson County sheriff to whom Teena reported his case. After reporting his rape, Teena faced discriminatory treatment that ultimately resulted in him losing state protection against his rapists' threat of retaliation. In its brief, Lambda Legal defined hate crimes as those "motivated by hatred of or bias against the victim because of the victim's race, color, religion, national origin, ethnicity, gender, sexual orientation, *or* gender identity," and declared hate crimes a "nationwide epidemic."[37] The brief drew from FBI statistics showing a steady rise in hate crimes and notably pointed to the escalating numbers in Nebraska, most of which were attributed to bias based on race or sexual orientation.[38] More central to the case, the brief cited statistics about victims' underreporting due to their fear of retaliation at the hands of the perpetrators and a distrust of the police and the criminal justice system. Lambda Legal viewed the prevalence of hate crimes as linked to victims' fear that reporting a crime would result in retaliation and that police would not come to their aid, citing Teena's murder as a prime example.

If Teena's murder emphasized the role of police neglect and discrimination in perpetuating a cycle of hate crime violence, Matthew Shepard's murder transformed the national and international awareness of gay men's vulnerability to violence and hate crime legislation. A white gay college student at the University of Wyoming, in the city of Laramie, Shepard was lured by two men he met at a gay bar to a parking lot. They then kidnapped him, tortured him, and left him for dead in the freezing cold. A mountain biker discovered Shepard naked and tied to a fence eighteen hours later, and after five days, Shepard succumbed to his injuries. Media attention was drawn to the brutality of the violence and to the Albany County sheriff's statement that Shepard may have been beaten because he was gay.

Communities in Laramie and across the nation held vigils for Shepard. Protesters in New York City staged a "political funeral" that ended in the arrest of hundreds. Prominent politicians and actors attended a candlelight vigil held by the Human Rights Campaign on the steps of the US Capitol. The day before Shepard's funeral, the US House of Representatives approved a resolution condemning the murder.[39] In his 1999 State of the Union address, President Bill Clinton stated that discrimination or violence based on sexual orientation is wrong and should be illegal, and he called on Congress to make the Hate Crimes Prevention Act "the law of the land." The act was reintroduced to Congress that same year, but it ultimately failed, despite support for hate crimes protections for sexual minorities by the majority of Americans. The Matthew Shepard and James P. Byrd Jr. Hate Crimes Prevention Act (Byrd was a Black man who was brutally murdered by three white men, two of whom were associated with white supremacist groups, in Jasper, Texas, in 1998) did not pass until 2009 because some lawmakers believed there were laws already in place to address the crimes outlined in the bill and that the bill might violate free speech for those speaking out against the LGBTQ community for religious reasons. However, naming the act after Matthew Shepard underscored the significant role played by the legacy of anti-queer violence in making this act the law of the land.

In its guide to state implementation of the act, the Human Rights Campaign declared it "a significant victory in the fight for equality for lesbian, gay, bisexual, and transgender people."[40] If we consider Shepard's legacy, however, we can see how forms of difference other than sexual orientation and gender identity came into play. Arguably, the case garnered national attention and calls to amend the law because of Shepard's whiteness and his legibility as a gay male. The focus on Shepard's death as a sexual-orientation-related bias crime eclipsed the assailants' subsequent involvement in racially motivated violence. Shepard's assailants brutalized two Latino youths after assaulting Shepard, calling attention to how, like in the Teena case, racism also created the conditions for Shepard's murder. Race undoubtedly played a role in Shepard's uptake as a symbol of the gay rights movement and hate crimes as a national problem that needed to be remedied through the extension of state protections. Unlike Teena, whose gender identity was not understood by the media and largely described as cross-dressing and deception, Shepard's gay male identity was easier for society to digest. The complex matrix of power that made Shepard a target for violence and an ideal victim remains unmarked in hate crimes legislation based on bias against a single group.

More than that, the act's limitation lay in the need to prove beyond a reasonable doubt that bias motivated a violent act. However, the act gave the US Department of Justice authority to investigate and prosecute violent crimes based on bias. It provided grants to states and local communities to cover the expenses of these investigations and prosecutions. It also funded local programs to combat hate crimes committed by juveniles and to train law enforcement to prevent and better handle these cases. It only covered acts of violence and did not protect against hate speech. To enforce these laws, civil rights attorneys not only needed to identify a homophobic or transphobic actor but also to prove that the actor directed their violence toward a specific group (often through speech) to establish a violent act as a hate crime. This requirement discounts the fact that homophobia and transphobia in society make these communities vulnerable and that individual social actors expressing these views need not be present for a bias-motivated attack to occur. Focusing on passing a federal hate crimes law as a significant victory for LGBTQ equality does little to fight systemic inequality. It also leaves people who face inequality based on multiple and interconnected forms of difference on the edges of the fight for equality.

The debates over and responses to the murder of twenty-five-year-old Black trans woman Amanda Milan revealed how systemic oppression and negotiating multiple forms of difference make trans women of color more vulnerable to harm. The debates also revealed that the law cannot fully adjudicate or remediate violence targeting Black trans women. According to the New York County District Attorney's Office, Milan was fatally stabbed after "a dispute developed" involving three men on June 20, 2000.[41] A police detective interviewed by the *New York Times* also stated that the murder resulted from a "dispute," dismissing Milan's aunt Diana Dyer McKee's account of the event as a hate crime: "I think it was a hate crime, and anyone who is trying to call it anything else is simply wrong."[42] McKee and other family members who were interviewed misgendered Milan even as they understood, as Milan's cousin Tammika L. Clark explained, that Milan's life was taken because "their way of life is not going to sit well with any of us."[43]

In July of that year, New York governor George E. Pataki signed a bill that imposed harsher sentences for crimes motivated by racial, religious, ageist, and homophobic bias. The bill did not include bias against trans people. The district attorney indicted all three men involved in Milan's death, but not for a bias crime.

Milan's murder mobilized trans communities, in part because it happened on the heels of the unsolved murders of three trans sex workers in Harlem over the course of fourteen months between 1997 and 1998, including Black teenager Ali Forney. The community held a memorial service and march and erected a shrine in honor of Milan. Octavia St. Laurent (of *Paris Is Burning* fame) delivered the eulogy, reportedly asking how many of us have to die before the community recognizes that we are not expendable.

Despite cosponsoring the memorial service and march, the Human Rights Campaign (HRC) declined to financially support the vigil at the trial of Milan's murderer. In their correspondence regarding the request, HRC field directors stated, "HRC's resources are being strategically spent on legislative efforts, including preparing for reintroduction of the federal Hate Crimes Prevention Act that would give federal authorities jurisdiction over hate crimes motivated by 'real or perceived gender.'"[44] In her response to HRC, Sylvia Rivera, president of Street Transgender Action Revolutionaries (STAR), which reformed in the wake of Milan's murder, stated, "HRC bears responsibility for forgetting the fact that we [trans people] have lives, feelings, and blood just like other human beings. Your people had no problem [at Stonewall] using the anger of our people who gave their all, who had nothing to lose, who brought you out of the closets. We still have nothing to lose, and we are still giving our all."[45] Despite these setbacks, Milan's death became a unifying event in the trans of color community.

These competing legal, familial, and activist accounts show the limits of hate crimes sentencing laws for protecting people like Amanda Milan. They reveal how bias, even the bias created because of the mainstreaming of LGBTQ advocacy groups like the Human Rights Campaign—exemplified by its strategic shift toward legislative efforts focused on gender identity rather than grassroots protests as forms of intersectional resistance—made Milan vulnerable. Milan's stigmatized identity as a Black transsexual made her a target of law enforcement officers and street harassment, and made her only marginally accepted by her family.

The marginalization of trans people from the workforce and subsequent participation in sex work also made Milan vulnerable. New York City's "Quality of Life" policing campaign, which cracked down on street-level offenses and increased police harassment of trans women assumed to be sex workers, also made her vulnerable. So did racial stereotypes about Black people, and Black men in particular, as dangerous criminals. Law enforcement officers' designation of the crime as resulting from a "dispute" rather than hate may reveal their bias against trans people, but more importantly it reveals that designating the cause of Milan's murder and adjudicating it based on that cause does not mean that the broader social and structural forces that made her vulnerable did not also come into play.

As her friend Octavia St. Laurent concluded in her eulogy, "Death will not be the last word for Amanda Milan."[46] Milan was an aspiring fashion designer and dreamed of one day being able to afford gender-affirming surgery. She was described as having a "welcoming smile dabbed with glossy red lipstick" and as a "full-figured Beverly Johnson look-alike."[47] She lived in uptown Manhattan with her Pomeranian, Ashley. Her mother told the *New York Amsterdam News* that she was "the joy of her life" and a "gift and a treasure" from God who "she could enjoy and rejoice in."[48] Milan's aunt, Diana Dyer McKee, said she gave Milan "unconditional love" during her childhood. Milan and her two closest friends of ten years, Kim and Simone, were described by community members as being "thick as thieves."[49] She was well-liked in the trans community, many of whom were also sex workers, and often assisted those in need. One friend remembered how Milan had helped her when she was near-homeless and assisted her in enrolling in school. Milan traveled to Milan, Paris, and London, and kept company with a fashionable crowd. She believed in standing up for yourself. Her friend Patra described her attitude toward life: "Her philosophy was, ameliorate yourself from mental slavery, stand up and be who you are, play that role. . . . She believed there is no justification in living a life of lies if deep down in your heart you know who you are."[50]

Octavia St. Laurent's question about how many Black trans women have to die before the community recognizes their value could also be directed to Black communities. The Million Man and Woman Marches in the mid- to late 1990s embodied a political shift in Black communities to an increased emphasis on personal responsibility and internal transformation that omitted the pressing political concerns facing Black LGBTQ people, who were already marginalized in predominantly white LGBTQ social movements. As we've seen, one pressing issue that Black LGBTQ people faced was violence. In the failure of Black communities to mobilize around issues like homophobic and transphobic violence, these fights were left to mainstream LGBTQ organizations that, ultimately, advanced a rights-based approach to ending hate crimes that did not consider the broader range of issues Black communities faced. Black queer and trans people's "feelings of being simultaneously squeezed between and invisible within both the Black and gay communities" are further revealed when examining their participation and marginalization in the marches that mobilized masses of African Americans in the mid-1990s.[51] The emphasis on internal transformation that guided these marches would change in the mid-2000s when Black religious leaders encouraged African Americans to become more vocal actors in petitioning the state to defend heterosexual marriage, scapegoating Black LGBTQ people in support of the federal government's moral agenda.

### MARCHING ON WASHINGTON

The Million Man March organizers' call for Black men to take their places as leaders of their families and communities raised questions about the gender and sexual norms that undergirded Black politics. Were the families and communities in question presumed to be heterosexual? Were queer families and communities included in this vision of national unity? Black gay men offered diverging responses to these questions.

Black gay activist Courtney Williams remembered the march as inclusive of sexual minorities. He participated in a pre-march rally with speeches by Black gay leaders such as Keith Boykin of the National Black Gay and Lesbian Leadership Forum and Ken Reeves, the openly gay mayor of Cambridge, Massachusetts. Williams marched with his best friend, Jeffrey Mason. Mason's straight brother marched in solidarity with the two gay men.[52] The rally participants walked to the National Mall donning T-shirts with slogans such as "I Am a Man" and "As proud of our gayness as we are of our blackness," the former a reference to the 1968 Memphis sanitation workers' strike and the latter the slogan for the National Coalition of Black Gays and Lesbians. Black gay men were often viewed as being unaffected by the political turmoil "real" Black men faced because homosexuality was seen by many Black leaders and their constituents as a psychopathological response to white supremacy. Therefore, it is significant that those present not only participated in the march but also embraced the Black gay men who participated with them.

Though some Black gay men appreciated how the march redeveloped bonds, others critiqued its limited political platform. Black queer scholar Robert F. Reid-Pharr, who attended the march, criticized the march leaders' emphasis on the personal responsibility of men to fix the "broken" Black family—imagined as the primary unit of the Black nation—as failing to hold the state accountable for the socioeconomic conditions of Black communities. Reid-Pharr related this political message to the pathologizing rhetoric of US politicians and policymakers, most famously espoused in Daniel Patrick Moynihan's 1965 report, which blamed single Black mothers and the breakdown of the Black family structure for their outsize numbers on the welfare rolls. Moreover, Reid-Pharr argued that the call for "heroic Black masculinity to restore order in our various communities," and the organizers' request that Black women stay home, left Black gay men marginal within this self-help movement because it was rooted in a vision of the heterosexual, male-dominated Black family.[53] This left Black gay men with a choice to reject the march because of homophobia and misogyny, to repair this flawed vision through Black gay visibility and representation, or to attend and voice their criticism after the fact.

Black gay visibility and representation are particularly salient issues since no Black gay or bisexual men spoke on the stage. Cleo Manago, founder of the Black same-gender-loving advocacy group Black Men's Xchange, was prepared to speak but was removed from the program.[54] Black political leaders who had previously supported lesbian, gay, and bisexual people, like march organizer Benjamin Chavis, veteran civil rights activist the Reverend Joseph Lowery, and longtime Black activist Jesse Jackson, did not mention LGBTQ rights in their speeches. Though there were no outright expressions of homophobia by march speakers, the omission of Black sexual diversity at the march attested to Black queer men's marginalization within this united Black male community. As historian Deborah Gray White argues, "Had any of these speakers seen Black LGBTs as integral to the community they were addressing, their remarks and actions might have been more inclusive."[55] Despite these major oversights, some Black gay men, like

Williams and Reid-Pharr, chose to go to the march, though they experienced it in different ways.

Many Black women supported the march, and leading Black women activists and artists like Rosa Parks, Dorothy Height, Dr. Betty Shabazz, and Maya Angelou spoke on the stage, demonstrating their investments in repairing the heterosexual, middle-class family, viewing it as integral to Black liberation. After all, one of the agenda items for the march was atonement for the mistreatment and neglect of Black women. In his speech, Jesse Jackson mentioned gender equality as one facet of the Black nationalist agenda.

Another example of how gender and sexuality were incorporated into the Black male political agenda was when a march speaker brought up the subject of AIDS. Nation of Islam minister of health Abdul Alim Muhammad boasted about his research with Barbara Justice on the drug Kemron, a purported cure for AIDS. As proof of the success of the drug after four years of drug trials, Muhammad brought to the stage two Black men who claimed that they were no longer HIV-positive, which was received by the audience with vocal affirmation and thunderous applause. This moment represented a shift in Black leaders' response to HIV/AIDS as infections among heterosexual Black women and men changed the face of the epidemic. The presumed heterosexuality of the men brought to the stage coupled with the omission of LGBTQ issues among speakers suggests that the disproportionate impact of HIV/AIDS on Black gay and bisexual men, especially in Washington, DC, was not part of the agenda. Despite the fact that the Million Man March raised issues of gender and sexuality, its organizers pushed a political agenda that conditioned community reconciliation on the restoration of the heterosexual family and male leadership.

Two years later, Black women organized the Million Woman March, which had an estimated higher attendance than the Million Man March. Held October 25, 1997, in Philadelphia's Love Park, Million Woman March organizers, led by local organizer Phile Chionesu and small business owner Asia Coney, themed the event "Repentance, Restoration and Resurrection," mirroring the emphasis on spiritual renewal that guided the Million Man March. The event included an actual march and a political rally and had more of the feeling of a street festival. Like the earlier march, the women's march emphasized restoring the family as an essential step in strengthening Black communities.

The Million Woman March departed from the Million Man March in that it did not solicit or receive the endorsement of traditional Black churches, Black elite institutions, or Black civil rights organizations, a choice made to maintain its grassroots origins. This decision caused internal division among the leadership regarding whether to solicit corporate donors and the role of prominent African American women in march planning.[56] March organizers did, however, receive early support and endorsement from the Nation of Islam. March leaders relied on local organizers in other cities—including some who helped organize the men's march—to get people to Philadelphia, since many potential attendees complained that the march planning was disorganized.[57] Even though there were disagreements within the group and problems organizing the march, the organizers' grassroots aspirations showed that they wanted to shift the focus from state and cultural institutions and corporate interests, and put more emphasis on group self-reliance.

White noted that their focus on self-help and personal transformation was ironic given the economic decline under the Reagan and Bush administrations, and that President Bill Clinton's pledge to end "welfare as we have come to know it" produced the conditions for Black women's political mobilization.[58] Still, the march promoted social justice alongside its focus on personal responsibility and internal transformation. The host of the event, actor Jada Pinkett, coupled her discussion of the significance of the heterosexual family with condemnation of the two hundred thousand "sistas" incarcerated. African American writer Richard Wright's daughter, Julia Wright, came from France and called on the crowd to hold Philadelphia leaders accountable and for the release of political prisoner Mumia Abu-Jamal. Former Black Liberation Army member Assata Shakur, who fled prosecution in the United States, sent a message to be read from her exile home of Cuba. Minister Louis Farrakhan, one of the few men who spoke at the march, issued a statement condemning violence against women, rape, and incest. In her keynote address, Congresswoman Maxine Waters, a Democrat of California, called for an investigation of the alleged CIA involvement with the drug traffickers who brought crack into Black communities, more government funding for HIV/AIDS (which she deemed the biggest killer of Black women at the time), and self-definition amid the stereotypes of Black women on welfare, citing a range of statistics on Black women's success, health outcomes, and workforce participation.

Despite its broad political platform, the religious tenor of the march, as evidenced by the theme, also produced adverse effects for the Black lesbian and bisexual women who attended. Black lesbian and bisexual women's decisions about whether to participate were shaped early on when gospel singers Angie and Debbie Winans of the legendary Winans family announced their plan to sing their single "Not Natural" at the event. The song was a response to increasing lesbian and gay visibility in popular media and repeated the popular refrain in Black churches that homosexuality was incompatible with biblical scripture. The song's circulation on the radio airwaves was met with irate calls from gay and lesbian individuals and groups, and some parishioners boycotted it after it was performed at Black churches across the country. The program committee chairwoman for the march, Paula S. Peebles, who claimed to have no previous knowledge of the Winans' plans to sing the song or about the controversy surrounding it, told the *Philadelphia Inquirer* that the march was an interdenominational event with no single religious perspective, also adding that the march "is not dealing" with issues of sexual orientation.[59] Though the march organizers ultimately asked the Winans not to sing the song, news coverage of their plan to sing it and the program chair's omission of issues of sexual orientation speak to the environment that the march produced for Black queer women.

Black lesbians like Sheila Alexander-Reid, editor of *Women in the Life* magazine, said she felt the event was positive overall but found some of the rhetoric to be less than inclusive. In an editorial cowritten with staff writer Straight from LA, Alexander-Reid called the rhetoric of the march "divisive," even though it was supposed to ensure sisterhood across sexualities. They described the intolerance promoted at the march as "scary for those of us considered outside of the mainstream."[60] Several readers of *Women in the Life* who attended the march responded to Alexander-Reid and Straight from LA's editorial with mixed responses about whether they truly felt the bonds of sisterhood they had sought from the march.[61] Though the editorial and its responses do not explicitly mention homophobia, the extensive coverage of the march in a Black lesbian–themed magazine reveals the stakes of sexual minority participation. The cheering crowd seemed to support the heteronormative notions of racial authenticity and family that some march speeches relied on. If these mass political mobilizations were symbols of Black unity, then Black lesbian, gay, and bisexual people held a nominal place within that unified body.

In his speech at the march, comedian and civil rights activist Dick Gregory called the Black family one of the strongest Black institutions, alongside the church. Both of these institutions marginalize Black LGBTQ people. This was exemplified in the 2004 Re-Ignite the Legacy march, which bolstered the Bush administration's faith-based initiatives aimed at strengthening heterosexual marriage and family. Bishop Eddie Long, who presided over New Birth Missionary Baptist Church in the Atlanta metropolitan area, called for Black churches across the nation to become more vocal political actors on issues such as banning same-sex marriage, reforming education and health care systems, and creating economic opportunities. To further promote this mission, Long and the Reverend Bernice King, the youngest daughter of the Reverend Martin Luther King Jr., co-organized a march in Atlanta, starting at the late civil rights leader's gravesite and ending at Turner Field.

The December 11 march drew an estimated 20,000 to 25,000 people, including 100 pastors from across the nation.[62] Long led the march carrying a torch lit by the eternal flame at King's tomb. Beginning the peaceful march at MLK's gravesite, calling it "Re-ignite the Legacy," and co-organizing it with Bernice King all signaled Long's intent to continue the "principals, morals, and ideals" that guided the late King's civil rights activism.

An estimated fifty predominantly Black gay and lesbian counterprotesters gathered at a nearby corner after being displaced by the police several times and chanted "Hey, hey! Ho, ho! Homophobia has got to go!" as the marchers passed. Long published an op-ed in the *Atlanta Journal-Constitution* newspaper addressing critics of the march, writing, "Critics say that the march was against the principles, morals and ideals of the late Rev. Martin Luther King, Jr. They have singled out the church's position to support a constitutional amendment for the protection of marriage between one man and one woman as our sole issue and even speculated that King would not have taken such a stance. . . . I do believe, however, that he would not have been silent for what he believed was right."[63]

Georgia had a Defense of Marriage Act in place since 1996, and in the month prior to the march Georgia voters had ratified a constitutional ban on gay marriage. These existing laws made counterprotest organizers question if, in addition to his message of bigotry, Long was scapegoating gays to support the moral agenda of then president George W. Bush's administration.[64] Long's ministry had received a $1 million faith-based "individual development" grant from the US Administration for Children and Families that year.[65]

The counterprotesters found allies in other prominent civil rights leaders such as the Reverend Joseph Lowery and Congressman John Lewis, both of whom condemned the march.[66] Black state legislators predicted that the march would have little impact since the Republican Party refused to take up issues important to the Black community and brought up how Coretta Scott King, the widow of Martin Luther King Jr., was a supporter of gay civil rights.[67] A majority of Black state lawmakers voted against Georgia's gay marriage ban, and Representative Tyrone Brooks, a Democrat of Atlanta, and the Reverend Timothy McDonald III, head of the African American Minister's Leadership Conference, were plaintiffs in the case to strike down the ban. Despite state legislators' predictions about the impact of this individual march, the Bush administration's faith-based funding initiative held sway with many African American voters. African American support for Bush grew slightly, with more substantial gains in battleground states, helping to secure Bush's reelection.[68] These unprecedented federal awards to Black churches coupled with the administration's support for banning gay marriage helped reshape Bush's image among traditionally Democratic African Americans.

African Americans took center stage again in California's 2008 referendum on gay marriage. Proposition 8, the ballot measure overruling the California Supreme Court case that legalized same-sex marriage in the state, passed in the November state elections with 52 percent of the vote, taking away a right granted only six months earlier.[69] The passage of Prop 8 pitted African Americans against the cause of gay rights, since national election poll data showed that 70 percent of African Americans voted in favor of it. After its passage, news media outlets blamed Black people, citing their religious beliefs as the cause of their homophobia. Protect Marriage (Yes on 8), an alliance of conservative and religious groups that led the campaign in support of Prop 8, worked closely with Black churches across the state, encouraging ministers to deliver sermons in favor of the ban. Black lesbian journalist and activist Jasmyne A. Cannick opined that it was the failure of the white gay community to reach out to Black people that was partially to blame for the passing of the ballot measure.[70]

Cannick's notion of outreach extended to the question of whether the right to marry was a priority among Black lesbian and gay communities whose identities were marginalized by what she called the "gay/Black divide": "The way I see it, the white gay community is banging its head against the glass ceiling of a room called equality, believing that a breakthrough on marriage will bestow on it parity with heterosexuals. But the right to marry does nothing to address the problems faced by both Black gays and Black straights. Does someone who is homeless or suffering from HIV but has no health care, or newly out of prison and unemployed, really benefit from the right to marry someone of the same sex?"[71] Cannick's question revealed the limits of legal reform. She indicted the white gay community for its narrow focus on marriage rights, a political platform that did little for Black LGBTQ people whose primary concerns were survival in the face of illness and poverty.

The concerns raised by Cannick did not stop LGBTQ activists from pursuing marriage rights as one of its primary campaign issues. In 2013, LGBTQ people made significant progress with the repeal of the 1996 Defense of Marriage Act (DOMA), which defined marriage as between a man and a woman and denied same-sex couples the right to adopt children and the legal recognition of partnership needed to petition for custody of children, hospital visitation rights, or child support in divorce proceedings.

The racial politics underlying this victory were witnessed in the response of the Black voters who formed the Democratic Party's base. African Americans who voted in record numbers for the first Black president of the United States, Barack Obama, were forced to confront the "gay/Black" divide when the Obama administration announced it would no longer defend a federal law banning same-sex marriage because it considered the legislation unconstitutional. During his first election campaign, Obama backed DOMA. Then, in 2010, Obama signed the repeal of the "Don't Ask, Don't Tell" federal policy banning lesbians, gays, and bisexual people from openly serving in the military, and he announced his evolving views of same-sex marriage. Obama's shifting position on gay rights brought the gay/Black divide to the center of American politics, and DOMA would ultimately be struck down by the Supreme Court in 2013, paving the way for the legalization of same-sex marriage in *Obergefell*.

## CONCLUSION

The legal victory in *Obergefell* coincided with the Black Lives Matter movement, a social media campaign against police brutality targeting African Americans that began after the death of Black teenager Trayvon Martin at the hands of community watchman George Zimmerman in Sanford, Florida, in 2012. The campaign reached its apex with the death of Black teenager Michael Brown at the hands of the police in Ferguson, Missouri, in 2014. That this movement was led by queer feminists was no accident: it drew from Black lesbian feminist and Black AIDS activism in the 1970s and 1980s that mobilized around the most marginal members of Black communities, rejecting the politics of respectability that would require a victim to be free of social stigma to deserve community outrage and state accountability in the face of injustice.

Yet, the urgent political issues facing Black communities required LGBTQ movement participants to focus on cisgender, heterosexual Black men and boys in the fight for racial justice, and less so on marginalized gender and sexual minorities. The Black LGBTQ organizations that fought alongside the broader Black community in the Black Lives Matter movement had to do so knowing that some Black community members did not view their struggles as gender and sexual minorities as linked to struggles for racial justice.[72] Some Black community members viewed racial discrimination as distinct from, and more pressing than, gender and sexual discrimination. The simultaneity of these movements revealed the ongoing marginalization of gender and sexual minorities in Black movements for racial justice and Black LGBTQ people's marginalization in the mainstream LGBTQ rights movement.

Black people's continued struggle against racial discrimination in law enforcement demonstrated how white gay and lesbian campaigns for equal protections under the law did little to remedy the systemic inequalities that have made Black LGBTQ people vulnerable because of their race as well as their genders and sexualities. In her op-ed responding to the Prop 8 controversy, Cannick challenged white gay advocacy groups' belief that "winning the battle for gay marriage" would "symbolically bring about equality for everyone": "That may seem true to white gays, but as a Black lesbian, let me tell you: There are still too many inequalities that exist as it relates to my race for that to ever be the case."[73] Cannick opined that it was not only a matter of including Black LGBTQ people in struggles for equality. Rather, it was the failure of mainstream gay rights activists to organize based on a broad political platform that could include inequality in education, the workforce, policing, and incarceration, among other societal systems. Cannick's comments mirrored those of Rivera and St. Laurent in their indictment of the narrow political interests of mainstream LGBTQ rights organizations.

The Black Lives Matter movement went a long way toward ending the gay/Black divide by focusing on the various forms of difference within each of these categories. Forces from within the movement, including the #SayHerName and #BlackTransLivesMatter campaigns, pushed for more inclusion. Political pressure from Black feminist and trans organizations prompted movement leaders to consider the history and current incidences of police violence against Black cis and trans women, with the Stonewall rebellion being one of the most obvious examples of this history. Moreover, this movement sought to dismantle the gay/Black divide by pushing African Americans who had not yet transformed their views on LGBTQ people and viewed them as outside of the community and not subject to the same forms of discrimination as Black people. The movement's eventual call for *all* Black lives to matter moved us closer to the political vision that

St. Laurent and Rivera called for—a movement that might have saved Amanda Milan's life.

Black Lives Matter activists did not seek legal reform. They sought to transform the racist, sexist, biphobic, homophobic, and transphobic society that made Black LGBTQ people more vulnerable to state violence in the form of policing and incarceration. They recognized that the state was one of the biggest perpetrators of violence against African Americans and that hate crimes statutes, same-sex marriage rights, and the right to serve openly in the military could do little to remedy this fact. The #AllBlackLivesMatter campaign showed that Black LGBTQ people could not rely on the state as the guarantor of rights and that the racism embedded in the law could not be eliminated by hate crime laws. In so doing, they demonstrated how the single-issue focus of the mainstream gay rights movement perpetuated inequality in its failure to address the multiple and interconnected forms of oppression that devalued Black queer and trans lives.

# AFTER WE'VE CREATED
# OUR OWN HISTORY

B lack queer filmmaker Cheryl Dunye's film *The Watermelon Woman* (1996) tells the story of Cheryl, a video store clerk and videographer who searches for a Black queer past.[1] She watches the 1930s film *Plantation Memories* and becomes intrigued by the "mammy" character, Elsie, credited as "The Watermelon Woman." Cheryl sets out to learn more about the woman in the film, interviewing her own mother and friends of the family and visiting libraries and independent archives. Eventually, Cheryl discovers that the woman's name is Fae Richards, and she is a "sapphic sister."

Among its themes, *The Watermelon Woman* dramatizes the search for Black queer history as Cheryl encounters the racial, gender, and sexual power dynamics that underlie archival research. For example, the grassroots lesbian archive Cheryl visits lists Black women's archival records separately. The library separates research on women in film from research on Blacks in film. And there is the matter of Fae's misnaming in the film credits. Cheryl finally finds answers in the personal archive of Fae's lover. The film culminates with Cheryl presenting her findings, providing photographs, film footage, and a voiceover narrating Fae's life. At the film's end, the viewer learns that Fae is a fictitious character, famously displaying a title card with the line, "Sometimes you have to create your own history. The Watermelon Woman is fiction." Dunye's mockumentary made history as the first feature film directed by a Black lesbian. Scholars and cultural critics continue to teach and write about the film for the powerful lessons it teaches about power, silence, and erasure in the Black queer historical archive.

*The Watermelon Woman* suggests that its protagonist, Cheryl, had to create Black queer history from fiction because archival records do not exist. Using constructed photographs, film footage, and a fictionalized character, Dunye confronts the marginalization of Black queer people in the archive by constructing a fictive narrative. The recent visibility and recognition of Black queer and trans people suggests that there is no longer a need to fabricate our history. We as scholars continue to confront power relations in the archive, and the availability of archival records of Black queer history pales in comparison to those individuals and communities accorded more power. Still, there is a growing body of research on Black queer history and culture and increased recognition of the contributions of Black queer Americans, past and present.

What, then, is the importance of *A Black Queer History of the United States* if that history has received much more recognition? What happens when we no longer have to invent a Black queer past and can draw on a vast array of primary and secondary source material to reconstruct it? What new power dynamics must we confront if there are Black queer archives in mainstream libraries and grassroots archives? What happens when librarians are much more inclusive in their cataloging and view the contributions of Black queer Americans as culturally significant?

Since the release of *The Watermelon Woman*, there has been an explosion of Black queer media. Barry Jenkins's Academy Award–winning film *Moonlight* (2016) has marked the growing interest in and popularity of Black queer film and television. Among other works are Patrik-Ian Polk's *Punks* (2000) and *Noah's Arc* (2004), Rodney Evans's *Brother to Brother* (2004), Tina Mabry's *Mississippi Damned* (2009), and Dee Rees's *Pariah* (2010) and *Bessie* (2015). Black queer artists have made strides in the visual arts. Some notable figures include Mickalene Thomas, Kehinde Wiley, Texas Isaiah, Nina Chanel Abney, Tourmaline, and Jonathan Lyndon Chase. Musicians include Frank Ocean, Big Freedia, and Lil Nas X. Black queer writers such as Roxanne Gay, Jericho Brown, Janet Mock, and Danez Smith have published award-winning and critically acclaimed works of memoir and poetry. In theater, there is Branden Jacobs-Jenkins, Tarell Alvin McCraney, Robert O'Hara, Donnetta Lavinia Grays, and Aziza Barnes. Film and television actors include Raven-Symoné, Laverne Cox, Tessa Thompson, and Amandla Stenberg, among many others. These cultural producers are actively making Black queer history. In our current moment, Cheryl would not need to invent a Hollywood actress and likely would not encounter stereotypical monikers in the film credits.

Dunye has made six films since the release of *The Watermelon Woman,* including the award-winning made-for-television movie *Stranger Inside.* We want to look at one of these later works to address our questions about the continued importance of reconstructing a Black queer past. *Black Is Blue* (2014) shows Dunye's continued interest in questions about history and power.[2] The narrative short follows Black, a young Black transgender man living on the streets of Oakland, California, amid the tech boom in the San Francisco Bay Area in the 2010s. The expansion of the tech sector was accompanied by an increase in homelessness, housing displacement, and rent hikes. The rapid gentrification of the Bay Area transformed Oakland's character; it pushed the low-income residents of color, which helped create its cultural identity, to the surrounding suburbs. The effects of these large-scale transformations can be observed in Black's everyday life, as he now lives in his car despite working full-time as a security guard at an apartment complex.

In the interview that opens the film, Black addresses the stereotypes he faces as a homeless person by stating that he does not have an addiction or mental illness. The interview is interspersed with images of Black brushing his teeth in an empty parking lot, getting dressed in his car, and walking to the gym before heading to work. Black is also viewed with suspicion as a Black trans man. As he gets out of his car, he encounters a white man who watches him out of what appears to be fear. Black acknowledges this as another stereotype he meets daily. His self-consciousness in the initial interview shows how stereotypical perceptions of race, gender, and class influence his vulnerability as an underhoused Black trans man.

Black's character reflects the realities of contemporary Black trans life. He experiences discrimination in the housing market. In the film, he discusses how landlords do not want to rent to him because they see that he is living in his car. He feels anxious performing daily activities because of his identity. He takes extra precautions in the gym locker room because he "does not have the right anatomy." He meets a woman on the street who flirts with him, but he "does not get the digits."[3] Dating is difficult for him because he is excluded from women's spaces after his transition, as witnessed through his violent encounter with his ex-lover Deja and her friends later in the film. He risks rejection in the dating scene without an inclusive space that affirms his identity and desires.

Black's confrontation with Deja serves as the film's central dilemma. She has not seen Black since his transition. Black encounters Deja and her friends in the apartment complex where he works. When their paths cross, Deja feels romantically betrayed after seeing Black, crying, "You left me to become a man." Deja's friends then assault Black. His transmasculinity appears to be an affront to their claims to identity and belonging as queer women. After they flee the scene, Black's coworker Derrick discovers him lying on the ground, bruised and disoriented. Black's encounter with Deja and her friends calls forth memories of the past as a source of pain. Black's past is a source of pain because he feels Deja could have been the one, and he lost a friend group and space of belonging. We view Black's painful encounter with the past as a metaphor for our efforts to write a Black queer history of the United States, when that history has been characterized by pain, violence, loss, and betrayal. His transition from Blue (his name before transitioning) to Black suggests that his past does not dictate his present or future, but his feelings of loss and longing reveal his close ties to it.

Despite drawing the audience's attention to the systems of inequality that influence Black trans lives today, the movie portrays trans identity as a positive "attribute" of Black life that could help Black "climb." In her signature mockumentary style, Dunye intersperses the film's credits with talking-head interviews with the cast. Trans actor Andre Le Blanc discusses what it meant for him to play Black's cisgender Black male coworker Derrick. Derrick calls Deja and her Black lesbian friends "bulldaggers" after they arrive at the apartment complex where he and Black work. Black's assault by Deja's crew is worsened by the fact that Derrick witnesses it; Black cannot reveal to Derrick the dynamics of the situation. Derrick's limited worldview contributes to the hetero- and gender-normative social environment that makes Black's everyday life as a trans man difficult. The revelation of actor Le Blanc's trans identity destabilizes this reality and reveals possibilities of transforming it.

Similarly, the actress Lisa Evans, who plays Deja, discusses how difficult it is for her to determine whether her character is transphobic. Her self-critical perspective makes a different social interaction between Black trans men and Black lesbians possible. The final talking-head interview with Kingston Farady, who plays Black, further establishes the film's future orientation. Farady says that he does not view trans identity as a minority status but as an "attribute" that he believes will help him "climb." Here again, Dunye blurs the distinction between fact and fiction. This time it is not about creating a Black trans past but about reorienting the viewer toward the future of Black life, crafted through self-invention. Black's present and future are linked to yet distinct from the history he is reminded of through his encounter with Deja. *A Black Queer History of the United States* similarly shows how Black queer and trans life is not wholly determined by histories of racial, gender, sexual, and economic marginalization. We document how Black queer and trans Americans have created their own histories and forged pathways for future generations.

Like Dunye, we blur fact and fiction to address the gaps in the archive. The historical archive has not yielded the kind of pleasurable and consensual experiences of same-sex desire represented in neo–slave narratives. These texts, like the talking head interviews in *Black Is Blue*, interrupt and destabilize the violence of the archive. Through fiction, we can glimpse how erotic touch became a tool of survival and an assertion of humanity among the enslaved. We also follow Dunye in our play with names to broaden the meaning of blackness from its association with a history of racial and sexual domination. Dunye's Black broadens the meaning of blackness to encompass trans identity. We have sought to expand dominant notions of blackness so that gender subversion becomes central to histories of racial freedom. A trans reading of the Crafts' and Cathay Williams/William Cathay's stories helps us account for gender variance in the Black past, which would not be possible if we followed the historically specific identity categories the archive imposes.

Black's persistent awareness of his transgender identity may seem like a personal struggle. If we read Black as embodying the broader African American experience, then we can reflect on how his hyper-vigilance connects to the image of the race. The white man's apparent fear of Black conjures historical stereotypes of Black men as predatory and criminal. It also channels moments in African American history when, under the white gaze, Black queer people have had to worry about how their gender identities and sexual practices might confirm the stereotypes used to justify Black disenfranchisement. Looking back at the experiences of prominent queer and trans intellectuals in the Black freedom movement, we can see how the character Black's encounter speaks to the pressure to conform to Euro-American gender and sexual norms. This pressure often comes at the expense of one's own gender and sexual freedom.

Even when the needs of Black queer and trans people have been disregarded and their desires implicitly discouraged by heterosexual Black communities, they have found ways to create unique forms of cultural expression. In fact, our marginal locations have proved to be fertile grounds for creativity. Farady reconfigures the meaning of trans identity as a positive attribute that will help him reach his goals. We have shown how queerness and transness have been positive attributes in the development of a rich Black cultural tradition and Black liberation movements. Black queer people have contributed to musical genres like the gospel, blues, and hip-hop in ways that have been critical to the survival of Black people. Works by artists such as Bessie Smith, Frankie Knuckles, and Tim'm T. West have provided critical tools of resistance to the racism, heterosexism, and transphobia that have marginalized all Black people.

Black queer resistance has not only emerged through individual acts of cultural expression. It has also gained expression through collective acts of political resistance. Black longed for the community of women he lost after he transitioned. Rather than viewing Black's transition as a reason to reinforce differences between Black lesbians and Black transmen, we can look toward the broad and coalitional political platforms advanced by Black lesbian feminists in the 1970s. Black lesbian organizations like Combahee River Collective (CRC) saw their struggles as Black lesbians as connected to the struggles of other marginalized people. The CRC provided precedent for the All Black Lives Matter campaign by affirming the inherent value in the most marginal members of the Black community.

The All Black Lives Matter campaign provides an antidote to a history of racial and trans marginalization in the mainstream LGBTQ movement. If anyone should have benefited from the Stonewall rebellion, it should have been Black trans people like the character Black. Racial and trans justice have not been historically centered in the queer movement, leaving Black trans people to negotiate the dangers of the public sphere on their own. This also applies to the legacies of the Black liberation movement—especially in Oakland, the birthplace of the Black Panther Party. Black liberation has been historically preoccupied with the free movement of Black bodies in public space. Civil rights activists' push for desegregation and the Black Panther's inclusion of freedom from prisons and jails in its ten-point program are clear examples of this. Eliminating the "color line" has long been a focus of African American politics. Yet, the gender and sexual norms that have upheld the color line have been underexamined, which has resulted in the curtailment of the civil rights of Black trans people like Black.

The Black community's failure to address the discrimination and brutality faced by some of its most marginal members has left mainstream movements to address issues like anti-queer and anti-trans discrimination and violence through legal reform. Legislative reform does not address the systemic inequalities affecting Black queer and trans people. The legal right to same-sex marriage granted in 2015, one year after the release of *Black Is Blue*, would do little to remedy the systems of inequality that left Black underhoused and brutalized by his former peers. The mainstream queer movement's turn to the law and law enforcement to achieve equality has inadvertently advanced queer rights while reproducing racial inequality. These laws would not eliminate the stereotypes of Black men as criminals that surface in Black's encounter with the white man at the beginning of the film.

Black's experiences illustrate how Black queer and trans people have been squeezed between mainstream Black and queer social movements. In this book, we have centered Black queer and trans voices rather than keeping them confined to the tight space between these movements. We have shown how, despite their multiple marginalization, Black queer and trans people have crafted selves, communities, cultural expression, and political analyses that would appear to be impossible given the histories they inherited. Their variant identities and behaviors have served as important elements in their quests to liberate themselves and all Black, queer, and trans people.

A Black Queer History of the United States provides important lessons for the present and future. As we were writing this book, education nonprofit the College Board was piloting a new AP course in African American studies, which would provide high school students with college credit in the field before their enrollment in an accredited university. Controversy arose over the course curriculum, as some controversial topics, such as intersectionality, Black Lives Matter, and Black queer studies, were rumored to be cut from the curriculum. The controversy stemmed partly from the broader US political debate about the role of critical race studies in K–12 curriculums and the push from conservative leaders to cut aspects of these curricula they consider to be racially divisive.

As we reviewed the revised curriculum for the AP course, we noted that only Black gay civil rights activist Bayard Rustin and the Black lesbian activist group Combahee River Collective were included in a curriculum that included four hundred years of African American history. The inclusion of Black lesbian and gay people in the African American studies curriculum is evidence of the mainstream recognition of queer contributions. Still, the rumored excision of Black queer studies, intersectionality, and Black Lives Matter, all of which are rooted in Black queer liberation movements, reminds us of ongoing attempts to limit our knowledge of the expansive pathways toward liberation that Black queer people are devising.

In light of the ongoing marginalization of Black queer history in K–12 and higher education curricula, it remains essential for us to create our own histories. These histories are not solely born out of histories of collective marginalization. Rather, queerness and transness have served as key elements in fashioning new pathways toward Black liberation. Whether it has been through creative practices of naming and self-invention, embracing our most marginal citizens, resisting legibility and capture, creating venues and cultural forms through which we can come together, innovative practices of collective survival, or fierce critique and ordinary resistance, we have refashioned the meanings of blackness beyond its historical association with domination and devaluation. The film *Black Is Blue* reminds us that our encounters with the Black queer past may help us understand how the past has shaped our present, yet these encounters should not limit our understanding of what Black is or ain't but show what it most expansively can be.

# NOTES

**INTRODUCTION**

1. Marlon T. Riggs, dir. *Black Is . . . Black Ain't: A Personal Journey Through Black Identity*, California Newsreel, 1995.

2. *Black Is . . . Black Ain't* (transcript), Signifyin' Works, 1995, https://newsreel.org/transcripts/black-is-black-aint-transcript.pdf.

3. Riggs, *Black Is . . . Black Ain't*.

4. Riggs, *Black Is . . . Black Ain't*.

5. "New York; Health Department Tests Urged in H.I.V. Scare," *New York Times*, November 8, 1997, https://www.nytimes.com/1997/11/08/nyregion/metro-news-briefs-new-york-health-department-test-urged-in-hiv-scare.html.

6. Riggs, *Black Is . . . Black Ain't*.

7. Riggs, *Black Is . . . Black Ain't*.

8. Riggs, *Black Is . . . Black Ain't*.

9. DeNeen L. Brown et al., "Slavery's Bitter Roots: In 1619, '20 And Odd Negroes' Arrived in Virginia," *Washington Post*, August 24, 2018, https://www.washingtonpost.com/news/retropolis/wp/2018/08/24/slaverys-bitter-roots-in-1619-20-and-odd-negroes-arrived-in-virginia/.

10. E. Carlton Winford, *Femme Mimics*, Winford, 1954, https://www.queermusicheritage.com/femme8.html, cited in *Zagria* (blog), December 2008, https://zagria.blogspot.com/2008/12/phil-black-190-1975-female-impersonator.html.

11. Thaddeus Russell, "The Color of Discipline: Civil Rights and Black Sexuality," *American Quarterly* 60, no. 1 (2008): 101–28.

12. Angelique Harris, "Review: Homosexuality and the Black Church," *Journal of African American History* 93, no. 2 (2008): 262–70.

13. Russell, "The Color of Discipline."

14. "Night Clubs Found Chief Vice Centres, *New York Times*, October 14, 1929, https://www.nytimes.com/1929/10/14/archives/night-clubs-found-chief-vice-centres-committee-of-fourteen-in-its.html.

15. Lucious Limpwrist, "'Les Girls' Had a Ball at Rockland, Honey!" *New York Age*, December 7, 1957.

16. Russell, "The Color of Discipline," 101.

17. Russell, "The Color of Discipline," 103.

18. "Picketing the Ball," *New York Amsterdam News*, December 7, 1962; Elyssa Maxx Goodman, *Glitter and Concrete: A Cultural History of Drag in New York City* (Toronto: Hanover Square Press, 2023), 64.

19. "Shake Dancer Postpones Sex Change for Face Lifting," *Jet*, August 6, 1953, p. 19.

20. Clare Sears, "This Isn't the First Time Conservatives Have Banned Cross-Dressing in America," *Jacobin*, March 15, 2023, https://jacobin.com /2023/03/cross-dressing-law-united-states-history-drag-bans.

21. Tony Gild, "Tripping the Light Fantastic and the Funmakers Ball," *National Insider*, April 20, 1969, pp. 12–13.

22. Sears, "This Isn't the First Time Conservatives Have Banned Cross-Dressing in America."

23. Willie Sabb, "My Mother Was a Man," *Ebony*, November 1953, 80, at Internet Archive, https://archive.org/details/sim_ebony_1953-06_8_8 /page/75/mode/1up?q=%22GeorgiaBlack."

24. Russell, "The Color of Discipline."

25. "The Man Who Lived 30 Years as a Woman," *Ebony*, November 1975, p. 85, reprinted from *Ebony*, October 1951.

26. Sabb, "My Mother Was a Man," 80.

27. "The Man Who Lived 30 Years as a Woman."

28. Mark Stein, *The Presidential Fringe: Questing and Jesting for the Oval Office* (Lincoln, NE: Potomac Books, 2020), 155.

29. Joe E. Jeffreys, "Joan Jett Blakk for President: Cross-Dressing at the Democratic National Convention," *TDR* 37, no. 3 (1993): 186, https://doi .org/10.2307/1146317.

30. Jeffreys, "Joan Jett Blakk for President."

31. Jeffreys, "Joan Jett Blakk for President," 187.

32. Jeffreys, "Joan Jett Blakk for President," 192.

33. Jeffreys, "Joan Jett Blakk for President," 194.

34. Joan Jett Blakk, interview by Owen Keehnen, published in *Chicago Outlines*, July 1992, https://www.owenkeehnen.com/interviews.

35. Bettina Aptheker, *The Morning Breaks: The Trial of Angela Davis* (Ithaca, NY: Cornell University Press, 1997).

36. "Exclusive: The '70s Revolutionary Icon Speaks Out," *Out*, February 1998, p. 67, https://www.out.com/out-exclusives/cover-gallery/2011/11 /16/1998#rebelltitem2.

37. Riggs, *Black Is . . . Black Ain't*.

38. Riggs, *Black Is . . . Black Ain't*.

39. Barbara Smith, "Why I Left the Mainstream Queer Rights Movement," *New York Times*, June 19, 2019, https://www.nytimes.com/2019/06 /19/us/barbara-smith-black-queer-rights.html.

40. Eric Marcus, interview with Barbara Smith, *Making Gay History* podcast, season 6, episode 3, first published November 21, 2019, https:// makinggayhistory.org/podcast/barbara-smith/.

41. Sherrel Wheeler Stewart, "Civil Rights Award Rescinded from Angela Davis After Jewish Community Objections," NPR, January 8, 2019,

https://www.npr.org/2019/01/08/683250815/civil-rights-award-rescinded
-from-angela-davis-after-jewish-community-objections.

**CHAPTER ONE: THE EROTIC LIFE OF COLONIALISM AND SLAVERY**

1. Martha McCartney, "Virginia's First Africans," in *Encyclopedia Virginia*, 2020, https://encyclopediavirginia.org/entries/africans-virginias-first/.

2. McCartney, "Virginia's First Africans."

3. Ivan Van Sertima, *They Came Before Columbus: The African Presence in Ancient America* (New York: Random House, 2003), 16.

4. Omise'eke Natasha Tinsley, "Black Atlantic, Queer Atlantic: Queer Imaginings of the Middle Passage," *GLQ: A Journal of Lesbian and Gay Studies* 14, nos. 2–3 (June 1, 2008): 191–215, https://doi.org/10.1215/10642684-2007-030.

5. See, for example, Sowande' M. Mustakeem's important history, *Slavery at Sea: Terror, Sex, and Sickness in the Middle Passage*, in which she describes how captive women, regardless of age, "were regularly exposed to violence as seafarers sought to hold complete dominance over their personal lives." Sowande' M. Mustakeem, *Slavery at Sea: Terror, Sex, and Sickness in the Middle Passage* (Urbana: University of Illinois Press, 2016), 86.

6. Harriet A. (Harriet Ann) Jacobs, *Incidents in the Life of a Slave Girl, Written by Herself*, ed. Lydia Maria Child (Thayer and Eldridge, 1861), republished by Townsend Press in 2004, available at https://www.gutenberg.org/ebooks/11030. See also Don Romesburg, ed., *The Routledge History of Queer America* (New York: Routledge, 2018), for a discussion of sexuality and the archives of slavery.

7. Treva B. Lindsey and Jessica Marie Johnson, "Searching for Climax: Black Erotic Lives in Slavery and Freedom," *Meridians* 12, no. 2 (2014): 189, https://doi.org/10.2979/meridians.12.2.169.

8. John Hope Franklin and Alfred A. Moss Jr., *From Slavery to Freedom: A History of African Americans* (New York: Knopf, 2000), 86.

9. Van Sertima, *They Came Before Columbus*.

10. *The Papers of Thomas Jefferson, Vol. 1, 1760–1776*, ed. Julian P. Bond (Princeton, NJ: Princeton University Press, 1950), 243–47, https://www.loc.gov/exhibits/declara/ruffdrft.html.

11. Tinsley, "Black Atlantic, Queer Atlantic."

12. *The Papers of Thomas Jefferson*, 243–47.

13. Mustakeem, *Slavery at Sea*.

14. David Root, *A Fast Sermon on Slavery. Delivered April 2, 1835, to the Congregational Church and Society in Dover, N. H. By David Root, Pastor* (Dover: Enquirer Office, April 2, 1835), 11, archived by HathiTrust Digital Library, https://hdl.handle.net/2027/loc.ark:/13960/t6tx3fj4t?urlappend=%3Bseq=7.

15. Root, *A Fast Sermon on Slavery*.

16. US History Scene, "Gender and Race in the Antebellum Slavery Debates," *US History Scene* (blog), https://ushistoryscene.com/article/gender-race-slavery/, accessed January 23, 2025.

17. US History Scene, "Gender and Race in the Antebellum Slavery Debates."

18. Harriet E. Wilson, *Our Nig: Or, Sketches from the Life of a Free Black*, illustrated edition, ed. Henry Louis Gates Jr. and Richard J. Ellis (Westminster: Vintage, 2011).

19. Patrice D. Douglass, "Whither the Queer History of Slavery?" in *The Cambridge History of Queer American Literature*, ed. Benjamin Kahan (Cambridge: Cambridge University Press, 2024), 79, https://doi.org/10.1017/9781108918725.005.

20. Aliyyah I. Abdur-Rahman, "'The Strangest Freaks of Despotism': Queer Sexuality in Antebellum African American Slave Narratives," *African American Review* 40, no. 2 (2006): 226.

21. Emily A. Owens, *Consent in the Presence of Force: Sexual Violence and Black Women's Survival in Antebellum New Orleans* (Chapel Hill: University of North Carolina Press, 2023), 51.

22. *The Papers of Thomas Jefferson*, 243–47.

23. Thomas A. Foster, *Rethinking Rufus: Sexual Violations of Enslaved Men* (Athens: University of Georgia Press, 2019), 3–4.

24. *Sexuality and Slavery: Reclaiming Intimate Histories in the Americas*, ed. Daina Ramey Berry and Leslie M. Harris (Athens: University of Georgia Press, 2018), 112.

25. Jacobs, *Incidents in the Life of a Slave Girl*, 53.

26. Jacobs, *Incidents in the Life of a Slave Girl*, 178.

27. Jacobs, *Incidents in the Life of a Slave Girl*, 178–79.

28. Abdur-Rahman, "'The Strangest Freaks of Despotism,'" 231.

29. Jacobs, *Incidents in the Life of a Slave Girl*, 179.

30. Jacobs, *Incidents in the Life of a Slave Girl*, 179.

31. Jacobs, *Incidents in the Life of a Slave Girl*, 179.

32. Abdur-Rahman, "'The Strangest Freaks of Despotism,'" 232–33.

33. Abdur-Rahman, "'The Strangest Freaks of Despotism,'" 233.

34. Jacobs, *Incidents in the Life of a Slave Girl*, 84–85.

35. Gloria Wekker, "Mati-ism and Black Lesbianism: Two Idealtypical Expressions of Female Homosexuality in Black Communities of the Diaspora," *Journal of Lesbian Studies* 1, no. 1 (December 15, 1996): 11–24, https://doi.org/10.1300/J155v01n01_03.

36. Jewelle Gomez, *The Gilda Stories* (San Francisco: City Lights Publishers, 2016).

37. Gomez, *The Gilda Stories*, xii.

38. Gomez, *The Gilda Stories*, 13.

39. Gomez, *The Gilda Stories*, 16.

40. Douglass, "Whither the Queer History of Slavery?" 73.

41. Robert Jones Jr., *The Prophets* (New York: G. P. Putnam's Sons, 2021), 10.

**CHAPTER TWO: BY ANY OTHER NAME**

1. William Still, *The Underground Railroad: A Record of Facts, Authentic Narratives, Letters &c., Narrating the Hardships, Hair-Breadth*

*Escapes and Death Struggles of the Slaves in Their Efforts for Freedom*, rev. ed. (Philadelphia: People's Publishing Co., 1879), 183, available at https://www.loc.gov/resource/rbc0001.2019gen24984/.

2. Still, *The Underground Railroad*, 2.

3. Still, *The Underground Railroad*, 185.

4. Hortense J. Spillers, "Mama's Baby, Papa's Maybe: An American Grammar Book," *Diacritics* 17, no. 2 (1987): 65–81, https://doi.org/10.2307/464747.

5. Daphne A. Brooks, "Introduction," in William W. Brown et al., *The Great Escapes: Four Slave Narratives* (New York: Sterling Publishing, 2007).

6. William Wells Brown, "William Wells Brown Describes the Crafts' Escape," *The Liberator*, January 12, 1849, available at Documenting the American South, https://docsouth.unc.edu/neh/craft/support1.html.

7. Aliyyah I. Abdur-Rahman, "'The Strangest Freaks of Despotism': Queer Sexuality in Antebellum African American Slave Narratives," *African American Review* 40, no. 2 (2006).

8. Josephine Brown, *Biography of an American Bondman* (Boston: R. F. Wallcut, 1856), available at https://archive.org/details/biographyofameri00brow/page/n3/mode/2up

9. William Craft and Ellen Craft, *Running a Thousand Miles for Freedom, Or, The Escape of William and Ellen Craft from Slavery*, 1860, available at https://www.gutenberg.org/ebooks/585.

10. Barbara McCaskill, *Love, Liberation, and Escaping Slavery: William and Ellen Craft in Cultural Memory* (Athens: University of Georgia Press, 2015), 25.

11. Mattie Udora Richardson, "No More Secrets, No More Lies: African American History and Compulsory Heterosexuality," *Journal of Women's History* 15, no. 3 (2003): 63–76.

12. "William Cathay's Enlistment Document," November 15, 1866, available at https://www.nabmw.org/cathay-williams.

13. "Cathay Williams Story," *St. Louis Daily Times*, January 2, 1876, available at https://www.nabmw.org/cathay-williams.

14. "William Cathay's Discharge Document," October 14, 1868, available at https://www.nabmw.org/cathay-williams.

15. DeAnne Blanton, "Cathay Williams: Black Woman Soldier, 1866–1868," *Minerva* 10, nos. 3–4 (1992): 1–12.

16. Blanton, "Cathay Williams."

17. AFP, "Josephine Baker: France's Adopted Black Superstar Immortalised," RFI, November 22, 2021, https://www.rfi.fr/en/josephine-baker-france-s-adopted-black-superstar-immortalised.

18. AFP, "Josephine Baker."

19. AFP, "Josephine Baker."

20. Daina Ramey Berry and Kali Nicole Gross, *A Black Women's History of the United States* (Boston: Beacon Press, 2020), 179.

21. "(1963) Josephine Baker, 'Speech at the March on Washington,'" *BlackPast* (blog), November 3, 2011, https://www.blackpast.org/african

-american-history/speeches-african-american-history/1963-josephine-baker
-speech-march-washington/.

22. Kevin Mumford, "Opening the Restricted Box: Lorraine Hansberry's Lesbian Writing," *OutHistory*, https://outhistory.org/exhibits/show/lorraine-hansberry/lesbian-writing, accessed January 24, 2025.

23. Imani Perry, *Looking for Lorraine: The Radiant and Radical Life of Lorraine Hansberry* (Boston: Beacon Press, 2018), 92.

24. Lorraine Hansberry, "Letter," *The Ladder* 1, no. 11 (August 1957), Lorraine Hansberry Literary Trust, https://www.lhlt.org/i-think-it-about-time-equipped-women-began-take-some-ethical-questions-which-male-dominated-culture.

25. Hansberry, "Letter."

26. "Lorraine Hansberry: Letters to 'The Ladder,'" Illinois History and Lincoln Collections, June 4, 2018, https://publish.illinois.edu/ihlc-blog/2018/06/04/lorraine-hansberry-letters-to-the-ladder/.

27. Perry, *Looking for Lorraine*, 90–91.

### CHAPTER THREE: ON THE OUTS

1. W. E. B. Du Bois, "The Talented Tenth," in *The Negro Problem: A Series of Articles by Representative American Negroes of To-Day* (New York: James Pott & Co., 1903), 33.

2. Derrick P. Alridge, "Atlanta Compromise Speech," in *New Georgia Encyclopedia*, 2004, https://www.georgiaencyclopedia.org/articles/history-archaeology/atlanta-compromise-speech/.

3. Du Bois, "The Talented Tenth," 44.

4. Du Bois, "The Talented Tenth," 33.

5. W. E. B. Du Bois, "The Criteria of Negro Art," *The Crisis* 32 (1926): 290–97.

6. Major Jackson, "Countee Cullen and the Racial Mountain," *Boston Review*, March 27, 2013, https://www.bostonreview.net/articles/countee-cullen-and-racial-mountain/.

7. Yolande Du Bois to W. E. B. Du Bois, "Letter from Yolande Du Bois to W. E. B. Du Bois," Correspondence, Manuscripts, W. E. B. Du Bois Papers (MS 312), October 1935, Special Collections and University Archives, University of Massachusetts Amherst Libraries, https://credo.library.umass.edu/view/full/mums312-b076-i372.

8. Yolande Du Bois to W. E. B. Du Bois.

9. Yolande Du Bois to W. E. B. Du Bois.

10. W. E. B. Du Bois, "Statement of W. E. B. Du Bois on the Divorce of Countee Cullen and Yolande Du Bois, ca. March 31, 1930," Announcements, W. E. B. Du Bois Papers (MS 312), May 23, 1929, Special Collections and University Archives, University of Massachusetts Amherst Libraries, https://credo.library.umass.edu/view/full/mums312-b056-i448.

11. Cathy J. Cohen, "Punks, Bulldaggers, and Welfare Queens: The Radical Potential of Queer Politics?" *GLQ: A Journal of Lesbian and Gay Studies* 3, no. 4 (May 1997): 437–65, https://doi.org/10.1215/10642684-3-4-437.

12. Cathy J. Cohen, *The Boundaries of Blackness: AIDS and the Breakdown of Black Politics* (Chicago: University of Chicago Press, 1999).

13. W. E. B. Du Bois, *The Souls of Black Folk*, ed. Brent Hayes Edwards (London: Oxford University Press, 2009), 3.

14. Cookie Woolner, *The Famous Lady Lovers: Black Women and Queer Desire Before Stonewall* (Chapel Hill: University of North Carolina Press, 2023).

15. Marcus A. Brooks and Earl Wright, "Augustus Granville Dill: A Case Study in the Conceptualization of a Black Public Sociology," *Sociology of Race and Ethnicity* 7, no. 3 (July 2021): 318–32, https://doi.org/10.1177/2332649220942253.

16. Quoted in Brooks and Wright, "Augustus Granville Dill," 320.

17. Brooks and Wright, "Augustus Granville Dill," 324–25.

18. Simon D. Elin Fisher, "Pauli Murray's Peter Panic: Perspectives from the Margins of Gender and Race in Jim Crow America," *TSQ: Transgender Studies Quarterly* 3, nos. 1–2 (2016): 95–103, https://doi.org/10.1215/23289252-3334259.

19. Pauli Murray, "Oral History Interview with Pauli Murray," interview G-0044, February 13, 1976, 37–38, Southern Oral History Program Collection (#4007), Southern Historical Collection, Wilson Library, University of North Carolina at Chapel Hill, https://docsouth.unc.edu/sohp/G-0044/excerpts/excerpt_8638.html#citing.

20. Murray, "Oral History Interview with Pauli Murray," 46.

21. Murray, "Oral History Interview with Pauli Murray."

22. Murray, "Oral History Interview with Pauli Murray," 48.

23. Glenda Gilmore, "'Am I a Screwball, or Am I a Pioneer?' Pauli Murray's Civil Rights Movement," in *Profiles in Leadership: Historians on the Elusive Quality of Greatness*, ed. Walter Isaacson (New York: W. W. Norton & Co., 2010), 267.

24. Gilmore, "'Am I a Screwball, or Am I a Pioneer?'"

25. Bayard Rustin, "Nonviolence vs. Jim Crow," in *Time on Two Crosses: The Collected Writings of Bayard Rustin*, ed. Donald Weise and Devon Carbado (Jersey City, NJ: Cleis Press, 2003), 4.

26. Donald Weise and Devon Carbado, "Introduction," in Rustin, *Time on Two Crosses*, xxvii; George Chauncey Jr., "An Interview with George Chauncey, Jr.," in Rustin, *Time on Two Crosses*, 302.

27. Kevin Mumford, *Not Straight, Not White: Black Gay Men from the March on Washington to the AIDS Crisis* (Chapel Hill: University of North Carolina Press, 2016), 11.

28. James Baldwin, "Letter from a Region in My Mind," *New Yorker* 94, no. 36 (1962): 30–39.

29. Baldwin, "Letter from a Region in My Mind," 11–13.

30. James Baldwin and Richard Goldstein, "'Go the Way Your Blood Beats': An Interview with James Baldwin," in *James Baldwin: The Last Interview; and Other Conversations* (Hoboken, NJ: Melville House, 2014), 73.

31. James G. Thompson, "Should I Sacrifice to Live 'Half-American'?" *Pittsburgh Courier*, January 31, 1942.

32. Daryl Michael Scott, *Contempt and Pity: Social Policy and the Image of the Damaged Black Psyche, 1880–1996* (Chapel Hill: University of North Carolina Press, 1997), 94.

33. Gunnar Myrdal, *An American Dilemma: The Negro Problem and Modern Democracy* (New York: Harper & Bros., 1944), xivii.

34. Myrdal, *An American Dilemma*.

35. Khalil Gibran Muhammad, *The Condemnation of Blackness: Race, Crime, and the Making of Modern Urban America, with a New Preface* (Cambridge, MA: Harvard University Press, 2019), 276–77.

36. Muhammad, *The Condemnation of Blackness*, 277.

37. Joanne Meyerowitz, "'How Common Culture Shapes the Separate Lives': Sexuality, Race, and Mid-Twentieth-Century Social Constructionist Thought," *Journal of American History* 96, no. 4 (March 1, 2010): 1057–84, https://doi.org/10.1093/jahist/96.4.1057.1084.

38. Meyerowitz, "'How Common Culture Shapes the Separate Lives,'" 1078.

39. Daniel Patrick Moynihan, *The Negro Family: The Case for National Action*, Office of Policy Planning and Research, US Department of Labor, March 1965, https://www.dol.gov/general/aboutdol/history/webid-moynihan.

40. Moynihan, *The Negro Family*.

41. Ellen Herman, *The Romance of American Psychology: Political Culture in the Age of Experts* (Berkeley: University of California Press, 1995), 214.

42. Alvin Poussaint, "Sex and the Black Male," *Ebony*, August 1972, 117–18.

43. Poussaint, "Sex and the Black Male"; Darius Bost, "Evidence of Being: Urban Black Gay Men's Literature and Culture, 1978–1995," PhD diss., University of Maryland, 2014, 190.

44. Joanne Meyerowitz, *How Sex Changed: A History of Transsexuality in the United States* (Cambridge, MA: Harvard University Press, 2002), 62.

45. GerShun Avilez, *Radical Aesthetics and Modern Black Nationalism* (Champaign: University of Illinois Press, 2016), 7.

46. Cherise A. Pollard, "Sexual Subversions, Political Inversions: Women's Poetry and the Politics of the Black Arts Movement," in *New Thoughts on the Black Arts Movement*, ed. Lisa Gail Collins and Margo Natalie Crawford (New Brunswick, NJ: Rutgers University Press, 2019), 173–86.

47. George Bliss, "'Welfare Queen' Jailed in Tucson," *Chicago Tribune*, October 12, 1974.

48. "Alleged 'Welfare Queen' Is Accused of $154,000 Ripoff," *Jet*, December 19, 1974, 16–17.

49. John Fialka, "Reagan's Stories Don't Always Check Out," *Register-Guard*, February 9, 1976.

50. Julilly Kohler-Hausmann, "Welfare Crises, Penal Solutions, and the Origins of the 'Welfare Queen,'" *Journal of Urban History* 41, no. 5 (2015): 756–71, https://doi.org/10.1177/0096144215589942.

51. Ange-Marie Hancock, "Contemporary Welfare Reform and the Public Identity of the 'Welfare Queen,'" *Race, Gender, and Class* 10, no. 1 (2003): 37.

52. Evelynn M. Hammonds, "Toward a Genealogy of Black Female Sexuality: The Problematic of Silence," in *Feminist Theory and the Body: A Reader*, ed. Janet Price and Margrit Shildrick (Edinburgh: Edinburgh University Press, 2022), 93–104.

53. National AIDS Treatment Advocacy Project," HIV & Black Women," https://www.natap.org/2006/HIV/031506_03.htm, accessed May 20, 2025.

54. *The Oprah Winfrey Show*, season 20, "A Secret Sex World: Living on the Down Low," April 16, 2004, ABC-TV.

55. Ruby Tapia, Jeffrey McCune, and Jennifer Devere Brody, "Dangerous Profiling: Recent Media Representations of Black Male Sexuality," in *Black Sexualities: Probing Powers, Passions, Practices, and Policies*, ed. Juan Battle and Sandra L. Barnes (New Brunswick, NJ: Rutgers University Press, 2009), 128.

56. Ann Cvetkovich, *An Archive of Feelings: Trauma, Sexuality, and Lesbian Public Cultures* (Durham, NC: Duke University Press, 2003), 94.

57. Hammonds, "Toward a Genealogy of Black Female Sexuality."

CHAPTER FOUR: WERK!
1. Langston Hughes, "The Negro Artist and the Racial Mountain," *The Nation* 122, no. 3181 (June 23, 1926): 602–4.

2. Hughes, "The Negro Artist and the Racial Mountain."

3. Journalist and Bessie Smith biographer Chris Albertson notes that while the date of her birth is unverified, it is likely that she was born April 15, 1894, which is the date found on her marriage certificate.

4. Chris Albertson, *Bessie* (New Haven, CT: Yale University Press, 2005), 15.

5. Carla Williams, "Smith, Bessie (1894–1937)," 2015, GLBTQ Archive, www.glbtqarchive.com.

6. K. Allison Hammer, "'Just like a Natural Man': The B.D. Styles of Gertrude 'Ma' Rainey and Bessie Smith," *Journal of Lesbian Studies* 23, no. 2 (April 3, 2019): 279–93, https://doi.org/10.1080/10894160.2019.1562284.

7. Lucille Bogan, "B.D. Woman's Blues," 1935, quoted in Hammer, "'Just like a Natural Man,'" 279.

8. According to his obituary published in the *Los Angeles Times*, "By marrying the spiritual uplift of church-schooled lyrics to the physical energy of blues-fired music, Dorsey was able to reach his audience in ways that even the greatest preachers couldn't." In J. D. Considine, "An Appreciation: Dorsey's Gospel Music Gave the Devil His Due," *Los Angeles Times*, January 27, 1993. Dorsey is not known to be queer, but he collaborated with numerous queer musicians as a blues composer and accompanist, and as a gospel composer.

9. Pianist Willie Love noted about Broadnax, "Little Axe couldn't sing low, because he had a relatively high voice. It wasn't falsetto, it was naturally high. So somebody had to sing the bottom." In Anthony Heilbut, *The Fan*

*Who Knew Too Much: Aretha Franklin, the Rise of the Soap Opera, Children of the Gospel Church, and Other Meditations* (New York: Knopf, 2012).

10. Gayle Wald, *Shout, Sister, Shout! The Untold Story of Rock-and-Roll Trailblazer Sister Rosetta Tharpe* (Boston: Beacon Press, 2007), 68–70.

11. Tyina Steptoe, "Big Mama Thornton, Little Richard, and the Queer Roots of Rock 'n' Roll," *American Quarterly* 70, no. 1 (2018): 55–77.

12. "Sir Lady Java Fights Fuzz-y Rule Nine," *Los Angeles Advocate*, no. 3 (November 1967): 1.

13. "Sir Lady Java Fights Fuzz-y Rule Nine."

14. Treva Ellison, "The Labor of Werqing It: The Performance and Protest Strategies of Sir Lady Java," in *Trap Door: Trans Cultural Production and the Politics of Visibility*, ed. Reina Gossett, Eric A. Stanley, and Johanna Burton (Cambridge, MA: MIT Press, 2017), 1–21.

15. "'Double-Sexed' Defendant Makes No Hit with Jury," *Chicago Daily Defender*, April 4, 1957.

16. "'Double-Sexed' Defendant Makes No Hit with Jury."

17. "Brutality 'Twist,'" *Chicago Daily Defender*, October 13, 1969.

18. "Brutality 'Twist.'"

19. Gillian Frank, "Discophobia: Antigay Prejudice and the 1979 Backlash Against Disco," *Journal of the History of Sexuality* 16, no. 2 (2007): 276–306.

20. Frank, "Discophobia."

21. Sharon Davis, *Mighty Real: Sharon Davis Remembers Sylvester* (Bank House Books, 2014), 39–40.

22. Chris Parker, "Tim'm West: Rhymes with Homo Side," *Creative Loafing*, May 21, 2008, https://creativeloafing.com/content-160883-tim-m -west-rhymes-with-homo-side.

23. Scott Poulson-Bryant, "'Put Some Bass in Your Walk': Notes on Queerness, Hip Hop, and the Spectacle of the Undoable," *Palimpsest: A Journal on Women, Gender, and the Black International* 2, no. 2 (2013): 214–25.

24. Poulson-Bryant, "'Put Some Bass in Your Walk.'"

25. Deep Dickollective, *On Some Other*, Sugartruck Recordings, released 2007.

26. Jenna Wortham, "How Janelle Monáe Found Her Voice," *New York Times Magazine*, April 19, 2018, https://www.nytimes.com/2018/04/19 /magazine/how-janelle-monae-found-her-voice.html.

27. Wortham, "How Janelle Monáe Found Her Voice."

28. Wortham, "How Janelle Monáe Found Her Voice."

29. Samantha Riedel, "Visionary Singer-Songwriter Janelle Monáe Has Come Out as Nonbinary," *Them*, April 21, 2022, at Internet Archive, https://web.archive.org/web/20220421184335/https://www.them.us/story /janelle-monae-nonbinary-coming-out.

**CHAPTER FIVE: COMING TOGETHER**

1. Although sexual entrapment in bars was less common for women than men, women's bars were often targeted for anti-prostitution raids. See

Christina B. Hanhardt, *Safe Space: Gay Neighborhood History and the Politics of Violence* (Durham, NC: Duke University Press, 2013), 28.

2. George Chauncey has estimated that between 1923, when the New York state legislature outlawed homosexual cruising as a form of disorderly conduct, and 1963, when gay activists and allies persuaded Mayor John Lindsay to end the police department's use of entrapment, more than fifty thousand men were arrested for cruising in bars, streets, parks, and subway washrooms in New York City alone. See George Chauncey, "The Forgotten History of Gay Entrapment," *The Atlantic* (blog), June 25, 2019, https://www.theatlantic.com/ideas/archive/2019/06/before-stonewall-biggest-threat-was-entrapment/590536/.

3. Treva Ellison, "From Sanctuary to Safe Space: Gay and Lesbian Police-Reform Activism in Los Angeles," *Radical History Review* 135 (2019): 97, https://doi.org/10.1215/01636545-7607845.

4. Alex Ross, "Harry Hay, John Cage, and the Birth of Gay Rights in Los Angeles," *New Yorker*, June 25, 2021, https://www.newyorker.com/culture/cultural-comment/harry-hay-john-cage-and-the-birth-of-gay-rights-in-los-angeles.

5. "Statement of Purpose for Vanguard," *Vanguard Magazine: The Magazine of the Tenderloin* 1, no. 1 (August 1996), available at Digital Transgender Archive, https://www.digitaltransgenderarchive.net/files/cz30ps69r.

6. "Sweep In," *Vanguard Magazine: The Magazine of the Tenderloin* 1, no. 2 (October 1996): 4, available at Digital Transgender Archive, https://www.digitaltransgenderarchive.net/files/q237hr95t.

7. Sylvia Rivera, "Queens in Exile, the Forgotten Ones," in *Street Transvestite Action Revolutionaries: Survival, Revolt, and Queer Antagonist Struggle* (Bloomington, IN: Untorelli Press, 2013), 49.

8. Sylvia Rivera, "People fail to realize that the Stonewall was not a drag queen bar. It was a white male bar for middle-class males to pick up young boys of different races. Very few drag queens were allowed in there because if they had permitted drag queens into the club, it would have brought the club down. That would have brought more problems to the club. It's the way the Mafia thought, and so did the patrons. So the queens who were allowed in basically had inside connections. I used to go there to pick up drugs to take somewhere else. I had connections." Rivera, "Queens in Exile, the Forgotten Ones."

9. Marsha P. Johnson and Randy Wicker, *Making Gay History*, podcast, n.d., season 2, episode 1, https://makinggayhistory.org/podcast/episode-11-johnson-wicker/.

10. Johnson and Wicker, *Making Gay History*.

11. Johnson and Wicker, *Making Gay History*.

12. Johnson and Wicker, *Making Gay History*.

13. Patrick Hinds, "Uncovering the Stonewall Lesbian: Storme DeLarverie Was There That Infamous Night. Now She's Coming Clean," *Curve* 18, no. 1 (January–February 2008): 64.

14. Stephan L. Cohen, *The Gay Liberation Youth Movement in New York: "An Army of Lovers Cannot Fail"* (New York: Routledge, 2007), 2.

15. Melinda Chateauvert, *Sex Workers Unite: A History of the Movement from Stonewall to Slutwalk* (Boston: Beacon Press, 2014), 11.

16. Kimberly Springer, "The Interstitial Politics of Black Feminist Organizations," *Meridians* 1, no. 2 (2001): 163.

17. Springer, "The Interstitial Politics of Black Feminist Organizations," 164.

18. Patricia Romney, *We Were There: The Third World Women's Alliance and the Second Wave* (New York: Feminist Press at CUNY, 2021), 143.

19. *Feminist Manifestos: A Global Documentary Reader*, ed. Penny A. Weiss (New York: New York University Press, 2018), 256–57.

20. Combahee River Collective, "The Combahee River Collective Statement," in *How We Get Free: Black Feminism and the Combahee River Collective*, ed. Keeanga-Yamahtta Taylor (Chicago: Haymarket Books, 2017), 18.

21. Winifred Breines, *The Trouble Between Us: An Uneasy History of White and Black Women in the Feminist Movement* (New York: Oxford University Press, 2007), 118; Beverly Guy-Sheftall, ed., *Words of Fire: An Anthology of African-American Feminist Thought* (New York: New Press, 1995).

22. Audre Lorde, *Cables to Rage* (London: Paul Breman, 1970).

23. Barbara Smith, "A Press of Our Own Kitchen Table: Women of Color Press," *Frontiers: A Journal of Women Studies* 10, no. 3 (1989): 12, https://doi.org/10.2307/3346433.

24. Cherríe Moraga and Gloria Anzaldúa, "Introduction, 1981," in *This Bridge Called My Back: Writings by Radical Women of Color*, ed. Cherríe Moraga and Gloria Anzaldúa (Berkeley, CA: Third Woman Press, 2002), lii.

25. Sidney Brinkley, "Who's Who in Black Gay Politics," *Blacklight*, 1983, p. 12.

26. Sidney Brinkley reported that issues regarding lack of training as social activists, lesbians who were intolerant of the group's male-oriented attitudes, failures to address these concerns, and deception by and subsequent lack of faith in leadership left the DC Coalition demoralized. See Brinkley, "Who's Who in Black Gay Politics."

27. Beau Lancaster et al., "The History Missing from the LGBTQ Story Told During Pride Month," *Washington Post*, June 20, 2022, https://www.washingtonpost.com/outlook/2022/06/20/history-missing-lgbtq-story-told-during-pride-month/.

28. Darius Bost, "At the Club: Locating Early Black Gay AIDS Activism in Washington D.C.," *Occasion* 8 (2015), https://shc.stanford.edu/arcade/publications/occasion/race-space-scale/club-locating-early-black-gay-aids-activism.

29. Other Countries, "Proposal—Chicago Resource Center," 1988, p. 1, Other Countries Records, Box 1, Folder 38, Schomburg Center for Research in Black Culture.

30. *MMWR: Morbidity and Mortality Weekly Report* 30, no. 21 (1981).

31. Lawrence K. Altman, "Rare Cancer Seen in 41 Homosexuals," *New York Times*, July 3, 1981, https://www.nytimes.com/1981/07/03/us/rare-cancer-seen-in-41-homosexuals.html.

32. Centers for Disease Control and Prevention (CDC), "30 Years of HIV in African American Communities: A Timeline," 2011, https://stacks.cdc.gov/view/cdc/26102.

33. CDC, "First 500,000 AIDS Cases—United States, 1995," *MMWR*, November 24, 1995, https://www.cdc.gov/mmwr/preview/mmwrhtml/00039622.htm.

34. Walt Odets, *Out of the Shadows: Reimagining Gay Men's Lives* (New York: Picador, 2020).

35. CDC, "Fact Sheet—HIV Among African Americans," 2019, https://www.cdc.gov/nchhstp/newsroom/docs/factsheets/cdc-hiv-aa-508.pdf (URL no longer accessible).

36. An estimated 40 percent of ClubHouse's membership was lost to the disease. Bost, "At the Club," 8.

37. Tracy Baim, "NCBG: Building Black-Gay Coalitions," *GayLife*, March 28, 1985, https://outhistory.org/files/original/8f20a17f8abf95bcbb4b271b37813f03.jpg; Tristan Cabello, "NCBG-Chicago: The National Coalition of Black Gays," in *Queer Bronzeville, 1900–1985* (OutHistory), https://outhistory.org/exhibits/show/queer-bronzeville/part-4/ncbg-chicago, accessed January 15, 2025.

38. Baim, "NCBG: Building Black-Gay Coalitions;" Cabello, "NCBG-Chicago."

39. Darius Bost, "Black Lesbian Feminist Intellectuals and the Struggle Against HIV/AIDS," *Souls: A Critical Journal of Black Politics, Culture, and Society* 21, nos. 2–3 (2019): 180.

40 Quoted in Lou Chibbaro Jr., "AIDS Conference, Black Conference This Weekend," *Washington (DC) Blade*, October 7, 1983, 1; Darius Bost, *Evidence of Being: The Black Gay Cultural Renaissance and the Politics of Violence* (Chicago: University of Chicago Press, 2019), 29.

## CHAPTER SIX: SURVIVAL IS NOT A LUXURY

1. The US Park Police estimated the attendance to be two hundred thousand, while organizers believed it was well over three hundred thousand. Lou Chibarro Jr., "Our History of Marching on Washington," *Washington Blade*, June 11, 2017, https://www.washingtonblade.com/2017/06/11/history-marching-washington/.

2. Lena Williams, "200,000 March in Capital to Seek Rights and Money for AIDS," *New York Times*, October 12, 1987.

3. "Our Demands: March on Washington for Lesbian and Gay Rights," One Institute, October 11, 1987, https://www.oneinstitute.org/wp-content/uploads/2015/02/Our-Demands-March-on-Washington-for-Lesbian-and-Gay-Rights-Oct-11-1987.pdf.

4. "Our Demands: March on Washington for Lesbian and Gay Rights."

5. Williams, "200,000 March in Capital to Seek Gay Rights and Money for AIDS."

6. Associated Press, "Suit Over March Count Threatened," *Los Angeles Times*, October 18, 1995, https://www.latimes.com/archives/la-xpm-1995-10-18-mn-58397-story.html.

7. Louis Farrakhan, Million Man March National Organizing Committee, "Purpose of the Million Man March," in *Million Man March/Day of Absence: A Commemorative Anthology*, ed. Haki R. Madhubuti and Maulana Karenga (Chicago: Third World Press, 1996), 151.

8. Maulana Karenga, "The Million Man March/Day of Absence Mission Statement," *Black Scholar* 25, no. 4 (1995): 2–11, https://doi.org/10.1080/00064246.1995.11430749.

9. Courtney Williams, "Million Man March 20 Years Later," *Washington Blade*, October 1, 2015, https://www.washingtonblade.com/2015/10/01/million-man-march-20-years-later/.

10. Williams, "Million Man March 20 Years Later."

11. Dale Carpenter, "The Unknown Past of Lawrence v. Texas," *Michigan Law Review* 102, no. 7 (2004): 1482, https://doi.org/10.2307/4141912.

12. Carpenter, "The Unknown Past of Lawrence v. Texas," 1483.

13. Carpenter, "The Unknown Past of Lawrence v. Texas," 1502.

14. Carpenter, "The Unknown Past of Lawrence v. Texas," 1483.

15. Siobhan B. Somerville, "Queer Loving," *GLQ: A Journal of Lesbian and Gay Studies* 11, no. 3 (June 2005): 335–70, https://doi.org/10.1215/10642684-11-3-335.

16. Somerville, "Queer Loving."

17. Obergefell v. Hodges, 576 U.S. 644 (2015), US Reports, Supreme Court of the United States, 2015.

18. Journalist Markus Schmidt interviewed Bernard S. Cohen, who argued the Lovings' case in the Supreme Court: "The decision in Loving brought enough to encompass the principle involved in the gay marriage case. Because the constitutional principle involved is the same, the right to marry is a constitutionally protected right of liberty. I think it's that easy." In Markus Schmidt, "Loving v. Virginia Looms Large in Gay Marriage Case," *Richmond Times-Dispatch*, May 23, 2015, https://richmond.com/news/local/government-politics/loving-v-virginia-looms-large-in-gay-marriage-case/article_1818c5b1-4680-51ea-b53e-c14247ab4f6e.html.

19. Somerville, "Queer Loving," 335–36.

20. Marcus Anthony Hunter, "Race and the Same-Sex Marriage Divide," *Contexts* 12, no. 3 (August 2013): 74–76, https://doi.org/10.1177/1536504213499884.

21. Darryl Robertson, "Prof. Tera Hunter Explores the Meaning of Slave Marriage in New Book, *Bound in Wedlock*," *Vibe*, August 17, 2017, https://www.vibe.com/features/editorial/v-books-tera-hunter-bound-in-wedlock-532767/.

22. National Park Service, Presidential Proclamation on the Camp Nelson National Monument, October 26, 2018, https://www.nps.gov/cane/learn/pres-proclamation.htm.

23. Marc Stein, *Sexual Injustice: Supreme Court Decisions from Griswold to Roe* (Chapel Hill: University of North Carolina Press, 2013), 45.

24. "Queer Nation," flyer, n.d., Lesbian and Gay Community Center, New York, box 1, folder 3, Kearns Papers.

25. "Reward Letter," n.d., Lesbian and Gay Community Center, New York, box 1, folder 3, Kearns Papers.

26. "Friends of Marsha," flyer, n.d., Lesbian and Gay Community Center, New York, box 1, folder 3, Kearns Papers.

27. "Friends of Marsha."

28. "Justice for Marsha, Pack a Piece," flyer, n.d., Lesbian and Gay Community Center, New York, box 1, folder 3, Kearns Papers.

29. "Marsha P. Johnson: Gay/Lesbian Power Now," flyer, n.d., Lesbian and Gay Community Center, New York, box 1, folder 3, Kearns Papers.

30. Susan Turner et al., "An Evaluation of the Federal Government's Violent Offender Incarceration and Truth-in-Sentencing Incentive Grants," *Prison Journal* 83, no. 6 (2006): 364–85.

31. Suzanne M. Kirchhoff, *Economic Impacts of Prison Growth*, Congressional Research Service, 2010, p. 15, available at https://digital.library .unt.edu/ark:/67531/metadc501951/.

32. Erin J. McCauley, "The Cumulative Probability of Arrest by Age 28 Years in the United States by Disability Status, Race/Ethnicity, and Gender," *American Journal of Public Health* 107, no. 12 (December 2017): 1977–81, https://doi.org/10.2105/AJPH.2017.304095.

33. Dean Spade, *Normal Life: Administrative Violence, Critical Trans Politics, and the Limits of Law* (Durham, NC: Duke University Press, 2015), https://doi.org/10.1215/9780822374794.

34. "Deadly Deception," *Chicago Tribune*, January 17, 1994, https:// www.chicagotribune.com/1994/01/17/deadly-deception/.

35. Jennifer Devere Brody, "Boyz Do Cry: Screening History's White Lies," *Screen* 43, no. 1 (March 1, 2002): 93, https://doi.org/10.1093/screen /43.1.91.

36. C. Riley Snorton, *Black on Both Sides: A Racial History of Trans Identity* (Minneapolis: University of Minnesota Press, 2017), 180–81.

37. Lambda Legal, Brief of Amici Curiae in Support of Brandon Teena, Brandon v. Richardson County, 624 N.W.2d 604 (Neb. 2001), Supreme Court of Nebraska, April 15, 2004.

38. Lambda Legal, Brief of Amici Curiae in Support of Brandon Teena, 6.

39. Beth Loffreda, *Losing Matt Shepard: Life and Politics in the Aftermath of Anti-Gay Murder* (New York: Columbia University Press, 2001), 21.

40. Human Rights Campaign, *A Guide to State-Level Advocacy Following Enactment of the Matthew Shepard and James Byrd, Jr. Hate Crimes Prevention Act*, 2014, p. 4, https://hrc-prod-requests.s3-us-west-2 .amazonaws.com/files/assets/resources/HRC-Hate-Crimes-Guide-2014.pdf.

41. New York County District Attorney's Office, "News Release," December 22, 2000, at Internet Archive, https://web.archive.org/web/20100 616065113/http://manhattanda.org/whatsnew/press/2000-12-22.shtml.

42. Nina Siegal, "Watershed of Mourning at the Border of Gender," *New York Times*, July 24, 2000, https://www.nytimes.com/2000/07/24 /nyregion/watershed-of-mourning-at-the-border-of-gender.html.

43. Siegal, "Watershed of Mourning at the Border of Gender."

44. Correspondence between HRC, STAR, and Sylvia Rivera regarding a STAR request for HRC to financially support the Amanda Milan vigil, February 23, 2001, Queers Without Borders Archive, https://issuu.com /queerswithoutborders/docs/star_and_hrc.

45. Correspondence between HRC, STAR, and Sylvia Rivera.

46. Siegal, "Watershed of Mourning at the Border of Gender."

47. Nina Siegal, "The Crying Game," *Salon*, June 20, 2001, https:// www.salon.com/2001/06/20/milan/.

48. Vinette K. Pryce, "Rainbow of Solidarity for Slain Transsexual Woman," *New York Amsterdam News*, July 27, 2000.

49. Siegal, "The Crying Game."

50. Siegal, "The Crying Game."

51. Hunter, "Race and the Same-Sex Marriage Divide."

52. Williams, "Million Man March 20 Years Later."

53. Robert F. Reid-Pharr, "It's Raining Men: Notes on the Million Man March," *Transition* 69 (1996): 38.

54. Cleo Manago, "Black Same-Gender-Love, Represented at Historic 'Millions More Movement' Podium," *Cleomanagosblog* (blog), October 15, 2005, https://cleomanagosblog.livejournal.com/1298.html.

55. Deborah Gray White, "Out and on the Outs: The 1990s Mass Marches and the Black and LGBT Communities," in *Connexions: Histories of Race and Sex in North America*, ed. Jennifer Brier, Jim Downs, and Jennifer L. Morgan (Champaign: University of Illinois Press, 2016), 289.

56. White, "Out and on the Outs."

57. White, "Out and on the Outs."

58. White, "Out and on the Outs."

59. Kristin E. Holmes, "Controversy Following Duo to March," *Philadelphia Inquirer*, October 16, 1997.

60. Sheila Alexander-Reid, "Editorial," *Women in the Life*, November 1997, 10.

61. Alexander-Reid, "Editorial," 11.

62. Ryan Lee, "Bishop Eddie Long's Anti-Gay March Through Atlanta," *Georgia Voice*, September 24, 2010, originally published December 17, 2004, https://roughdraftatlanta.com/2010/09/24/flashback-bishop-eddie -longs-anti-gay-march-through-atlanta/.

63. Eddie Long, "New Birth Missionary Baptist March: King Would Defend His Beliefs; So Must I," *Atlanta Journal-Constitution*, December 19, 2004.

64. Lee, "Bishop Eddie Long's Anti-Gay March Through Atlanta."

65. Peter Wallsten, Tom Hamburger, and Nicholas Riccardi, "Bush Rewarded by Black Pastors' Faith," *Los Angeles Times*, January 18, 2005, https://www.latimes.com/archives/la-xpm-2005-jan-18-na-faith18-story.html.

66. Lee, "Bishop Eddie Long's Anti-Gay March Through Atlanta."

67. Lee, "Bishop Eddie Long's Anti-Gay March Through Atlanta."

68. Wallsten, Hamburger, and Riccardi, "Bush Rewarded by Black Pastors' Faith."

69. Karl Vick and Ashley Surdin, "Most Calif. Blacks Backed Proposition 8," NBC News, November 7, 2008, https://www.nbcnews.com/id /wbna27584685.

70. Jasmyne A. Cannick, "The Gay/Black Divide," *Los Angeles Times*, November 8, 2008, https://www.latimes.com/archives/la-xpm-2008-nov -08-oe-cannick8-story.html.

71. Cannick, "The Gay/Black Divide."

72. Isabella Grullón Paz and Maggie Astor, "Black Trans Women Seek More Space in the Movement They Helped Start," *New York Times*, June 27, 2020; Kiara Brantley-Jones, Steve Osunsami, and Ashley Schwartz-Lavares, "Black Trans Lives Matter: Activists Call for Inclusion in Racial Justice Movement," ABC News, October 20, 2020, https://abcnews.go .com/US/black-trans-lives-matter-activists-call-inclusion-racial/story?id =73571954.

73. Jasmyne A. Cannick, "No-on-8's White Bias," *Los Angeles Times*, November 8, 2008, https://www.latimes.com/opinion/la-oe-cannick8 -2008nov08-story.html.

**CONCLUSION**

1. *The Watermelon Woman*, dir. Cheryl Dunye, Dancing Girl, 1996.

2. *Black Is Blue*, dir. Cheryl Dunye, 13th Gen., 2014.

3. Dunye, *Black Is Blue*.

# INDEX